TECHNICAL WRITING
FOR TEAMS

TECHNICAL WRITING FOR TEAMS

The STREAM Tools Handbook

Alexander Mamishev
Sean Williams

IEEE PRESS

A JOHN WILEY & SONS, INC., PUBLICATION

Published by John Wiley & Sons, Inc., Hoboken, New Jersey.
Published simultaneously in Canada.

For general information on our other products and services or for technical support, please contact our Customer Care Department within the United States at (800) 762-2974, outside the United States at (317) 572-3993 or fax (317) 572-4002.

Wiley also publishes its books in a variety of electronic formats. Some content that appears in print may not be available in electronic formats. For more information about Wiley products, visit our web site at www.wiley.com.

Library of Congress Cataloging-in-Publication Data:

Mamishev, Alexander, 1971–
    Technical writing for teams using STREAM tools / Alexander Mamishev, Sean Williams.
        p. cm.
    ISBN 978-0-470-22976-7 (pbk.)
    1. Technical writing.   I. Williams, Sean, 1970–   II. Title.
    T11.M3357 2010
    808′.0666—dc22

                                                                    2009041786

Printed in the United States of America.

CONTENTS

3. DOCUMENT DESIGN 35

5. PLANNING, DRAFTING, AND EDITING DOCUMENTS   85

7. ASSURING QUALITY WRITING   161

PREFACE

Business processes change continuously, becoming increasingly automated, especially in such areas as customer interaction, order handling, and marketing. Collaborative teams are now formed across continents, and everyone—from individuals to small businesses to global corporations—has to operate in this increasingly interconnected world to maintain their competitiveness. The field of research and development is no exception: the processes of producing and managing knowledge change as new information technology tools become available. One of these processes, the production of manuscripts—journal articles, conference papers, technical reports—is one of the most important activities in scientific and technical organizations and this process, too, has become highly automated.

Recognizing these changes, our goal for this book is to provide technical teams with tools that allow them to streamline their collaborative writing activities. Ultimately, this approach will not only increase the overall productivity of the group but will also enhance the quality of the output, the creativity in the organization, and the ability of team members to interact with each other.

In this book, we cover several key areas of manuscript generation: writing, editing, proofreading, formatting, and file management. Unlike most other writing manuals, we place specific emphasis on teams rather than on individual writers. Therefore, we address such areas as team dynamics, training, separation of duties, and workflow, while also focusing on the tools that will help team members collaborate more successfully.

One example of a team centered approach is the way we tackle writing quality. Becoming a great technical writer is a lifelong process. The rewards of writing well are great: winning large technical bidding contracts, getting your work published in highly respected journals, rapidly developing and protecting your intellectual property. With all due respect to many who have preceded us, like Strunk and White, we feel that today we have an opportunity to improve writing by focusing attention on specific areas that need improvement rather than discussing writing *in general*.

In short, this book presents a system that enables collaborative authors to unlock the potential of teams in creating the highest quality documents in a minimum amount of time.

Chapter 1 introduces the philosophy behind this book by examining the need for the system we present in subsequent chapters. The chapter offers a historical account of how our perspective has evolved, discusses why writing teams need a good "writing system," and introduces the system itself. This chapter does not teach any skills, so your team can scan it quickly or even skip it entirely if you want to move directly into an outline of the system, which we present in Chapter 2.

We have dubbed the collection of approaches in this manual *STREAM Tools*, which stands for **S**cientific and **T**echnical w**R**iting, **E**diting, and file **M**anagement. In addition, we developed a "minimum subset" version of *STREAM Tools* to meet the needs of busy collaborators who do not have the time or desire to learn the entire system. The manual you are reading is the current embodiment of *STREAM Tools*, a system that continues to grow and evolve as more groups begin to use the system.

There are two options in learning *STREAM Tools*: one for experienced writers and the other for the beginners. Experienced writers already know how equations should look and why a figure caption should be on the same page as the figure itself. These experienced writers can learn the basics of *STREAM Tools* in a quick 30-minute overview and will then be ready to co-author manuscripts with their colleagues using the system. Chapter 2 presents the shortest possible introduction to *STREAM Tools* by providing the minimum set of instructions that ensure reasonable compatibility among multiple writers.

Newer authors, as well as more experienced authors with little experience in collaborative writing, should consider reading Chapter 3, which integrates the document management advice specific to Microsoft Word with a general tutorial for achieving consistent formatting in your documents. This chapter outlines how different elements of a manuscript—such as figures, tables, or equations—should be managed and why a particular way of managing the elements will produce effective documents. The list of the most typical mistakes made by previous generations of beginners is included. Finally, Chapter 3 contains a collection of advanced tips and tricks at the end of each section to help experienced authors work even more efficiently.

Chapter 4 addresses how collaborators can integrate bibliographic databases into their projects. As writing teams conduct their research and develop their projects, inevitably they construct a large database of sources. This chapter outlines a method both for compiling these databases and also general procedures for drawing on the database as the team constructs its documents.

Chapters 5, 6, and 7 take a step back from the "Quick Start" approach and offer more detailed guidance on issues confronting writing teams. Chapter 5 presents a system for planning, drafting, and editing documents, which, in a way, provides the container for the entire system of *STREAM Tools* outlined in this book. For example, Chapter 5 discusses important concerns such as analyzing audiences, organizing content and naming files, and annotating documents using electronic editing tools. Guidelines and checklists for each of these stages of collaboration accompany the discussion so that teams can be sure they are operating as efficiently as possible.

Chapter 6 presents a detailed discussion of what components are necessary for successful writing teams. Like Chapter 5, this chapter contains multiple subtopics such as understanding how teams work, how to manage the work of teams, and how to work successfully at a distance. While experienced collaborative authors will have had some experience with these principles, we encourage all readers to review this chapter since it explicitly articulates a series of approaches that most authors have only intuitively learned. Most importantly, this chapter outlines a series of questions and methods for managing teams to maximize their effectiveness, and each set of concerns is accompanied by checklists and guidelines that serve as a quick reference guide for busy teams.

Most writers will find Chapter 7 to be a good review of quality writing. This chapter presents some of the most common challenges faced by technical writing teams and gives examples of these challenges. This chapter addresses the mechanics of writing, such as constructing strong sentences, choosing the best words, and punctuating for clarity. While the content of this chapter might seem like adornment when compared to the "real" work of writing, efficient writing processes must attempt to get things right the first time to avoid rewriting (at best) or confusion among co-authors (at worst).

Chapter 8, the final chapter, presents a business case for using *STREAM Tools* and addresses "frequently asked questions." The chapter also includes some success stories about *STREAM Tools* that supplement the business case and demonstrate why the method can be so valuable for writing teams.

Our overarching purpose is to enable your team to begin writing quickly, efficiently, and with high quality, so we do not present extensive resources, references, and exercises throughout the book. Instead, we present many "take away documents" to help facilitate your process—checklists and guidelines that can be used separately from the book itself—as well as including a list of resources in most chapters so that interested readers can study these materials if they have time.

Finally, we invite you to visit the website that accompanies this book for additional information and to join the growing community of users already successfully collaborating using *STREAM Tools*. The central satellite website is streamtoolsonline.com. From there you can follow web links to additional websites.

ACKNOWLEDGMENTS

We would like to thank many individuals for their participation in various stages of this project. First, we would like to thank our families for their patience and understanding.

We would like to thank Professors David Farkas of the University of Washington and Kelli Cargile Cook of Texas Tech University for their constructive feedback at the early stages of this project, as well as Professors Kirk St. Amant and Mark Haselkorn for their assistance in working with the IEEE Professional Communications Society.

We also would like to thank our students, those who were among the first to try and then help refine various collaborative writing techniques described here, and those who helped us conceive of the content that appears throughout. In particular, we would like to thank Julia Arp, Jill Bunch, Sarah Hershman, Kathy Jeep, Amy Jessee, Bing Jiang, Nels Jewell-Larsen, Xiaobei Lee, Jessica Lisenby, Matthew Nelson, Chih-Hsu Peng, Gabriel Rowe, Pamela Saunders, Meagan Schuver, Kishore Sundara-Rajan, Amanda White, Brian Verhoeven, Min Wang, Kenneth Yuen, and Aaron Zielinski.

Our thanks also go to the IEEE Press staff: Cathy Faduska, senior acquisitions editor who helped formulate this project; Steve Welch, acquisitions editor who patiently worked with us as we defined our team and roles; and Jeanne Audino, project manager, who supervised the project through completion stages.

1

INTRODUCTION

In a given week, I probably only do about 15 minutes of real, actual work.
—Office Space (1999)

1.1 IN THIS CHAPTER

This chapter discusses the motivation behind the collaborative technical and scientific writing approach presented in this book. We touch upon the history and development of *STREAM Tools* and discuss common problems encountered by technical and scientific writers in order to set the stage for why *STREAM Tools* will help your team write better and more efficiently. In part, this introductory chapter should persuade you of the value that a structured, software-enabled approach to team writing brings to your projects. It should also enable those who already see the value of such an approach to best make a case for such a system to their collaborators.

Overall, this chapter is an elaborate expansion of the notion that as little time as possible should be spent dealing with the more mundane aspects of the writing process—such as formatting and redundant editing—in order to leave more time and resources for creativity and rigor in research and development.

If your team is ready to begin using *STREAM Tools* right away because you already believe in the value of standardizing your group's approach to writing or have experienced the challenges of collaborative authorship without such a system, then reading this chapter is probably unnecessary. Skip directly to Chapter 2 and begin there to initiate your writing project.

1.2   OUR AUDIENCE

Our audience includes scientists, engineers, technical managers, students, professors, grant writers, and administrative assistants—technical professionals who produce complex documents as part of their jobs, especially those who work and write in teams. In principle, any technical professional can utilize *STREAM Tools*, whether working alone or in a team, but since the majority of complex technical work occurs in teams, we emphasize the ways that *STREAM Tools* can help multiple collaborators streamline their writing activities.

Finally, all members of our audience share some characteristics regardless of their position, title, or specialization: they are busy professionals who demand excellence and efficiency and wish to maintain great relationships with their collaborators. *STREAM Tools* enable our audience to meet each of these objectives.

1.2.1   A Few Horror Stories

First, we would like to include several anecdotes about the challenges that led ***us*** to begin thinking about ways that we could improve our own collaborative writing. Some readers will readily identify with our stories and could quickly contribute their own similar accounts. Here are a few stories to set the stage:

Professor Mamishev, University of Washington:
We were submitting a large multi-university proposal to the National Science Foundation. The lead writer was at another institution. I sent my contributions to the proposal and was waiting for the compiled version of the manuscript to review. When the file finally arrived, I realized that some critical figures were taken out during the editing stage. Without these figures, the ideas were not communicated clearly. I wrote a new version, with the figures included and text shortened to keep the total length of this portion unchanged. Even though there were still many days left before the submission, the reply from the lead writer was adamant: "We have already numbered the figures, and at this point it would be too much work to change the structure of the manuscript." Needless to say, we did not get funded at that round.

Professor Mamishev:
Having almost had completed my Ph.D. dissertation at MIT, I had to tie up some loose ends in my graduate education. One of them was submitting a report to the foundation that had sponsored my dissertation research for one year. The requirements from the foundation were very clear, and the foundation officers were adamant—the report should be in Microsoft Word format. This would not have been a big deal, except that I wanted to adapt materials from my dissertation, which was written in LaTeX, a

typesetting system widely used at MIT. More than 700 pages of non-stop entertainment. That is, if you consider design of fringing electric field sensors entertainment. I did ... Anyway, I had to bite the bullet and sit in front of the computer screen for two days straight reformatting chapters, sections, figures, and equations, finally producing a document that looked pretty much exactly like a few chapters of my thesis—the content did not change at all. Two days of my life. I felt that they could have been better spent.

Professor Williams, Clemson University:

A few years ago, I was hired as an outside expert to help a large bank organize some of their internal documentation regarding a specific internal product. The team I led, composed of a group of subcontractors and a group from the bank, had a very short timeframe in which to deliver our project since the product was going to be rolled out to the entire company in three months. At that time, the subcontracted technical writers were located in three different states, the client was in another state, and I was in the fifth state—all of which made face-to-face collaboration nearly impossible. To complicate matters, the documents provided by the bank were in "old" word processing formats like Word Perfect; some were handwritten on paper; yet others were in PowerPoint, Microsoft Word, or Adobe PageMaker. Finally, the documents contained large numbers of figures and tables, all of which were numbered inconsistently at best. Combine the complexity of the documents we received with the multitude of formats, plus the challenges of working at distance and the pressures of completing the project under a tight deadline and you can imagine the stress the team felt as we squandered hours debating how we would produce the final document set and in what software package. Let's just say that the result of this chaos was that I have not been invited to bid on another project for this client.

Gabe Rowe, large semiconductor manufacturing firm:

I often write technical memos for the company I work for, but I am one of the few employees who use autonumbering for figures, tables, and cross-references, or who takes advantage of Styles and Formatting options. I am able to make a small change and quickly shoot out a new version of the memo while other people have to go through and manually update all of the references to figures. It's funny. These Microsoft Word shortcuts are old technology, but very few people know how to use them. It makes me think that there really should be more training on this kind of stuff.

Nels Jewell-Larsen, graduate student, University of Washington:

In my first year of graduate school, I only had to write short conference papers and simple reports, so there were no difficulties putting them together. Once I had to write a thesis, things suddenly changed. For several days, I was struggling with the document formatting, completely abandoning all other aspects of the project. There were so many figures, tables, and references to keep track of. At this point, I had no choice but to learn the document design principles used by more senior graduate students in our lab.

Kishore Sundara-Rajan, graduate student, University of Washington:

During my first year of graduate school, I was required to submit a literature search report for a class. I had written a five-page paper, and during one of the numerous revisions of the paper, I introduced new figures and citations in the middle of the text. This required that I renumber all of the following figures and references in the manuscript, and I was positive that I had managed to do that just fine. I was surprised when the professor gave me a low grade and returned the paper with a note that I hadn't entirely understood the field. It turned out that I had not changed a few citations and reference to the figures in the body of the text during the changes and as a result, that paper was incomprehensible. I could have saved myself a lot of time and pain had I adopted an auto-numbering system. Needless to say, once I began using the system, my 130-page master's thesis was a breeze to edit and revise.

These situations demonstrate why a system like *STREAM Tools* can be helpful. Yet, on the other hand, some might argue that their experiences with collaborative writing have been more positive and, in fact, we've had good experiences as well. But our purpose in telling these stories is to encourage people to look beyond their personal desktop. Perhaps everything is running smoothly in your office or with your specific team, but is it true for your organization? Perhaps you have mastered the tools of the writing trade, but your students or junior colleagues spend enormous amounts of time preparing their documents and therefore are not as productive as they could be. Maybe you do not worry about writing efficiency because your organization has administrative assistants who pick up the loose ends, but if you looked closely, perhaps the hidden costs are mounting up. In all, this book hopes to outline a process, *STREAM Tools*, that will be useful across your organization, to all those impacted by writing, so that everyone can work more successfully, regardless of their level.

1.2.2   Some History

Most technical writing guides are not tied to any particular software practices. They follow a sensible philosophy: "Here are your audience analysis paradigms, your composition principles, and your grammar rules and you can use your favorite software to put your ideas down on paper." In this book, we depart from those other guides and explicitly recommend that writing teams utilize Microsoft Word. We recommend Microsoft Word primarily for practical reasons: it is simply the easiest to use, the most widely available, and it has enough functionality to meet the needs of nearly every collaborative research team. Why struggle within your team to decide which software packages to use when others have already done it for you? We also recommend Microsoft Word because *STREAM Tools* uses a holistic approach in which considerations of grammar and style are closely linked to other aspects, such as editing, collaborative writing, document design, and document management; Microsoft Word enables each of these aspects with relative ease.

Even with these arguments, some of our more dedicated LaTeX users might require a bit more persuasion, so let's start with a brief history about the evolution of LaTeX and Microsoft Word and then attack a few myths.

Let's start with the 1980s. Early versions of Microsoft Word were running on computers that could not hold a large document in RAM. Writers could only work with small documents with limited graphics, and even then, the operating system crashed frequently and unpredictably. At that time, writers designed a document in a text file using an HTML-like language and then compiled it into a postscript file that would then output to a printer as formatted in the markup. At that time, "serious" academic writers chose LaTeX for their scholarly work and reserved Microsoft Word for letters, memos, short papers, and other ephemeral communications. As computers became more powerful and software companies eliminated bugs from mainstream typesetting packages, Microsoft Word started gaining ground with writers of large manuscripts.

At the same time, document management systems evolved from passing floppy disks among team members to sending emails, placing files on FTP servers, and using sophisticated collaborative environments like wikis or SharePoint. Today, all these methods coexist in some form (floppy disks have been replaced by USB flash drives). While the myriad of choices available for document management are not bad in themselves, it poses a serious challenge to collaborating groups. Incompatibility of writing processes and document design methods slows down manuscript production enormously.

Computerized offices have also led to the elimination of most secretaries and typists from the workforce. Two decades ago, technical professionals would rely on highly trained secretarial staff to ensure that their writing adhered to proper form. Typed manuscripts would be prepared for offset printing by yet another set of professionals, who possessed a detailed knowledge of fonts, margins, Greek letters, serifs, line widths, etc.—the multitude of details that make up a professional publication. Today, the burden of such knowledge rests squarely on the shoulders of technical and scientific professionals, as in most cases, the professional submits the manuscript directly to an audience without intervening document production experts.

1.3 THE NEED FOR A GOOD "WRITING SYSTEM"

Given the complexities presented by collaborative writing situations, adopting a good writing system will enable your team to work more efficiently and produce higher quality documents. In short, technical and scientific writing teams often struggle to produce their documents because they get wrapped up in debates about details—debates that greatly slow down document production, but in the end, have little impact on the document's final quality. Dozens of methods, tricks, and practices for streamlining the writing process evolve in different research groups as each team seeks to maximize the time they spend on their research and development activities. Each time a member joins a new project team, all of those "rules" must be relearned, slowing down the writing process. In addition, publishers, journal editors, and conference organizers develop sets of rules most suitable for their fields, adding further complications to the strategies that teams create. Adhering to the standards of a particular academic society is important. Your work will not be read—no matter how good it is—unless it meets the requirements of a publisher or a particular society. We'd wager that most teams would prefer to spend time on matters more profound than debating which software package to use or which set of conventions to follow. Unfortunately, in reality, many teams spend inordinate amounts of time on these very tasks they'd like to avoid.

Given the challenges faced by research groups, providing a standardized framework for approaching collaborative writing practices is quite important. For example, the same text and graphical information must often be adapted for research reports, conference papers, theses, proposals, presentations, and internal memos. Additionally, multiple authors, communicating electronically, might contribute to these documents, making an effective, well-organized writing system essential for creating a successful document.

Check any of these statements that apply to you:

— I spend excessive amounts of time formatting documents.

— I need to write a long manuscript (thesis, book) and I am finding it difficult to keep track of document structure and numbered items, such as figures, tables, and references.

— My boss (advisor, professor) is never happy with my writing.

— I spend excessive amounts of time editing documents written by my subordinates, and yet they never seem to improve.

— Just as soon as my subordinates (graduate students, grant writers) get adequate training, they leave for other jobs and the writing process haunts me again.

— Our collaborators use all kinds of word-processors—LaTex, Microsoft Word, Open Office, plain text, Google Docs, etc.—which makes it rather difficult to merge material from different contributors.

— Our group frequently misses manuscript (paper, report, proposal) submission deadlines.

— Our papers and proposals often get rejected due to low quality of writing, even though the content is quite good.

— Our institutional knowledge (group knowledge, tribal knowledge) gets lost because of high turnover of group members.

— We need an effective process to reuse our existing documents (legacy content).

No matter where you find yourself in your career, developing strategies to manage many of the problems noted above will help propel you to success. The techniques presented in this book will help you overcome the challenges previously noted and enable you to improve both the quantity and quality of the manuscripts generated within your organization. *STREAM Tools* will not only help you to manage your regular workload, but it may also help you advance in your career as those around you begin to see your success at managing complex writing projects.

1.4 INTRODUCING *STREAM TOOLS*

1.4.1 What is *STREAM Tools*?

STREAM Tools is a collection of best practices for use by scientific and technical writers. *STREAM Tools* also utilizes an integrated approach to collaborative writing in which specific software tools are integrated with writing quality and team interaction through a flexible collection of stand-alone modules that enable users to choose elements most relevant to their work. Although many *STREAM Tools* elements are valuable for individual writers, the system is most beneficial when every collaborator in a

STREAM Tools

	Writing Quality	Document Design	File Management
Focus	Style Grammar Content Adherence to standards	Time-effectivenes, especially with long documents Camera-ready output Making sure that writing quality is not hindered by typesetting issues	Re-use of legacy content Simultaneous content generation by multiple contributors
Methods	Coded feedback Continuous improvement Layered editing Checklists	Autonumbering of figures, tables, headings, etc. Paragraph style control Advanced equation editing Shared references databases	Network file-sharing Version management and naming conventions Workflow optimization
Software	Microsoft Word	Microsoft Word MathType EndNote or Reference Manager CorelDraw or Visio	Wiki Sharepoint Google Docs

Figure 1.1. Overview of *STREAM Tools*

team adopts it. With *STREAM Tools*, the whole is greater than the sum of the parts. Figure 1.1 shows the overall structure of *STREAM Tools*. The *STREAM Tools* system addresses three areas: Writing Quality, Document Design, and File Management. Within each area, writers are asked to go through an evaluative process, first determining the *focus* of their efforts, in other words, identifying the areas that need most improvement. After that, the writers learn the *methods* most applicable to addressing their specific areas of need. Finally, the writers select the *software* most suitable for the selected methods. Each writing group is unique and will benefit from a unique and custom-tailored combination of tools. *STREAM Tools* is meant to help with the process of choosing the best tools for each specific group.

1.4.2　Why Use *STREAM Tools*?

STREAM Tools enables your team to be more efficient, achieving maximum results with minimum effort. While developing *STREAM Tools*, we observed a number of organizations and found that writers waste a staggering amount of time on tasks that could be streamlined and automated.

Tables 1.1, 1.2, and 1.3 provide specific examples of problems encountered specifically by science and engineering authors and the solutions provided by *STREAM Tools*. While reading this book, you may choose to select the areas of your most pressing need and go directly to the sections indicated in the right column, or you could read the material consecutively and apply these principles to your work more generally. Either way, you will find that utilizing *STREAM Tools* can help free up your time to focus on things that matter.

While teams will ultimately produce manuscripts and push them out the door, the losses due to inefficient organizational practices far exceed the time spent overcoming the challenges listed in these tables. The inefficient practices shown in these tables can cause excellent ideas to be rejected, moved lower in priority in patent filings, or in extreme cases, people could lose their jobs. Conversely, continuous improvements in all areas of one's profession, including writing and publishing, gives individuals and organizations an advantage in a highly competitive world.

1.4.3　The Software of *STREAM Tools*

1.4.3.1　Recommended Packages. *STREAM Tools* integrates closely with specific software packages because these programs are both widely available and easy to use. Microsoft Word is necessary, of course, since the templates used by *STREAM*

TABLE 1.1. Writing Quality Problems

Problem	Solution	Sections	Page Numbers
Senior team members spend too much time correcting grammatical errors instead of focusing on core issues	Coded feedback notes with pointers to reading sections for improvement	2.3; 5.4.5.2	19, 122
"Learning grammar" is a daunting and overwhelming task	Focusing on the most critical areas for improvement hand-picked by an expert	2.3; 5.4.5.2	19, 122
Lack of adherence to organization (company, society) style	Planning and coordination stage among project participants	5.2; 5.3	87, 94
Writer's block	Using structured techniques for overcoming writer's block	5.3.5.1	107
Getting lost in the document complexity	Using template files with auto-numbering features Using Outline view Using color-coding for different types of text	2.4; 3.2; 5.3; 5.4	22, 36, 94, 116

TABLE 1.2. Document Design Problems

Problems	Solutions	Sections	Page Numbers
Difficult to keep track of numbered items Manual re-numbering wastes time	Automatic numbering of headings, equations, figures, tables, and literature citations	2.4, 3.2	22, 36
Conversion from single-column to double-column format	Conscientious use of styles throughout the manuscript	3.3.2	65
Conversion from single numbered equations, figures, and tables to dual-numbered equations, figures, and tables (e.g., Figure 8 becomes Figure 3.2) and vice-versa	Template captions and bookmarks that switch with on a quick selection of options	3.2.2.5	45
Typing complex mathematical equations	Using MathType	2.4.2.2	26
Mouse-free typing of equations	Learning MathType keyboard shortcuts	2.4.2.2, 3.2.2.5	45
Compatibility with TeX and LaTeX users	Entering coded output into TeX and LaTeX documents Generating equations in source LaTeX documents with MathType	3.2.2.5	45

TABLE 1.3. File Management Problems

Problems	Solutions	Sections	Page Numbers
One collaborator blocking others from working across the document	Real-time checking out of documents	5.4.1.3; 6.5	118, 152
Version leapfrogging	File naming conventions Document check-out	5.4.1.3; 6.5	118, 152
Effective use of legacy content	Creating annotated collections of manuscripts	5.4.1.1	116
Incompatible software	Using the same basic set of software tools Teaching everyone on the team basics of *STREAM Tools*	1.4.2; 1.4.3	8, 8
Providing timely feedback to members	Effective use of document-sharing systems	2.5.3; 5.4.5.2; 6.5	34, 122, 138
Circular editing	Layered editing	5.4; 5.5	116, 128

Tools are developed in that environment (for a complete discussion of why *STREAM Tools* uses Microsoft Word and not LaTeX, see section 1.4.3.2). However, writers frequently need equation, graphics, and bibliographic software as well, and since the purpose of *STREAM Tools* is to enable writing teams to get to work quickly and effectively, we recommend software below for each of these purposes.

STREAM Tools Commandment #1:
Team members should use compatible tools.

MathType is an enhanced version of the built-in Equation Editor in Microsoft Word. If you have many equations, it is worth switching to MathType, because it provides better graphics, more options, more streamlined keyboard shortcuts, and an ability to export equations in TeX/LaTeX, should you wish to maintain compatibility with these packages. The website is http://www.dessci.com/en/products/MathType/; a 30-day trial version is available.

CorelDraw is an excellent package for engineering drawings. It has an easy-to-use interface and outputs quality line art. If you do not have any organizational preference for your graphics software, use CorelDraw. The website is www.corel.com; a 30-day trial version is available.

Visio is another frequent choice for line art drawings. It is simpler than CorelDraw, but not as powerful. It is more frequently available in standard computer configurations. Both CorelDraw and Visio are adequate for users with very little experience in graphic design. The website is http://office.microsoft.com/en-us/visio/default.aspx; a 60-day trial version is available.

If, on the other hand, your organization has professional graphics specialists, then you are likely to have various 3D (three-dimensional) CAD (computer-assisted design) packages, Adobe Illustrator, or other programs used by professional graphic designers. These are fine packages, but are less useful to everyone on the writing team, due to the steep learning curve that comes with using them.

An example of the other extreme of graphics packages is the Windows application Paint. While extremely simple to use, it only produces bitmap output, and is not really suitable for formal scientific and engineering documents, such as journal papers or patents.

EndNote is the leading database software for searching and managing literature citations. EndNote allows for quick online searches and subsequent storage of massive numbers of references. With some extra effort, a research group can create and maintain one common database in a particular field of interest, to be used by all members of the group.

EndNote provides essentially the same functions as **Reference Manager**. Just like with the metric and British systems, there is overhead in maintaining compatibility between the two equivalent products. However, since groups of researchers have adopted both technologies, they will probably coexist for the foreseeable future. It would be wise to check whether your potential collaborators are already using one of the two packages. The website for both packages is www.refman.com.

1.4.3.2 A Brief Comparison of Microsoft Word vs. LaTeX: History and Myths.
The choice of a document design system is a huge decision for any organization. In light of the struggle writers face over which software to pick as they compose their documents, we offer some commentary in this section on the advantages and disadvantages of both Microsoft Word and LaTeX. Our goal is to demonstrate not just

the differences, but also to show why using Microsoft Word will make your writing team more efficient and effective.

Two fundamentally different systems dominate the market for producing research and technical documents: Microsoft Word and LaTeX (or TeX for the most proficient users). Microsoft Word is based on the principle of "What You See Is What You Get" (WYSIWYG); that is, the writer can immediately see where on each page the text, figures, equations, etc., that he or she adds will appear. One can start using Microsoft Word within seconds as it requires little start-up time; most computer users have now become familiar with Microsoft Word due to its overwhelming dominance of the general word processing market.

LaTeX, on the other hand, requires entering the text and the references to all graphical elements into a coded text file, which then is compiled into a final document. The principles of LaTeX are quite close to those of HTML, where the presentation of content and the content itself are separate. The software handles the pagination, spacing, margins, orphan control, figure placement, and many other small details, and so the document looks professional even when prepared by a novice. In addition, LaTeX is greatly suited for writing large manuscripts. Even a thousand-page book full of graphics can be compiled with LaTeX using very modest hardware.

The downside is that many people are not familiar with LaTeX and it is difficult for people to learn the software. In collaborative groups where members belong to different organizations, or in large research groups where members have diverse backgrounds, it is nearly impossible to get everyone to learn LaTeX. Besides, the team's time is best spent on research and innovation, not learning software packages. Because LaTeX has a steep learning curve and because many people simply don't have time to learn yet another software package, *STREAM Tools* employs Microsoft Word as the foundation for collaboration. The methods described in this book rely only on Microsoft Word. You simply cannot get a typical nontechnical person started on LaTeX in 30 minutes, whereas it is entirely feasible to get a typical nontechnical person started on *STREAM Tools* in 30 minutes.

Given this general background, let's examine various issues surrounding the use of Microsoft Word and LaTeX in some detail. First of all, the compatibility between the two systems leaves much to be desired. Although there are software converters that take a Microsoft Word file as an input and then output a LaTeX-compatible file (and vice versa), the formatting of complex documents is not well preserved in the conversion steps. Much like a computer translation from a foreign language, extensive human corrections are necessary in order to guarantee the quality of the final result.

A second issue is that different fields use different tools, and since most research teams now span disciplines, deciding on a single authoring tool becomes critical. For example, in business, law, medicine, and most professional communication, Microsoft Word unquestionably dominates. However, LaTeX is the frequent choice in certain fields of hard sciences, like mathematics, physics, or engineering. Professionals in these fields are comfortable with the technical complexity associated with the text file that looks like a computer program and, more importantly, scientists and engineers frequently need to manipulate large quantities of equations and graphics.

As long these two groups do not need to collaborate, there is no problem. However, most complex research and innovation now requires interdisciplinary teams. For example, a sizeable biomedical instrumentation research project may require input from medical doctors, engineers, statisticians, lawyers, technical writers, and even patients. It is just not realistic to expect all these participants to give up their expectations of WYSIWYG convenience and instead learn to compile their documents using a rather complex set of rules.

In spite of the practical concerns associated with forcing team members to learn LaTeX, one commonly encounters the opinion in many academic settings that LaTeX solves all typesetting problems; some aficionados will not step away from it under any pressure. A fraction of people who hold this position are justified in their view because, indeed, they stand to lose too much by this conversion. For example, a tightly knit team composed of a professor and three graduate students who publish only in specialized journals indeed might be better off with LaTeX. However, in most cases, the decision to use multiple incompatible packages in the same collaborative group is driven by habit rather than a judicious choice: the team leaders choose the system based on tradition, personal preference, local user knowledge, or institutional support rather than what will produce the highest quality product most effectively.

To demonstrate why some authors might prefer LaTeX, and then to demonstrate why we encourage using Microsoft Word, let's examine some of the advantages of each package and then debunk a few myths that arise from the differences.

The Advantages of LaTeX over Microsoft Word
- LaTeX enforces proper typesetting, especially for inexperienced writers. The math symbols are italicized, equations are numbered, and figures are properly captioned because the templates take care of it. By contrast, inexperienced Microsoft Word users have plenty of opportunities to divert from proper typesetting options.
- LaTeX is stable. It does not crash much and has low machine memory requirements. Microsoft Word, especially with large documents, requires both memory and speed.
- LaTeX software packages are forward and backward compatible. LaTeX manuscripts written in 1988 compile in 2008 with few or no problems. In previous years, backward compatibility of Microsoft Word was especially problematic and numerous issues still arise today.
- Automatic figure positioning is far more efficient in LaTeX than in Microsoft Word.

In short, LaTeX does provide some advantages over Microsoft Word, particularly for very long and very complex technical documents. However, Microsoft Word also has advantages.

The Advantages of Microsoft Word over LaTeX
- Microsoft Word is ubiquitous. In most cases, co-writing with groups from different companies or across industry and academia is a lot easier with Microsoft Word than with LaTeX.

- Such features as spell check, grammar check, WYSIWYG, track changes, word count, line numbering, and the manuscript marking system are more powerful and convenient with Microsoft Word.
- Microsoft Word is easier to use for novices.
- Microsoft Word now has many handy multi-authoring tools built in.
- Reuse of figures and text is easier when using Microsoft Word and PowerPoint together (as opposed to LaTeX and PowerPoint).

Naturally, experienced writers tend to prefer one package or the other. Often, these opinions are a result of not being adequately informed about software capabilities. The following section examines some common misconceptions.

Myth: Only LaTeX should be used for scientific writing. Microsoft Word just does not have proper tools to manipulate figures, form equations, etc.

Reality: This might be true for highly specialized areas of mathematics. For most engineering and science disciplines, however, Microsoft Word is adequate, as long as it is used effectively.

Myth: LaTeX is good for writing long manuscripts, whereas Microsoft Word is good for memos and short papers.

Reality: This used to be true when computers crashed frequently and had slow processors. In the last few years, however, creating manuscripts of several hundred pages, filled with figures and equations, became feasible and easily manageable with Microsoft Word.

Myth: In LaTeX, one can write equations without leaving the keyboard, whereas in Microsoft Word, one needs to use the mouse all the time.

Reality: This is not quite true. A handy add-on to Microsoft Word, MathType, provides keyboard shortcuts that allow writing equations with only the keyboard. However, since an option of using the mouse is available, many people never invest their time into learning keyboard shortcuts.

All things considered, we contend that Microsoft Word can now be used in the majority of collaborative writing projects in technical settings because it now has nearly the same capabilities as LaTeX. Most importantly, for getting the team collaborating right away, Microsoft Word requires little training time because it is so ubiquitous. Since a primary goal of this book is to provide tips and techniques for those who want to be efficient and effective in their collaborative work, we focus strictly on how to use Microsoft Word for team collaborations as the core of *STREAM Tools*.

1.5 HOW TO USE THIS BOOK

This book is written primarily for technical professionals who need to create complex documents on a regular basis. The techniques presented here allow technical writers to focus on developing superior content and meeting the needs of their audiences rather than inventing collaboration strategies or spending extraordinary time formatting documents. The benefits of this streamlined approach to group writing permeate all levels of the organization, saving time, facilitating effective communication, and improving work quality.

Let us have a look at how different groups of readers will benefit from adopting *STREAM Tools*.

If you are an *undergraduate student or novice employee*, you have a lot to learn. Start by experimenting with the Quick Start guide in Chapter 2; get a feel for it. As your writing tasks become increasingly complex, go through material in Chapters 3 and 4, selecting elements of interest from the book's table of contents. As you become more experienced and want to understand how to create more powerful documents, study Chapter 5 to learn about the full system and Chapter 6 to learn about successful collaboration in writing teams. Finally, to refine your writing style and grammar, peruse Chapter 7 initially, and then find a mentor who can identify your writing weaknesses. Return to each chapter's material based on your mentor's feedback, internalizing material in small chunks.

If you are a *graduate student*, a *postdoctoral researcher, bench scientist/engineer*, or the *technical writer on a product team*, you can follow the same pattern as an undergraduate student, except that you may be able to do so with much less guidance. You are likely to be the catalyst for implementing *STREAM Tools* in your organization—undergraduates and novice writers do not yet have to write long and complex formal documents, and executive advisors with many responsibilities tend to be less occupied with this kind of work on a daily basis. So, if you are in this group, we recommend beginning with Chapters 2, 3, and 4 but paying close attention to Chapters 5 and 6 because these chapters are more strategic than the "Quick Start" chapters and position you well to become a manager or group leader.

If you are a *professor* or a *leader of a technical group*, you stand to benefit from adopting the system perhaps more than anyone else. By adopting *STREAM Tools*, you will be able to process material received from peers and subordinates more effectively, thus producing better papers, proposals, books, and reports. You will also save tremendous amounts of time for yourself by coding and properly directing your feedback during manuscript editing stages. You will be able to avoid excessive coaching on mundane and trivial aspects of professional writing, focusing on content instead of form. You should thoughtfully read Chapter 1 in order to judge the importance of *STREAM Tools* for your group, master Chapter 2, and assign someone in your organization to master the techniques covered in Chapters 3 and 4. You should be aware of the overall process outlined in Chapter 5 as well as the importance of collaboration, as outlined in Chapter 6. Each of these chapters presents concerns that are your responsibility as you ensure the quality not just of the project, but also of the relationships among employees. Finally, become aware of the material presented in Chapter 7, so that you can effectively use the *STREAM Tools* Editorial Mark-up Table (STEM Table).

If you are an *administrative assistant* in charge of composing documents or a *professional grant writer* who uses material from multiple sources, then you should be

TABLE 1.4. Classification of Writers with Respect to *STREAM Tools*

Category	Description
Novice	An inexperienced team member. Does not know how to use *STREAM Tools*, has weaknesses in many areas of technical writing.
Outsider	An expert in his or her field, sometimes the most experienced member of the team; however, not familiar with *STREAM Tools* and therefore has difficulty integrating with the group writing efficiently.
User	User can use *STREAM Tools* methods and templates with some guidance from more experienced team members. User knows what to do and follows the established procedures.
Expert	Expert can teach (and convince) collaborators to use *STREAM Tools* for the benefit of the group. Expert, unlike User, knows not only what to do, but also what NOT to do when using *STREAM Tools*. In other words, an Expert has enough experience to be able to judge which options and techniques will work best for his or her organization.
Wizard	Wizard has a deep understanding of *STREAM Tools* principles and software methods that enables him or her to create new templates and modify basic techniques to meet the needs of his or her organization.

most interested in Chapters 2 through 5, which will enable you to streamline the process of compiling complex documents with input from many parties.

If you are a *course instructor,* you should be able to use this book either as a core text or as a supplement, depending on your audience. Professional audiences may have much less interest in basic grammar discussions and may want to get immediately to the heart of *STREAM Tools*. College students, on the other hand, will benefit from rigorous treatment of traditional technical writing material, and are likely to enjoy *STREAM Tools* as an integral element of group course assignments.

With respect to *STREAM Tools*, we could broadly organize writers into five categories: Novices, Outsiders, Users, Experts, and Wizards, as seen in Table 1.4.

From the perspective of maximizing productivity, most members of a collaborating group should be either Users or Experts, while a small number of Wizards can take care of advanced issues, such as making new templates for everyone to use. In many cases, it may be advisable for an organization to invite an outside Wizard in to streamline a specific process. After that, operations should run smoothly as long as there is at least one Expert in the organization. There should also be a quick and painless process for training Outsiders to the level of Users.

Invariably, the deployment of open-ended systems like *STREAM Tools* leads to unexpected implementations, and so we cannot predict all possible uses of the proposed tools and techniques. However, it is our hope that each reader will take the suggestions we present as a foundation to build upon and expand, developing systems that will help you meet your organization's needs.

EXERCISES

Exercise 1.1. Conduct a critical review of your writing practices. Respond to the following questions:

(A) Do you practice productive and sustainable writing habits? These include knowing your own preferred writing process, writing early and often, and knowing when and where to seek help with your writing or revisions.

(B) What fraction of total writing time do you spend on routine tasks, such as manual numbering and formatting, editing trivial grammatical errors, or converting text from old documents to new ones?

(C) What fraction of your time goes into actual writing—the generation of new text?

(D) How much time do you spend procrastinating or dealing with writer's block?

Exercise 1.2. Conduct informal interviews with your colleagues. Identify their answers to the questions in the previous exercise.

Exercise 1.3. Conduct an informal meeting with your colleagues (co-workers, classmates). Do they have any "horror stories" to share from their own writing experiences? Do you think these stories could have been avoided with proper planning and use of tools?

Exercise 1.4. Review Figure 1.1 either individually or as a group. Based on the problems you identified in previous exercises in this chapter, determine critical focus areas for your writing challenges. Keep this list for the future, so that you can decide whether different tools that you plan to learn are applicable to you.

Note: This exercise is especially valuable for the group. An individual may intuitively decide whether or not a specific tool is useful to him or her, but as a group member, you may simply not be aware of the scope and scale of problems your group members are facing. Therefore, taking time to assess the overall distribution of skills and habits among group members helps tremendously. You may discover in group discussions that some of the problems may be solved with quick fixes using shared knowledge of team members, and yet other problems will require a systematic approach and substantial efforts.

QUICK START GUIDE FOR
STREAM TOOLS

Colette: No. Follow the recipe.
Linguini: But you just said that ...
Colette: [interrupts] No, no, no, no. It was his job to be unexpected. It is our job
to follow the recipe.

—Ratatouille (2007)

2.1 IN THIS CHAPTER

Consider this chapter to be "*STREAM Tools* 101." Essentially, this chapter provides a basic overview of the practices that are necessary for a novice to begin interacting productively with other users of *STREAM Tools*. The primary intent of this chapter, then, is to provide introductory instruction for novices to quickly grasp the *STREAM Tools* method and therefore begin collaborating immediately with more experienced colleagues.

Since this chapter is a quick start guide for new *STREAM Tools* users, we do not expect your team to read it sequentially. We have organized this chapter into modules,

Technical Writing for Teams: The STREAM Tools Handbook, by Alexander Mamishev and Sean Williams
Copyright © 2010 Institute of Electrical and Electronics Engineers

so that you can read each section as a stand-alone unit that outlines a particular component of *STREAM Tools*. Depending upon which component you or your team leader feels is most important to learn immediately, you can begin with that section.

Following a general overview of the writing process, this chapter's modules—or sections—parallel the introduction to *STREAM Tools* presented in the previous chapter.

> ***To learn:*** the most crucial element of the writing quality tools, particularly the table that will enable your team to begin immediately editing and providing quality feedback on versions of your documents,
>
> ***Skip to:*** *Section 2.3. Introduction to Writing Quality Tools: The STREAM Tools Editorial Mark-up Table.*

> ***To learn:*** the process for using templates, autotext, and cross-referencing to design elements in documents including headings, equations, figures, and tables,
>
> ***Skip to:*** *Section 2.4. Introduction to Document Design Tools.* Learning these tools will ensure that your team can produce consistently formatted documents with minimum effort.

> ***To learn:*** the methods for ensuring that team members work on the most current versions of documents, do not "leap frog" content, and always have access to the content they need,
>
> ***Skip to:*** *Section 2.5. Introduction to File Management: Optimizing Your Workflow.*

Since this chapter is a "Quick Start Guide," it omits all discussions of why things are done a certain way, any possible exceptions, and all possible differences in writing styles among disciplines and individuals. If you have a good reason to depart from the techniques suggested in this chapter, you can do so, as long as you understand the effect of your deviations and coordinate with your co-authors. In general, though, we recommend sticking with the systems outlined in this chapter until you become closely familiar with *STREAM Tools*.

2.2   A GENERAL OVERVIEW OF THE WRITING PROCESS

STREAM Tools represents a systematic way of moving through the writing process that ensures quality content and attractive documents by employing efficient processes. In order for *STREAM Tools* to be the most effective for your team, it helps to understand a bit about the writing process as a whole. *STREAM Tools* seeks to enable and automate parts of the writing process, but it does not substitute for the process itself, which generally follows the stages below:

1. ***The Definition Stage.*** This stage marks the beginning of the document creation process where the team outlines initial plans for the project. This stage includes, for example, holding a kick-off meeting to analyze the audience, formulating the purpose, and selecting the right combination of *STREAM Tools*. The *STREAM Tools* components dedicated to this activity are fully articulated in Section 5.2.

2. ***The Preparation Stage.*** This stage marks the initial developments and skeleton of a document and assigns responsibility for actual writing. This stage includes, for example, evaluating historical documents, creating a file repository, drafting an outline of the document, and assigning writing tasks to the team members. The *STREAM Tools* components dedicated to this activity are fully articulated in Section 5.3.

3. ***The Writing Stage.*** This stage marks the team's actual writing work as they draft sections, combine them, and revise. This stage includes, for example, entering legacy content, requesting that team members submit staged drafts, verifying that the document is moving in the right direction, compiling the whole document, and revising for content. The *STREAM Tools* components dedicated to this activity are fully articulated in Section 5.4.

4. ***The Completion Stage.*** This stage marks the end of the writing process where the team confirms that it has met the goals outlined in the early stages of the process and then submits the final document. This stage includes, for example, copyediting, soliciting external reviews, final submission, and analyzing the whole document development process. The *STREAM Tools* components dedicated to this activity are fully articulated in Section 5.5.

There are, of course, entire books published on the writing process and effectively moving through its stages. Different components of *STREAM Tools* facilitate the writing process, but these tools do not replace the well-designed writing process that skilled writers employ. *STREAM Tools* simply helps those writers do their work better.

2.3 INTRODUCTION TO WRITING QUALITY TOOLS: THE *STREAM TOOLS* EDITORIAL MARK-UP TABLE

Producing writing in multiple passes, where you cycle back through your work over and over again, constantly revising and improving—creating what are called "iterations" of a text—is essential for producing quality writing. If adopting an iterative approach is a key for individual writing, then employing an iterative strategy for group writing is absolutely necessary. Do not try to write the perfect document on the first attempt, and do not try to make all corrections after the first pass. Assuming your team can do either one of these things will produce frustration at best and poor documents and hard feelings at worst.

Therefore, we recommend that you sequence your editing tasks:

1. Read for content, while leaving a few occasional comments, like "c:\glob," in the initial paragraphs (the "c:\glob" mark and other basic editing comments from the *STREAM Tools* Editorial Mark-up Table appear in Table 2.1).

2. Shift from content to form, starting to address such issues as grammar, style, or appearance, leaving comments such as c:\casual.

3. Prepare your document for final distribution by carefully proofreading after your team has dealt with other editing issues.

TABLE 2.1. The Essential *STREAM Tools* Editorial Mark-up Table (STEM Table)

Comment	Abbreviation Deciphered	Meaning	Section in This Book	Page Numbers
c:	Comment	This is not a replacement text but rather a comment.	Self-explanatory	88
c: \AA	Analyze the audience	The document does not address the right audience.	5.2.3	22
c:\auto	Autonumbering	Implement autonumbering features.	2.4	162, 168, 170
c:\awk	Awkward	Sentence is awkward. Possibly word sequence, word selection, or sentence structure need to be changed.	7.2; 7.3; 7.4	162
c: \casual	Casual wording	The wording is too casual. People may talk like that, but this wording is not suitable for formal writing.	7.2	162, 85
c:\colloq	Colloquial	A colloquial expression. People talk like that, but they do not write like that	7.2; Chapter 5	107, 161
c:\EOI	End of iteration	The manuscript contains too many errors or, perhaps, the editor ran out of time. The editor stopped at the EOI point and expects the writer to learn from previous mistakes, apply them to the entire body of the manuscript, and bring it back for the next iteration.	5.3.5.1; Chapter 7	
c:\glob	Global change	A request to correct this type of a problem throughout the document. This comment is to be used in combination with other comments, when the same type of mistake occurs multiple times and the editor does not want to correct it every time.	Self-explanatory	
c:\gram	Grammatical error	A catch-all comment for grammatical errors.	Chapter 7	161
c:\model	Model document	Do you have a good model document after which current manuscript is structured?	5.3.1	95

TABLE 2.1. *Continued*

Comment	Abbreviation Deciphered	Meaning	Section in This Book	Page Numbers
c: \purp	Purpose	The purpose of this part of the document is not clear. Should it be persuasion, exposition, or instruction?	5.2.4	92
c: \pw	Poor wording	The sentence is poorly worded.	7.2	162
c: \pwt	Problems with terminology	Poor selection of terminology, could be confusing, misleading, or just plain incorrect	7.2.2.5	167
c: \rep	Repetition	Repetitive use of the same word or root	Self-explanatory	
c: \sp	Spelling	Incorrect spelling	Self-explanatory	
c:\struc	Structure	The document lacks proper structure.	5.3.3	101
c:\STH x.x	Writing for Research Teams	Read section x.x (for example, section 5.2) from this book, *Technical Writing for Teams: The STREAM Tools Handbook.*	Self-explanatory	
Written with a pencil	Regular comment	Changes can be made without a discussion.	Self-explanatory	
Written with a red pen	Talk to the reviewer about it	Usually, a complex subject nature that Requires a discussion	Self-explanatory	

These recommendations represent only the most elemental steps in the process of ensuring writing quality. The full discussion of ensuring writing quality tools appears in Chapter 5, and the editing process in particular appears in sections 5.4 and 5.5.

One key feature of *STREAM Tools* is what we call the *STREAM Tools* Editorial Mark-up Table, or *STEM* Table. The STEM Table is a great time saver. For a writing team just becoming familiar with the system, the STEM Table enables reviewers to provide quality feedback in a short amount of time while informing novice writers of exactly which topics they need to improve. The STEM Table also enables reviewers to provide consistent feedback because this tool utilizes a series of standardized marks as shorthand for common problems found in collaborative documents. In short, the STEM Table directs writers to problems in the manuscript, sometimes offering correction suggestions but more frequently identifying problems that the writers can then repair.

STREAM Tools Commandment #2:
Your boss is not your English teacher.

In Table 2.1, we present the basic version of the STEM Table, which includes the most frequent and useful entries. Granted, for a while, your team will have to refer to the symbols in the table until they immediately recognize the shorthand. However, once your team develops skill with using these symbols as they move through the editing process, your team will produce iterations of documents both more rapidly and with higher quality.

The STEM Table has two major purposes: to present those who review manuscripts with a set of shorthand comments that will speed up their feedback, and to present the writers of manuscripts with a resource that explains the comments on their writing. While we were in school—and English classes in particular—our instructors provided complex feedback in the margins or at the end of documents. However, in workplace writing, reviewers seldom have the time to provide extensive explanations for their commentary and, really, teaching is not the primary purpose of the feedback. When we review in workplace contexts, the main purpose is to improve the document, not necessarily the writer. The STEM Table enables both of these purposes to coexist—teaching and improving documents—because the commenting codes point out significant problems in a text *and* refer writers to an explanation of that commentary.

The commenting codes also cover a variety of concerns not addressed in standard notation symbols and these extend the opportunity for improving the document and coaching writers. For example, in standard editorial mark-up, no symbol exists for "Analyze the Audience", even though this particular concern represents one of the most significant potential issues with a document's effectiveness. Within the *STREAM Tools* Editorial Mark-up table, though, this and other significant issues carry a commenting code that reviewers can note quickly and that points writers to the part of this book that further explains that concept. In comparison to standard editorial text *or* standard instructional feedback, the STEM Table enables both quick review *and* coaching, improving on other types of editorial feedback in the workplace.

2.4 INTRODUCTION TO DOCUMENT DESIGN TOOLS

The document design components of *STREAM Tools* evolved from a consistent set of concepts. Each of these concepts, discussed in Section 2.4.1, enables writers to create document design elements such as headings, equations, figures, and tables. Each of these concepts reappears in the individual Quick Start instructions for creating elements in a document that begin in Section 2.4.2.1. Some readers might find it most useful to skip right to those instructions that begin in Section 2.4.2.1, but others might find it helpful to see the big picture first, which we present in Section 2.4.1. These instructions are written for Microsoft Word 2007. Other versions of Microsoft Word are very similar in their functionality, but the path to the menu selection buttons may be slightly different.

2.4.1 Important Fundamental Concepts

STREAM Tools typesetting rules, in their barebones form, can be reduced to four fundamental concepts or practices:

1. *Step 1.* Use template files to create your new manuscripts.
2. *Step 2.* Copy existing elements—headings, equations, figures, tables, and references—and paste the copy into a new location in the document to create a new element that maintains automatic numbering.
3. *Step 3.* Edit the element.
4. *Step 4.* Cross-reference elements, especially equations, figures, tables, and references to ensure they update automatically.

These practices apply across the entire system, regardless of the particular type of document or place in the document, and so they are worth explaining in a bit more detail. With just these fundamentals, you can begin experimenting with *STREAM Tools*.

2.4.1.1 *Step 1: Use Template Files to Create Your New Manuscripts.* If you plan to write a complex document, we highly recommended that you use a template file as the starting point rather than beginning with a blank document. A template file already has the settings and tools necessary for the time efficient development of a manuscript, which means that your team will not need to recreate formatting items such as heading styles. *STREAM Tools* employs three basic template files that are available at the project's website, streamtoolsonline.com, and other template files can be derived from the basic ones.

STREAM Tools Commandment #3:
Use document templates.

Review Table 2.2, "Templates Available for *STREAM Tools*," to determine which template is appropriate for your situation, then download the template most appropriate for your project and begin using it to create your new document.

By altering these basic templates, writers can create new, derived templates that not only possess all the qualities of a *STREAM Tools* template but also meet the requirements of a specific publisher or agency. Chapter 3 discusses this option in detail and provides examples.

2.4.1.2 *Step 2: Copy Existing Elements and Paste Them into a New Location.* It might seem strange to copy an existing element such as a heading, equation, or figure to create a new one, but fortunately, the *STREAM Tools* templates make

TABLE 2.2. Templates Available for *STREAM Tools*

Filename	Description
BasicTemplateSingleColumn.doc	A single-column template for short reports and papers, typically up to 20 or 30 pages.
BasicTemplateDoubleColumn.doc	A double-column template for camera-ready double-column papers, typically up to 10 pages.
BasicThesisOrBookTemplate.doc	A single-column template for long manuscripts, such as theses, books, or long reports. Main differences from the other two templates are: — Chapter number is included in the numbers of figures, tables, and equations (e.g., *Figure3.5* rather than *Figure 15*). — Templates for the front matter (preface, table of contents, etc.) and the back matter (appendices, index, etc.) are included.

it very easy to create a new element from an existing one. If you copy existing elements and then paste the copy into a new location, this maintains the "auto-numbering" of the element so that every time somebody adds an element such as a new heading, the entire document automatically updates all the numbers of each element.

> **STREAM Tools Commandment #4:**
> Use automatic formatting features.

Procedurally it looks like this:

1. Copy and paste the existing element to a new location (e.g., copy an existing figure and its caption, then paste the copy into a new location in the document).
2. Type new text into the placeholder copy (e.g., type in the new caption for a figure. *NOTE: Do NOT type over the automatic caption number*).
3. Press **Ctrl-A and then F9** to update the numbering (e.g., the numbering of figure captions).

You should notice that the number attached to your element has now been updated to reflect its sequence in the document. For example, if you copy Figure 1.1 into Chapter 3 of your document, and the new figure is the second figure in that chapter, it will now be numbered Figure 3.2.

2.4.1.3 Step 3: Edit the Element. The last stage of the general process is actually editing the elements. Recall that to create new elements, you copy a prior instance and then paste that copy into a new location in the document. This process leaves you with a duplicate of a prior element so the new element still needs to be edited.

Consider a heading, for example, which is the easiest element to create and alter. If you wanted to insert a "Step 4" heading, you would copy the "Step 3" heading above, and then paste the copy somewhere later. That would give you the new heading of "2.4.1.4 Step 3: Edit the element." Notice that the number of the heading has updated but the text has not. Therefore, you select the text of the heading, add some text like "Step 4: New Step" and then update the entire document by pressing **Ctrl-A and then F9.**

Conceptually, all elements work the same way: you copy an instance, paste it into a new location, and then edit that particular instance. Obviously, editing tables and figures will be more complicated because each of these has additional steps for ensuring the quality of the table or figure itself, but in principle, the process remains exactly the same: **copy** → **paste** → **edit** → **update.**

2.4.1.4 Step 4: Cross-Referencing Elements.
The final step in the process is to ensure that the numbering attached to elements updates automatically by adding cross-references. Imagine cross-referencing as asking Microsoft Word to remember that a particular element, like a figure's caption and number, is attached to a particular piece of text in the body. In other words, when you cross-reference the title and number of a figure with a reference to the figure in the body of the manuscript, Microsoft Word reads both references as one unit. When one changes, the items linked to the one you changed will update as well. For example, we could insert a cross-reference here and it would look identical to the heading text above: "Step 4: Cross-Referencing Elements."

And if, for some reason, the title of the heading changed to something like "Step 4: Linking Elements," the in-text reference would change to read exactly the same way—automatically when you update the document by pressing **Ctrl-A and then F9.** If this sounds a bit confusing, don't worry. In Section 2.4, we discuss the process for adding cross-references to elements (as well as the other steps in the process) and once you've done it once, you'll see how simple this is—and how much time it will save you! Now the complete process looks like this: **copy** → **paste** → **edit** → **update** → **cross-reference**.

2.4.2 Creating Elements in a Document

So far we have outlined the general concepts and processes used for *STREAM Tools*. In this section, we'd like to put you to work actually creating elements in a document. Each of the sections below describes the complete process for each of a document's major elements, moving from **copying** an old element, **pasting** it at new location, **editing** the element, **updating** the document to reflect new element numbering, and finally adding **cross-references** to the element as they are needed.

Note: Occasionally, formatting is not successful when you update your document after following steps 1–4. If this happens, try turning on Microsoft Word's "Formatting" view by clicking the paragraph symbol: ¶. This view uncovers hidden formatting commands in Microsoft Word. From this view, confirm that you have selected all appropriate formatting elements, including those just before and just after the element you copied.

2.4.2.1 Headings

To create a new heading element:
1. Copy an existing heading, *including* the line before the heading (otherwise you would be copying only the text, but not the style for this line).
2. Paste the heading at the new desired location.

To edit a new heading:
1. Replace the heading text as desired, but do not touch the heading number.

To cross-reference a heading:
1. Identify a place in the text where you'd like to refer to the heading.
2. Click **Insert → Cross-Reference**.
3. Select **Heading** in the *Reference Type* dialogue box.
4. Choose **Heading Number** Under **Insert Reference To**.
5. Uncheck **Insert as Hyperlink** and uncheck **Include above/below**.
6. Click **Insert**.

Now you'll see the heading number in the text where you placed your cursor in Step 1. Depending upon which type of reference suits your text best, you might also choose to include a cross-reference to the text of the heading as well. In this case, simply repeat the process above and then select **Heading Text** in the **Insert Reference To** box. To update your text, press **Ctrl-A** to select the entire text and then press **F9** to complete the update.

Note: The path within the menu differs slightly in different versions of Microsoft Word. This manuscript does not attempt to list minor differences in Microsoft Word menus. For example:
   Microsoft Word 2003 sequence: **Insert → Reference → Cross-Reference → Heading;**
   Microsoft Word 2007 sequence: **Insert → Cross-Reference → Heading.**

2.4.2.2 Equations

To create a new equation element:
1. Copy the entire line of the equation template.
2. Paste it to the new location.

To edit a new equation:
1. Double-click on the equation itself to edit it.
2. To cross-reference an equation, you must first create a bookmark.

Often, the equation editor in Microsoft Word will be inadequate to edit your equations; if this is the case, then we recommend using MathType as your equation editor. This more complicated process is described in Chapter 3.

To cross-reference an equation:
Creating a cross-reference for a new equation actually requires two separate stages. First, you have to create a bookmark for the equation, basically giving it a unique name and identifier. Then, you insert the cross reference to that bookmark (the unique identifier).

Stage 1: Create a bookmark:
1. Select the equation number on the right in the equation line.
2. Click **Insert → Bookmark.**
3. Give this bookmark a short descriptive name that starts with "eq," for example, eqNewtonsFirstLaw.

Stage 2: Cross-reference the equation using the bookmark:
1. Click **Insert → Cross-Reference**.
2. Under **Reference Type** click **Bookmark.**
3. Uncheck **Insert as Hyperlink**, unless you have a strong reason to have a hyperlink in your document.
4. Under **Insert Reference To** click **Bookmark Text**.
5. Pick the desired bookmark from the list and click **Insert**.

To update the equation press **Ctrl-A** and then **F9** and be sure to save your document as well.

2.4.2.3 Figures. In Microsoft Word, a figure graphic or picture is a separate object from a figure caption. The automatic numbering applies to captions, and the graphics are just objects that happen to be next to captions. Be sure that you keep specific graphics and their corresponding captions together because each figure really is the combination of the figure itself *and* the caption.

To make a new figure element:
1. Copy an existing graphic and the corresponding caption.
2. Paste them into a new desired location.

To edit the new figure:
Because each figure consists of two parts, the graphic and the caption, editing likewise requires that you edit each of the two parts. Therefore, editing the new figure occurs in two stages.

Stage 1: Editing the graphical element:
1. Delete the old graphic in the new location and paste a new graphic in its place.
(Note: For maximum compatibility between versions and writers, do not use

Paste. Instead, click **Home** → **Paste Special** → **Picture**). (There are exceptions to this rule, which you will discover when your figures start looking distorted.)

2. Right-click on the graphic to select it.
3. Click **Edit** → **Format Picture** → **Layout** → **In line with text** to properly align the graphic.
4. Adjust the graphic's size and centering as desired.
5. Click **OK**.

This process assumes that your graphic has been created and is ready to be inserted. Chapter 3 describes the full process of editing high quality graphics.

Stage 2: Editing the caption:
1. Delete the text of the prior caption.
2. Type the new text.

Note: Remember to preserve the figure number, because this is auto-text. For example, in the caption, "Figure 14. Experimental setup," you can replace the words "Experimental setup." Do not type in the field "Figure 14." The number will update automatically.

To cross-reference a figure:
1. Click **Insert** → **Cross-Reference**.
2. Under **Reference Type** click **Figure**.
3. Uncheck **Insert as Hyperlink**.
4. Under **Insert Reference To** click **Only Label and Number**.
5. Pick the desired figure from the list.
6. Click Insert.

To update the document with the numbering for the figure, press **Ctrl-A** and then **F9**, making sure to save your document after doing so.

2.4.2.4 Tables. The process for creating, editing, and cross-referencing tables is identical to that of figures. As far as Microsoft Word is concerned, the table itself is equivalent to a graphic since the table itself exists independently from the caption. One slight formatting difference is that table captions should appear *on top* of the table rather than below it, as in the case of a figure. That is, tables are labeled on top; figures are labeled on the bottom. The process below parallels that for a figure.

To make a new table element:
1. Copy an existing table and the table's caption
2. Paste them into a new desired location.

To edit the new table:

Because each table consists of two parts, the table array and the caption, editing likewise requires that you edit each of the two parts. Therefore, editing the new table occurs in two stages.

Stage 1: Inserting the table:

1. Delete the old table in the new location and paste a new table in its place.

or

1. Create a new table by selecting **Insert** → **Table** → **Insert Table** and then indicate how many columns and rows you'd like your table to contain.
2. Click **OK**.

Stage 2: Editing the caption:

1. Delete the text of the prior caption.
2. Type the new text.

Note: Remember to preserve the table number, because this is auto-text. For example, in the caption, "Table 14. Experimental setup," replace the words "Experimental setup." Do not type in the field "Table 14." The number will update automatically.

To cross-reference a table:

1. Click **Insert** → **Cross-Reference**.
2. Under **Reference Type** click table.
3. Uncheck **Insert as Hyperlink**.
4. Under **Insert Reference To** click **Only Label and Number**.
5. Pick the desired table from the list.
6. Click **Insert**.

To update the document with the numbering for the figure, press **Ctrl-A** and then **F9**, and be sure to save your document as well.

2.4.2.5 References (Literature Citations). Although Microsoft Word has built-in tools for automatic numbering and cross-referencing of literature citations, they are only suitable for small projects. For extensive group writing, it is highly advisable to equip everyone with a dedicated software package for this purpose. Two leading packages are EndNote and Reference Manager. Both programs are very similar, with a few differences.

If you are a novice in a group that already uses EndNote, follow the procedures below. These steps represent just an outline of possibilities, and you might need to reference the software manual or an experienced user to accomplish these steps.

1. Open the Microsoft Word file.
2. Make sure that the EndNote toolbar is visible.

3. Place the cursor at the location where you want to enter the reference.

4. Click on **Go To EndNote** to bring up the database software.

5. Search the Internet databases for references of your interest.

6. Enter these references into the group database.

7. Select references by clicking the corresponding checkbox.

8. Click on **Return To Word Processor.**

9. Click on **Insert Citation/Insert Selected Citation(s)**. The reference to your entry will appear in the text, and the literature citation itself will be at the end of the document.

10. Click on **Style** to select output style.

11. Click on **Update Citations and Bibliography** to update the list of references.

The reference to your entry will appear in the text, and the literature citation itself will be at the end of the document. Chapter 4 provides a more detailed discussion of bibliographic database management.

2.5 INTRODUCTION TO FILE MANAGEMENT: OPTIMIZING YOUR WORKFLOW

2.5.1 General Principles

By definition, when a team produces a document, there are numerous contributors. Pieces of the document fly back and forth as information is recycled, exchanged, and created depending on the document and the stage in the process. Mastering the process of building new manuscripts with multiple remote contributors is one of the most important elements of successful technical and scientific writing in organizations. In fact, this book itself demonstrates this claim since the authors created the entire book from locations separated by 3,000 miles!

STREAM *Tools* Commandment #5:
Use modern communication tools.

Many modern organizations already have discovered that they need to move past email as a method for exchanging files and have implemented shared drives on a network, retail products like SharePoint, proprietary groupware, or systems readily available on the Internet like Google Docs and wikis. Shared drives and SharePoint are typically provided by the information technology department of the organization and work well when every team member has immediate access to them. For teams from multiple organizations, wikis and Google Docs often work much better, because they can be set up in a matter of minutes and can be accessed by anyone.

While it is not possible for us to recommend one file management system for every group and organization, we would like to present here one of the most common and useful examples of file management, the "wiki." Therefore, in this section we provide a minimal starting guide for using PBworks, a free online resource.

2.5.2   Using a Wiki for File Management

In principle, using PBworks is simple:

1. Point your browser to **www.pbworks.com**.
2. Click **Try it Now**.
3. Select the Free plan (unless your group wishes to purchase a paid subscription).
4. Follow the wizard's steps to create your wiki.
5. Edit the introduction page by clicking on the **Edit tab**.
6. Create additional pages, if desired.
7. Invite team members by clicking **Settings** → **Users**, then typing their email addresses.
8. Begin creating/editing pages and uploading files.

Editing wiki pages is, for the most part, self-explanatory. Assuming you have given your team members writing privileges, they can click on the **Edit tab** and edit any individual page. Once you click on the **Edit tab**, text can be copied and pasted from programs such as Microsoft Word, while retaining most formatting, such as italics, font size, and headings. However, other features of Microsoft Word (such as automatic numbering) are non-transferrable. Once you have edited a page, be sure to click "Save" at the bottom of the screen to ensure your changes have been recorded. There is a link on each page to that page's edit history and users can subscribe to email notifications and/or RSS feeds to receive information about page updates. The page history gives a list of links to past revisions (noting, in particular, the time of each) with the additional option of comparing any two. It is worth noting, however, that this compare function only lists changes made to the content of a page, not to its formatting.

Your wiki will be searchable and you can view a complete list of pages at any time by clicking **View all pages**. Nevertheless, it would be a good idea to utilize some of PBworks' organizing features by placing pages in folders. To create a list of subfolders:

1. Click **Create New Folder** on the right side bar.
2. Name the folder.
3. Click on the named folder.
4. Create new pages in the folder by clicking **New** → **Create Wiki Page.**

Creating a list of folders (with links to those folders) on the front page and putting a directory page in each folder will simplify site navigation immensely. To create links between pages:

1. Navigate to the page where the link will be inserted.
2. Click the **Edit tab**.
3. Type some text or highlight some text that will serve as the link anchor.
4. Select **Insert link** to a new page on the right side menu.
5. Choose **PBworks Page** from the first drop down menu.
6. Choose the appropriate page from the second drop down menu.

Finally, to begin using PBworks for file sharing, your team will need to upload files to be shared with others. Below, in Section 2.5.3, we discuss version control of files by using naming conventions. However, to upload files:

1. Select the page where a link to the file will be located.
2. Click the **Edit tab** on the top of the page.
3. Select **images and files** from the right side menu.
4. Click **Upload files.**
5. Navigate to the appropriate file and select **OK**.
6. Place your cursor at a spot in the text or highlight some text that will be linked to the file.
7. Select the file from the right side menu and the text you highlighted will be underlined to indicate a link or the name of the document will appear where you placed your cursor.

This introduction simply discusses the most basic features to begin using your wiki quickly, but as you begin experimenting with PBworks, you'll discover that it contains many useful features not discussed here, such as inserting images and plugins (e.g., YouTube videos, tables of contents, etc.) by using the appropriate feature in the editor. For a complete list of plug-ins, visit http://usermanual.pbworks.com/Plugin-Information. Finally, as is the case with any software, particularly web-based software, these instructions might change at any time as the developers alter their services. However, PBworks has been stable for quite some time, with only minimal alterations to the basic scheme.

2.5.3 Version Control

Version control is very important when several people edit one manuscript, either sequentially or in parallel. Name your files in such a way that everyone on the team understands who worked on the document, and when they did the work. An example of a well-named document is: *TransactionsPaper-Dec6-2pm-imw.doc*. This file name indicates that you are looking at the draft of a certain transactions paper, last edited on December 6 at 2 pm by I.M. Writer. Each time a new author begins working on a document, the first action should be to change the name. In other words, if a second author were to begin working on the transactions paper cited above, that new author would:

1. Download the file from the wiki.
2. Resave the document with a new name on his or her own hard drive, for example, as *TransactionsPaper-Dec8-8am-nw.doc*.
3. Edit the document as necessary.
4. Upload the new document to the wiki.

In order to avoid "leapfrogging," no group member should be able to edit the file while someone else is working on it. In other words, only one writer should be working on one part of the document at any one time. One way to ensure your team members do not leapfrog is to create an entry in your wiki that looks like this

```
Filename: ProjectReportJun11dtw.doc
Status: Checked out by John
Description: This is the most recent version of our project
   report.
```

The words "Checked out by John" need to be entered manually by John when he starts working on the document after he has downloaded it. Two other possible entries for the Status field are "Available," meaning that the document is available for edits, and "Frozen," meaning that this document is not meant to be the subject to changes. All of the transactions on a document—each upload and associated author—should be recorded in your wiki so that the team has a history of the document's construction and associated authors. Therefore, your team members will need to be familiar with the procedures for editing pages in the wiki.

To summarize, the overall process for version control works this way:

1. Ensure that a document is available to be edited by checking its status in the wiki.
2. Download an existing file.
3. Edit the wiki text to indicate the document's status (e.g., "checked out").
4. Rename the document with the appropriate naming conventions.
5. Edit the text.
6. Upload the document to the wiki.
7. Edit the wiki to indicate the document's status (e.g., available).
8. Add commentary on the new version of the document indicating the work accomplished.

Your team might evolve some slightly different procedures and naming conventions, but, in principle, every team should use standardized naming conventions that show the version of a document and who worked on the document last and at what time. Your team should also develop a uniform plan for checking files in and checking files out, especially if you're using a wiki and not a formal document sharing program like SharePoint.

2.6 CONCLUSIONS

If you have read this chapter, you have now completed the Quick Start Guide to *STREAM Tools*. The Quick Start did not focus on explaining why things are done this way, or how the templates were created. The Quick Start does not differentiate between hard rules to be followed exactly and personal preferences that can be altered by experienced writers. Instead, the Quick Start enables you to quickly learn the most useful features of *STREAM Tools* in order to make your writing highly compatible with that of others who use the same system. If you wish to move beyond blindly following Quick Start rules, read on.

EXERCISES

Exercise 2.1. Download the file *BasicTemplateSingleColumn.doc*. Modify the template so that it has three figures, four equations, two tables, and six headings of different levels, all properly autonumbered. Use any of your past papers as a filler text. You should not worry about content, only formatting features.

Exercise 2.2. Download the file *BasicTemplateDoubleColumn.doc*. Modify the template so that it has three figures, four equations, two tables, and six headings of different levels, all properly autonumbered. Use any of your past papers as a filler text. Again, formatting features, not content, is important here.

Exercise 2.3.
(A) Create a private wiki on pbworks.com.
(B) Give access to your supervisor/instructor.
(C) Upload your modified templates (see Exercise 2.1 and Exercise 2.2), and create links to these two files on the Front Page of your wiki.
(D) Give these files status "Frozen."

Exercise 2.4. Proofread a classmate's document using shorthand comments from Table 2.1, the STEM Table.

Exercise 2.5. Address the comments from your classmates given in the previous exercise.

3

DOCUMENT DESIGN

Automated announcement: [ding] There are 1,200 minutes of productivity remaining until the weekend. [ding]

—Visioneers (2008)

3.1 IN THIS CHAPTER

This chapter dives into the details of document design, sequentially reviewing formatting and visual design aspects of headings, equations, figures, and tables. This chapter builds on Section 2.4, Introduction to Document Design Tools. Not everyone needs this chapter. If you are an experienced professional who already has *STREAM Tools* templates at your disposal (in other words, a User, according to the definition given in Table 1.4), you should only need to take a cursory look at the material in this chapter, probably in order to refer the less experienced members of your team to it. If you are a Novice, you stand to benefit a great deal from the visual design aspects discussed here. Finally, if you are an aspiring Expert, this chapter is essential for you, as it will enable you to lead your organization when it comes to document design.

Technical Writing for Teams: The STREAM Tools Handbook, by Alexander Mamishev and Sean Williams
Copyright © 2010 Institute of Electrical and Electronics Engineers

In several instances, the instructional approach taken in this chapter involves telling the reader "what not to do." For example, we found that going through a list of common mistakes turns a Novice into a budding User very quickly. For further personal growth, the generic advice we present in this chapter about designing your documents should be supplemented by specialized advice in your field. For example, the requirements for drawings in patent applications differ substantially from the requirements of a trade magazine.

One final note: we discuss references (literature citations) in Chapter 4. This important subject is treated separately in Chapter 4 because it requires a separate software package and is not applicable to all writers.

3.2 CREATING TEMPLATES

If you or your team members desire to create templates, you have probably already made the transition from Novice to User, and perhaps to Expert. Creating templates requires that you consider all the elements of a document and that you avoid common mistakes as you create your template. In the sections that follow, we step through the major document elements and present frequent mistakes to help you to avoid making them yourself. In other words, the purpose of this section is to enable you to create templates from scratch in the event that other *STREAM Tools* templates are not available for your purposes.

3.2.1 Headings

Definition: Headings are the titles of chapters, sections, and subsections.

3.2.1.1 *How to Create and Cross-Reference a Heading Template.* There are two ways to make headings:

1. Copy an existing template.
2. Create a new heading.

To reuse an existing heading by copying one already in a template, see Section 2.4.2.1.

To create a new heading:
1. Type the heading text where you want it in the document.
2. While keeping the cursor on this heading line, click on the **Styles** ribbon in the **Home** tab, and pick the heading level you want.
3. To update the numbering and the table of contents, press **Ctrl-A** and then **F9**. Alternatively, if you'd like to use a shortcut to the above three steps, you can simply type **Ctrl-Alt-*Number***, where the number corresponds to the heading level, to insert the next heading place-holder.

To cross-reference a heading:

1. Click **References** → **Cross-Reference** and select **Heading** from the drop-down menu.

2. Select desired heading for cross-referencing.

3. Select how much information you would like the cross-reference to include from the drop-down menu on the right. The most frequently used set of options for a typical writer is: *Insert reference to*: **Heading number**, uncheck *Insert as hyperlink*, and uncheck *Include above/below*. Naturally, those who write with the Web in mind may keep the option of inserting as a hyperlink. If you do not intend to use the hyperlink option, keeping the hyperlink on will only annoy you during future editing iterations.

3.2.1.2 How to Alter a Heading Template. Writing teams will often need to change the appearance of headings to meet the needs of a particular writing situation. The two most common changes include altering style (e.g., font and size), and altering format (e.g., numbering schemes).

To alter the heading style:

1. Highlight the heading.

2. Click the **Home** tab in the toolbar.

3. Select the heading level in the **Styles** ribbon.

4. Right click on the style and select **Modify**.

5. Alter the font, size, spacing, etc, in the dialogue box that appears.

6. Select **Automatically Update**.

Members of writing teams also frequently need to change the format of headings when using legacy content. For example, your team might need to change:

1. *Introduction.*

to the format:

Chapter 1. Introduction.

To alter the heading format:

1. Place the cursor on the heading text.

2. Click the **Home tab**, then press the arrow to the right of the numbering icon under **Paragraph**.

3. Select **Define New Number Format**.

4. In the *Number format* dialogue box, type the word "Chapter" before the auto-text number.

5. Arrange the spacing and punctuation around the auto-text as desired.

6. Click **OK** and **Yes** buttons to exit dialogue boxes.

3.2.1.3 Common Formatting Mistakes in Headings. The most common typesetting mistakes pertaining to headings include:

- *Manually numbering headings instead of creating automated templates.* While this approach works for short documents, it defeats the idea of automatic generation of the table of contents, and the automatic heading numbering. It also eliminates the ability to cross-reference the heading in text.
- *Excessive switching of fonts.* In most technical and scientific manuscripts, the font of the headings is the same as the font of the main text. Mixing serif and sans serif fonts in the same manuscript is generally not a good idea. Of course, if your publisher expects mixed fonts, follow their instructions.

3.2.1.4 Common Stylistic Mistakes for Headings. The following example contains several common stylistic mistakes. An analysis of these mistakes follows after the box. Shaded cross-bars indicate that this is an example that contains intentional errors.

1. Design

1.1. Mechanical Design

1.2. Electrical design

1.2.1. Wiring

Software Design

2. Fabrication Of Parts

....

PROBLEM 1: ORPHAN HEADINGS. The term *orphan heading* means that the list of headings on a certain heading level has only one entry. For example, heading 1.2.1 in the example above is an orphan. If there is no 1.2.2, then 1.2.1 should not exist. It is acceptable to have orphan headings during the writing stage, but it is important to make sure that no orphan headings exist in the final version of the manuscript.

PROBLEM 2: INCONSISTENT OR INCORRECT CAPITALIZATION. In the example above, both words are capitalized in heading 1.1, but only the first word is capitalized in the heading 1.2. Both capitalization schemes are frequently used, but writers should pick one and maintain consistency throughout the document by following a "style guide" (see Section 5.3.5.2).

In heading 2 of the example, the word "Of" is capitalized. The American English standard is to leave prepositions as lowercase ("and," "of," "for," etc.) and articles ("a," "the").

3.2.1.5 Tips and Tricks for Headings.

MAINTAIN THE TABLE OF CONTENTS UNTIL THE LAST MOMENT. Long journal papers and research proposals usually do not require a table of contents. However, your team should keep the table of contents in the manuscript until submission time. Doing so helps your team develop the structure of the manuscript as it evolves by presenting the team with a birds-eye view of the document. You can delete the table of contents right before submission.

ALTER SPACE BEFORE AND AFTER HEADINGS.

To change the automatic spacing before and after heading:
1. Click on the **Home** tab.
2. Right click on the **Styles** ribbon corresponding to the heading of interest.
3. Click **Modify** → **Format** → **Paragraph**, and then change spacing as desired in the *Spacing selection* boxes.
4. Click OK in the open dialogue windows to get back to editing mode.

Note: Occasionally, formatting is not successful when you update your document. If this happens, try turning on Microsoft Word's "Formatting" view by clicking the paragraph symbol ¶. This view uncovers hidden formatting commands in Microsoft Word. From this view, confirm that you have selected all appropriate formatting elements, including those just before and just after the element you copied.

3.2.2 Equations

Most technical documents contain multiple formulas, so writing teams must either create new equations from scratch or alter existing formulas. In this section, we describe the two most efficient ways of creating equations as well as an efficient method for editing them.

3.2.2.1 How to Create and Cross-Reference an Equation Template.

STREAM Tools uses two methods for creating equations:

1. Copy the template equation (recommended for most cases).
2. Create a new equation template.

To reuse an existing equation by copying the template equation, see Section 2.4.2.2.

An equation consists of the equation (formula) itself and the equation number associated with it (unless it is an inline equation). Inline equations can be entered using MathType or equation editor. This sub-section covers numbered equations. In most cases, publishers expect that the equation itself is centered in the line, and the equation number is right-justified and enclosed in parentheses on the same line, like this:

$$E = mc^2 \qquad\qquad (1)$$

The following sequence teaches you how to create a template of a centered, numbered equation from scratch. It is a long process, but remember that you will not normally go through this process for every equation in every document. Instead, you will reuse the template already created as outlined in Section 2.4.2.2. Creating a new template equation requires first inserting the equation and then numbering it.

To insert an equation object:
1. Click **Insert → Equation → Insert New Equation**.
2. Write your equation in the window that appears in the body of the document.
3. Click on the arrow to the right of the equation window.
4. Click **Save as New Equation**.
5. Name the new equation in the *Create New Building Block* dialogue box.
6. Create placeholder parentheses for the equation number, by typing them after the equation. The equation and the parentheses jump to the left side of the page and look like this:

$$E = mc^2 \quad ()$$

To create the equation number:
1. Place the cursor between the parentheses, and click **References → Insert Caption.**
2. Click the **New Label** button in the *Caption* dialogue box.
3. Create a new label "eq."
4. The dialogue box under *Caption* will read "eq 1."
5. Click **OK.**
6. The equation jumps back to the middle of the page and will look like this:

$$E = mc^2 \quad \textbf{(eq 1)}$$

1. Remove letters "eq" and space between them and the numeral 1.
2. The equation will look like this:

$$E = mc^2 \quad \textbf{(1)}$$

Note: "eq" is just an identifier; you could call it eq_grp1 instead and have multiple groups of equations that run independent of each other.

Adjust the font size and style of the caption to be consistent with the rest of your manuscript by clicking on the **Home tab** and then altering the font, size, etc. The equation will now look like this:

$$E = mc^2 \quad (1)$$

Now, you need to format the placement of the equation and its number.

1. Create a new style:
   a. Place a cursor on the equation line to the left of the equation box.
   b. Select **Home,** then **Styles**.
   c. Click the down arrow with the line above, ⬇, it to display the *More Options* dialogue.
   d. Select **Save Selection as New Quick Style**.
   e. In the box **Name** write a name for this style, for example "EquationLine."
   f. Click **OK**.
2. Now, modify the new style to provide the alignment:
   a. Confirm that your rulers are visible by selecting the **View** tab and then clicking the **Ruler**.
   b. Select the centering tab, ⬣, by clicking the tab selector available on the top of the left ruler until the centering tab selection appears.
   c. Place the centering tab on the ruler, in the middle of the line width.
   d. Now, select the right-justified tab, ⬛, and place it on the right side of the ruler.
   e. Enter two tab characters, one immediately before the equation but *not* in the equation box itself and one immediately before the left parenthesis of the caption.
3. Now, update the style:
   a. Click **Styles**.
   b. Right click the style called EquationLine.
   c. Select **Update the EquationLine to Match Selection**.
   d. Click **OK**. Your formula looks like this:

$$E = mc^2 \qquad\qquad\qquad (1)$$

Again, you should only go through this lengthy procedure to create the equation template once (or not at all, if you use the provided template). For all subsequent equations, copy the template to the new location and reuse it. The equation numbers will update automatically upon entering **Ctrl-A**, **F9**.

Cross-referencing of equations was covered in Section 2.4.2.2, but we repeat it here with additional details. It is important to notice that auto-numbered captions for equations, figures, and tables are all created in a similar way. However, the cross-reference method for equations is *different* from that for figures and tables because, in order to cross-reference an equation, first you need to create a bookmark.

To create a bookmark:
1. Select the number on the right in the equation line.
2. Click **Insert, Bookmark**. Give this bookmark a short descriptive name that starts with "eq," for example, eqNewtonsFirstLaw.
3. Click **OK**.

Then, to cross-reference the equation:
1. Click **Insert, Cross-Reference**.
2. Select *Reference type:* **Bookmark**.
3. Uncheck *Insert as hyperlink*.
4. Select *Insert reference to*: **Bookmark text**.
5. Pick the desired bookmark from the list.
6. Click **OK**.

3.2.2.2 How to Alter an Equation Template. The variety of alterations your team might make to the equation template depends upon the disciplinary requirements of your audience. However, two primary variations occur: switching from single to double columns in the manuscript, and switching from single numbering to dual numbering (e.g., changing from 1 to 1.1).

Switching from a single column to a double column (and back) manually is not a trivial task if you have many equations because the centering of equations and the alignment of equation numbers does not adjust automatically. In order to switch automatically, change the style settings in the equation template.

To switch to double columns:
1. Place the cursor on the line of one of the equations that will become the updated template.
2. Move the centering tab, , to the new desired location on the ruler in the center of the column.
3. Move the right-justified tab, , to the new desired location on the ruler in the column.
4. Now, update the style:

a. Highlight the new equation template.

b. In the **Styles** ribbon, right click the style called EquationLine.

c. Select **Update EquationLine** *to match selection.*

d. Click **OK**.

Long manuscripts such as books and dissertations require dual numbering of equations (as well as figures and tables). In order to switch between the dual-number style for longer manuscripts and a single-number journal style throughout the manuscript, follow this sequence.

To switch to dual numbering:

1. Click **References** → **Insert Caption**.

2. Pick the *Label* "eq."

3. Click the **Numbering** button.

4. Select your preferences for the appearance of the caption (single or dual, dash or period between the numbers, etc.).

5. Click **OK** in all dialogue boxes.

6. Press **Ctrl-A**, **F9** to update the cross-references.

3.2.2.3 Common Formatting Mistakes for Equations.

• *Sloppy centering and justification.* Setting the position of the equation and number with strings of tab or space characters does not work well for camera-ready manuscripts. When each element is a few millimeters off from the alignment position, the entire document looks sloppy.

• *Inconsistent variable sizes.* The font size of variables should be proportional to the size of text and the font size of variables in equations should be the same as the font size of the variables in the text.

• *Using different fonts in equations and in text.* Novices are notorious for ignoring font conventions for variables when they use Microsoft Word. With novices, it is not uncommon to see "*W*" in the equation, "W" in another part of text, and "*W*" in figure caption, all referring to the same variable. While the font selection does not matter in undergraduate homework, it is important in rigorous technical and scientific writing. The distinction, for example, between a matrix, vector variable, or scalar variable is maintained through proper font selection. Microsoft Word users must apply a conscious effort to maintain a consistent style.

Here is an example of poor formatting:

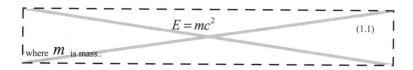

$$E = mc^2 \qquad (1.1)$$

where m is mass..

3.2.2.4 *Common Stylistic Mistakes for Equations.*

- *Incorrect cross-referencing.* In the middle of the sentence, the equation numbers should be placed in parentheses and referenced without the word "equation." The proper style for cross-referencing equations is:

> "… substitution of (3) into (2) yields (4)…"

Examples of improper style:

> "…substitution of equation 3 into equation 2 yields equation 4…"
>
> "…substitution of 3 into 2 yields 4…"
>
> "…substitution of [3] into [2] yields [4]…"

In the beginning of the sentence, the proper style is: "Equation 3 shows …"

- *Forgetting to define variables.* All new variables that appear in the equation should be defined in the text, immediately following the equation.
- *Using subscripts and superscripts incorrectly.* Large variations exist between disciplines for subscript and superscript font conventions. Be sure to check the conventions for your field.
- *Confusing bookmark names.* A bookmark "eq14" will not work well because the equation is not likely to be equation number 14 an hour later. A bookmark "newt" will not work well either because it is too short and will mix with other bookmarks (including non-equation bookmarks). A bookmark "eq:NewtonsFirstLaw" will work well. It has "eq:"—an equation identifier, and a clear description of what it is. Spaces are not allowed in bookmarks; capitalization of individual words is a convenient alternative.
- *Bookmarking the parentheses next to the equation number.* Most of the time, highlighting parentheses with the equation number while creating a bookmark makes it more convenient to cross-reference the equation in the text. However, some publishers expect equations to be referenced in the text as "Equation 5 shows…" instead of "(5) shows…", so including parentheses around "5" in the original bookmark will make typesetting more difficult. Therefore, parentheses should be kept as regular text both in the equation line and in the cross-referencing text.
- *Ambiguous display of units and use of incorrect units.* Although the standards for indicating units are delineated quite clearly for each scientific discipline,

many writers routinely ignore these standards. Conference committees are usually forgiving, and important publications are typeset by professionals who take care of errors automatically. On the other hand, with almost no additional effort you can follow the conventions of your field. Most technical publishers require the use of either SI (metric) units or, when necessary, dual units, including SI as well as other systems. Units representing ranges should be separated by the word "to," as opposed to ellipsis ("...") or dash ("-"). Examples:

Incorrect version	Correct version
... in the range from 200 to 400 lfm ...	... in the range of 1 m/s to 2 m/s (200 lfm to 400 lfm)
... the air velocity is 1-2 m/s ...	... the air velocity is 1 m/s to 2 m/s ...
... the air velocity is 1...2 m per second ...	... the air velocity is 1 m/s to 2 m/s ...

3.2.2.5 Tips and Tricks for Equations. If you have a lot of math in your manuscripts, your team should probably invest time in learning MathType and Microsoft Word keyboard shortcuts. Below is a list of frequently used shortcuts in both programs.

KEYBOARD SHORTCUTS IN MICROSOFT WORD. The following table lists some of the most useful keyboard shortcuts. Many other shortcuts are available and are listed in the help files for Microsoft Word.

Task	Shortcut
Apply Heading 1	Alt+Ctrl+1
Apply Heading 2	Alt+Ctrl+2
Bold	Ctrl+B or Ctrl+Shift+B
Copy	Ctrl+C
Cut	Ctrl+X
Field Codes	Alt+F9
Find	Ctrl+F
Hyperlink	Ctrl+K
Italic	Ctrl+Shift+I
Save	Ctrl+S
Subscript	Ctrl+=
Superscript	Ctrl+Shift+=
Undo	Ctrl+Z

KEYBOARD SHORTCUTS IN MATHTYPE AND MICROSOFT WORD 2003 EQUATION EDITOR.

Inserting Task

Task	Shortcut
Superscript	Ctrl+H
Subscript	Ctrl+L
Joint super/subscript	Ctrl+J
Underscript	Ctrl+T, U
Matrix template	Ctrl+T, M
nth root	Ctrl+T, N
Product	Ctrl+T, P
Summation	Ctrl+T, S
Absolute value	Ctrl+Shift+T,	
Root	Ctrl+R
Integral	Ctrl+I
Fraction	Ctrl+F
Slash fraction	Ctrl+/
Parentheses	Ctrl+(or Ctrl+9
Brackets	Ctrl+[
Braces	Ctrl+{
Overbar	Ctrl+Shift+Hyphen
Vector arrow	Ctrl+Alt+Hyphen
Tilde	Ctrl+~
Single prime	Ctrl+Alt+'
Double prime	Ctrl+Alt+"
Single dot	Ctrl+Alt+.

Inserting Space into Equations

Space Size	Shortcut
Zero space	Shift+Spacebar
1-point space	Ctrl+Alt+Spacebar
Thin space (one-sixth em)	Ctrl+Spacebar
Thick space (one-third em)	Ctrl+SHIFT+Spacebar

Inserting Symbols

Space Size	Shortcut
Arrow	Ctrl+K, A
Partial derivative	Ctrl+K, D
Infinity	Ctrl+K, I
Element of	Ctrl+K, E
Times	Ctrl+K, T
Not an element of	Ctrl+K, Shift+I
Contained in	Ctrl+K, C
Not contained in	Ctrl+K, Shift+C
Less than or equal to	Ctrl+K, <
Greater than or equal to	Ctrl+K, >

INSERTING GREEK CHARACTERS WITH THE KEYBOARD. When you're working in Equation Editor, typing **Ctrl+G** followed by a letter of the alphabet (shifted or not) inserts the corresponding Greek character. For example, **Ctrl+G, L** inserts, Γ.

ACCESSING SYMBOLS AND TEMPLATES WITH THE KEYBOARD. To access any palette, press **F2**, and then use the left and right arrow keys to move to the appropriate palette. When you reach the desired palette, press the down arrow key to open it. Select the desired item and press **Enter**. You may choose to record macros for the most frequent entries.

CONVERTING EQUATIONS FROM MATHTYPE TO TEX/LATEX. Some readers might need to maintain compatibility between their Microsoft Word documents and LaTeX documents because, for example, they have a subset of collaborators who use only LaTeX. MathType offers a convenient tool for converting Microsoft Word equations to LaTeX. To convert an equation from MathType to TeX or LaTeX, pick your preferences by clicking in the MathType window **Preferences, Translators, Translation to other Language (text).** After setting your preferences, copy your equation from the MathType window into TeX/LaTeX window using the standard **Ctrl-C/Ctrl-V** (copy/paste) commands.

ENTERING TEX OR LATEX DIRECTLY. Starting with Microsoft Word 2007 and concurrent recent versions of MathType, it is now possible to type TeX or LaTeX commands directly into equation editors. This long-awaited feature ameliorates the complaints of many LaTeX users who feel that it is important for them to enter math without using the mouse. In addition, incorporating TeX/LaTeX features will produce, generally speaking, the most professional-looking output.

Presenting the entire array of the TeX/LaTeX language is beyond the scope of this book. However, if you are a novice, you can rely on the shortcuts described below to get started and supplement them with an occasional point-and-click of the mouse. You can also use the Toggle TeX command (**Alt+**) to turn what you have typed into an equation. Use it again to edit the TeX language. If you use a lot of math, you will eventually memorize all the commands that you use frequently. As you increase your expertise with TeX, you might even arrive at a point where you discover commands and possibilities that are not well documented.

Greek Letters

LaTeX Symbol	LaTeX Command	LaTeX Symbol	LaTeX Command
α	\alpha	π	\pi
β	\beta	σ	\sigma
δ	\delta	μ	\mu
γ	\gamma	ϕ	\phi
ε	\epsilon	η	\eta
ω	\omega	κ	\kappa
λ	\lambda	θ	\theta

Greek Letters *Continued*

LaTeX Symbol	LaTeX Command	LaTeX Symbol	LaTeX Command
ρ	\rho	ψ	\psi
τ	\tau	υ	\upsilon
ξ	\xi	Δ	\Delta
χ	\chi	Γ	\Gamma
o	o	Π	\Pi
Σ	\Sigma	Φ	\Phi
Λ	\Lambda	Ξ	\Xi
Θ	\Theta	Ψ	\Psi
Ω	\Omega	φ	\varphi
Υ	\Upsilon	ζ	\zeta

Loglike Symbols

LaTeX Symbol	LaTeX Command	LaTeX Symbol	LaTeX Command	LaTeX Symbol	LaTeX Command	LaTeX Symbol	LaTeX Command
arcos	\arcos	csc	\csc	ker	\ker	min	\min
arcsin	\arcsin	deg	\deg	lg	\lg	Pr	\Pr
arctan	\arctan	det	\det	lim	\lim	sec	\sec
arg	\arg	dim	\dim	lim	\lim inf	sin	\sin
cos	\cos	exp	\exp	lim sup	\limsup	sinh	\sinh
cosh	\cosh	gcd	\gcd	ln	\ln	sup	\sup
cot	\cot	hom	\hom	log	\log	tan	\tan
coth	\coth	inf	\inf	max	\max	tanh	\tanh

Miscellaneous Symbols

LaTeX Symbol	LaTeX Command	LaTeX Symbol	LaTeX Command
$\surd$	\surd	$\forall$	\forall
$\spadesuit$	\spadesuit	∂	\partial
∞	\infty	$\natural$	\natural
$\blacktriangle$	\blacktriangle	$\exists$	\exists
$\blacktriangledown$	\blacktriangledown	$\aleph$	\aleph
∇	\nabla	$\parallel$	\parallel

Arrows

LaTeX Symbol	LaTeX Command	LaTeX Symbol	LaTeX Command
$\leftarrow$	\leftarrow	$\leftrightarrow$	\leftrightarrow
$\uparrow$	\uparrow	$\updownarrow$	\updownarrow
$\rightarrow$	\rightarrow	$\Leftrightarrow$	\Leftrightarrow
$\nearrow$	\nearrow	$\Rightarrow$	\Rightarrow
$\searrow$	\searrow	$\Downarrow$	\Downarrow
$\downarrow$	\downarrow	$\Uparrow$	\Uparrow

Binary and Operational Symbols

LaTeX Symbol	LaTeX Command	LaTeX Symbol	LaTeX Command
≤	\leq	*	\ast
≥	\geq	<	<
•	\bullet	>	>
∏	\prod	†	\dagger
Σ	\sum	|	\mid
◀	\blacktriangleleft	÷	\div
▶	\blacktriangleright	‡	\ddagger
≈	\approx	⊥	\perp
∈	\in	∉	\notin
≠	\neq	×	\times
⊕	\oplus	⊗	\otimes
≡	\equiv	ø	\oslash
∩	\bigcap	⊃	\supset
⊂	\subset	⊇	\supseteq
⊆	\subseteq	⊄	\subsetneq
±	\pm	∴	\therefore

> **Note**: Occasionally, formatting is not successful when you update your document. If this happens, try turning on Microsoft Word's "Formatting" view by clicking the paragraph symbol ¶. This view uncovers hidden formatting commands in Microsoft Word. From this view, confirm that you have selected all appropriate formatting elements, including those just before and just after the element you copied.

3.2.3 Figures

Since nearly every technical document contains figures, learning how to create and edit them efficiently should be one of your team's main document design goals. In the sections that follow, we discuss in detail the *STREAM Tools* method of creating and cross-referencing figures as well as the *STREAM Tools* method of altering a figure template.

3.2.3.1 How to Create and Cross-Reference a Figure Template. Before beginning your work with figures, it is important to understand that what we would consider one figure actually consists of two independent objects that happen to sit next to each other, the caption and graphic. Each of these are manipulated separately, but if you use the methods described below, the graphic and the caption will "travel" together in your document as one linked unit.

There are two ways to create figures:

1. Copy a template figure (recommended for most cases).
2. Create a new figure from scratch.

To reuse an existing figure by copying the template figure and caption, see Section 2.4.2.3. Section 2.4.2.3 also lists the entire procedure for copying and pasting graphics, so we won't cover that again here. *However*, remember to use **Paste Special** for line art (as opposed to Bitmaps) because using **Paste Special** gives you a chance to edit figures later without saving them to a separate file. Using **Paste Special** also increases the odds that your figure will remain compatible with the work of other writers. The most common selection that works well for **Paste Special** is *Picture (Windows Metafile)*, although this is not a foolproof selection. You may have to experiment with your pasting procedures to make the graphics look right.

Sometimes the fine features of the line art get distorted with **Paste Special**, and this problem can be fixed by inserting a .png file created by a graphics package (Corel Draw, for example). To insert a .png file, insert your cursor at the position where you'd like the image to appear, select the **Insert tab** → **Picture**, navigate to the image you'd like to insert and click **Insert**. The selected image will be placed at the position of the cursor. Most likely, your file size will grow more if you use .png source file rather than .wmf or .emf.

To cross-reference a figure once you have copied the template and pasted in a new graphic (or created one):

1. Click the **References Tab** → **Cross-Reference**.
2. Select *Reference type:* **Figure**.
3. Uncheck *Insert as hyperlink*.
4. Select *Insert reference to*: **Only label and number**.
5. Pick the desired figure from the list and click **Insert**.

3.2.3.2 How to Alter a Figure Template. Aside from altering the actual graphic in the figure, writers frequently need to edit the caption style or numbering style because the *STREAM Tools* templates use a different style. The steps for altering the figure template's caption styles appear below.

To CHANGE THE CAPTION STYLE. Of the needs for changing the figure templates, writers most often need to change the caption style. For example, your team might need to change the figure caption style from "Figure 1" to "Fig. 1." This change can be accomplished in several ways, but the most portable method is to manually change the caption's text from "Figure 1" to the text "Fig. 1" directly in the caption without creating a new label. After updating the entire document with **Ctrl-A**, **F9**, all cross-references will be updated according to the new style.

To CHANGE THE NUMBERING STYLE. While many different instances of changing a numbering style might occur, one of the most common is switching from a single number ("Figure 2") to a dual number ("Figure 2.1") This change occurs most often when writers transition from a shorter document such as a journal article or stand-alone report to a thesis or longer document that has several major sections or chapters. To change between the styles:

1. Select one of the caption numbers that you'd like to update.
2. Click the **References Tab** → **Insert Caption** → **Numbering**.
3. Select your preferences for the appearance of the caption in the dialogue box.
4. Click **OK** in all dialogue boxes and the caption changes to reflect the styles you chose.
5. Press **Ctrl-A**, **F9** to update the cross-references in the entire document.
6. Confirm that your changes have occurred in other parts of the document.

3.2.3.3   *Common Formatting Mistakes in Figures*

• *Forgetting to reference and explain the figure.* Each figure should be mentioned in the text *before* its first appearance in the manuscript and each figure should be explained in the text carefully to highlight the important points it shows. Finally, the figure should ideally be placed as closely as possible to the introductory and explanatory text.

• *Using excessive resolution.* Including a multi-megabyte photo when a much lower resolution option would suffice is not a problem when there are only a couple of images in the manuscript. However, if a document contains scores—or even hundreds—of images, having too many memory-hungry figures will become a problem for working with the document. In general try to keep your documents as lean as possible while retaining high enough resolution for the printing needs.

• *Using corrupted fonts.* Many mainstream plotting software packages label vertical axes in such a way that they look good on the screen but become corrupted when pasted into Microsoft Word. This problem most frequently occurs when writers produce figures using MS Excel. Why this happens is outside of the scope of this book, but below we will describe a sensible procedure to fix this problem when it occurs.

Suppose your source is Excel; you want to label the *x*-axis and the *y*-axis of a two-dimensional graph, add arrows and short comments to the picture, and paste the result into Microsoft Word. In the process, you discover that your *y*-axis looks unattractive in Microsoft Word, and that the arrow pointers have inexplicably moved to a different location. Your best option is fix the graphic in CorelDraw.

To Change a Graphic in CorelDraw.
1. Generate your plot, with axis titles and all other features in MS Excel.
2. Select and **Copy** the entire graph from MS Excel.
3. **Paste Special**, as **Picture (Metafile)**, into CorelDraw.
4. Click the **Ungroup** button.
5. Delete the corrupted elements.
6. **Select All**.
7. Click **Arrange** → **Convert to Curves**. You will not be able to edit your text directly after that. Instead, should you need to make changes, you will have

to remove the label, type new text, rotate it as needed, and convert it to curves again.

8. Select All.
9. **Copy** the entire graph from CorelDraw.
10. Switch to Microsoft Word. **Paste Special** your graphic, following the procedure described in Section 2.4.2.3.
11. Save your CorelDraw graph if you choose so. However, it is not necessary, as you will be able to copy this graph from Microsoft Word, put it back in CorelDraw, and edit it again—as long as you used **Paste Special** in the previous step.

Distorting the Figure. If the figure is too big or too small, change the size by pulling on the corner of the figure—not on the side—so that the height-to-width ratio is preserved. If you need to present several figures that are all exactly the same size:

1. Right click on the graphic.
2. Click **Format Picture**.
3. Pick the **Size** tab, change **Scale** to the same number for all figures.
4. Confirm that a checkmark appears in front of the **Lock Aspect Ratio** menu line.

Attempting to Use Figures with Textboxes. Figure captions and textboxes do not get along. A caption placed in a textbox is usually not seen by the Table of Figures, frequently does not follow auto-numbering settings, and can create many other problems. Therefore, avoid placing captions inside textboxes. The implications of this peculiarity can severely impact your documents. If you want to embed a figure side-by-side with text instead of using it to break up blocks of text, you have to resort to a multi-column approach rather than using textboxes. In this case, you would turn a portion of your single-column document into a double-column, with enough text to fill the left side of the page, and manually place the figure on the right side of the page. Alternatively, you can place your figures inside a table and then make the table borders invisible. The latter method offers you a bit more flexibility on figure sizing but takes longer to set up and does not work well with text/figure combinations. Giving up text-boxes might be quite difficult for some of your co-workers, but the efficiency gained by using auto-text features of Microsoft Word, especially when multiple people work on a document, far outweighs the benefits of using text boxes.

3.2.3.4 Common Stylistic Mistakes in Figures

Graphic Elements Are Too Small. As a general rule of thumb for figure elements, make sure that all elements in the figure are visible when the figure is shrunk to double-column paper format, in other words, when the figure spans only half-page width. If all elements are easily distinguishable in the double-column format, they will also be large enough for PowerPoint Presentations and bold enough for making photocopies. For each element, particularly check the following items:

- Line thickness
- Size of arrowheads
- Marker size (squares, dashes, triangles)
- Font size in graphs. Notice that default settings in MS Excel and Matlab lead to font sizes that are too small for double-column display.

USING A SERIF FONT TYPE. Unless specified otherwise by the publisher, use Arial or a similar font for labels in your figures. Whatever you use, the font should be sans serif, common and recognizable, not too narrow, and easy to read. The default Times New Roman is not optimal for figures because the serifs (the small lines at the end of each letter-stroke) become "gummed up" when reproduced. An important exception is figures for patents—requirements for those differ from general requirements for figures for journal and conference papers and books. Refer to the patent guidelines for these specifications.

USING COLOR INAPPROPRIATELY. Remember that publications are mostly black and white so that even if the original document contains color elements, readers will often print or reproduce a manuscript in black and white. Therefore, red and blue lines in the graphic that look great in Power Point will be indistinguishable in print. For the same reason, referring to a "red line" in the text is meaningless if your graph is black and white in the printed copy of the manuscript. Rather than using color for manuscripts destined for print, consider using non-color-based markers in your figures, such as hash marks or triangles, which can distinguish features in a way that is easily reproducible in black and white. You should still use colors in addition to using markers, in order for the graph to look its best when color viewing is available.

FUZZY IMAGES. Lines must be crisp. Use line art, not bitmaps, whenever possible.

"AS SHOWN IN FIGURE 1 …" The preferred usage is "Figure 1 shows…" or "… *explanatory text* (see Figure 1)."

MIXING LABELS AND CAPTION STYLES. One should pay attention not to mix labels, such as "Figure" and "Fig." in the same manuscript. This problem arises frequently, for example, when two conference papers are being combined into a journal paper. For ways to create consistency in your document, see Section 5.3.5.2.

MEANINGLESS OR REPETITIVE CAPTIONS. The caption "*Figure 12*. Temperature vs. Humidity" is not a good caption if temperature and humidity correspond to the axes already indicated in the graph. Whenever possible, captions should be concise and informative rather than simply descriptive, because the caption can add meaning or interpretation to the text. In the example above, a better caption would be *"Figure 12. Glass transition consistently takes place earlier than predicted by theory."* A good caption briefly summarizes the importance of the figure.

DUAL CAPTIONS. The default settings in plotting programs, such as MS Excel or Matlab, often place captions or titles above a figure, which are then incorporated into the figures themselves when they are imported into Microsoft Word. The figure in the manuscript should *not* be double-captioned. If this happens, touch up the figure by removing the caption in the native graphic. Additionally, the convention holds that figure captions should be below the graphic, not the above it, so, unless your publication guidelines specify otherwise, place figure captions below the graphic. (Note that table captions, on the contrary, are usually placed above the table.)

SHOWING A 3D PLOT FROM A BAD ANGLE. Three-dimensional plots must show salient features of the data rather than simply functioning to make figures "pretty." If a 3D component does not add to the information value of the figure, then eliminate the 3D aspect entirely. If, however, the 3D aspect does help readers discern the meaning of a figure, the plot should be rotated into the most advantageous viewing position. Likewise, multiple 3D plots with the same axes should be shown from the same angle for ease of comparison. In general, however, your team should seek to avoid 3D plots when possible, because they tend to confuse readers more than they assist with understanding. With that said, there are many cases when 3D representation is truly the most appropriate for the data.

3.2.3.5 *Tips and Tricks for Figures.*

Microsoft Word does not replicate some of the more powerful figure positioning capabilities of LaTeX and some of Microsoft Word's abilities might not be suitable for very long technical manuscripts. However, it is possible to overcome many limitations of Microsoft Word with clever formatting. We discuss the most important of these below.

ORPHAN CONTROL. The figure and its caption should stay on the same page. If part of a caption runs over to the next page, it is called an "orphan." The *STREAM Tools* template file is already formatted to prevent that from happening. However, if you've created a new template, and wish to enable orphan control (and we recommend you do), force the caption to attach to the graphic above it this way:

1. Select both the graphic and the caption.
2. In the **Paragraph** ribbon.
3. Select **Line and Page Breaks**.
4. Select the boxes **Keep with next** and **Keep lines together**.

As a result, you may end up with a block of white space on the previous figure. Unfortunately, we cannot recommend an elegant solution to this problem. Microsoft Word does not come even close to LaTeX when it comes to figure positioning. Our experience is that paragraph text may have to be moved around in the nearly final version of the manuscript in order to optimize figure placement. Despite this inconvenience, figure placement problems in Microsoft Word do not propagate too far into subsequent pages, whereas in LaTeX, a difficulty with placing one figure may affect many figures downstream.

FIGURE POSITIONING. The individual preferences (and publisher requirements) for figure positioning vary widely. The procedures described above work for figures that occupy the entire width of text and do not need to be pushed to the top or bottom of the document. In a single-column document, if the figure is narrow and page-space needs to be conserved, a viable option is to switch to a double-column format, either grouping two figures together or placing text to one side of a lone figure. An equally convenient method is to create a table with two rows and two columns, filling out the top row with graphics and the bottom row with the corresponding text captions. After that, make table borders invisible to give the document a more seamless appearance. In general, try to avoid mixing single and double column templates because it will add complication to your team's process.

Some users prefer to place figures with their captions inside textboxes. The advantage of this approach is that the textbox can be pinned to a specific location, for example, at the bottom of the page, allowing the remaining text to wrap around the figure. Unfortunately, while textboxes allow for better control of figure positioning, they are not compatible with figure caption auto-numbering. Until this problem is fixed in the software, we do not recommend using textboxes for figure positioning in long documents.

CROSS-REFERENCING A REMOTE FIGURE. If the figure is located far away in the manuscript, help the reader by using the style "Figure 18 on page 132 shows …" Naturally, the page number should be an auto-text. You can do it by clicking **References**, **Cross-reference**, selecting *Figure* in the *Reference type box*, and selecting *Page number* in the *Insert reference to box*. Ideally, however, your figures should be located as close to the text that describes them as possible to assist readers.

ERROR! MESSAGES. Unfortunately, automatic cross-referencing of figures and tables in Microsoft Word is far from foolproof. Often, the auto-text cross-references disappear during editing stages, and are replaced with text reading "**Error! Reference source not found.**" This happens most frequently when auto-text is copied to two locations and the references become ambiguous, colliding with each other. For example, suppose you begin with a piece of text that references Figure 4. You copy Figure 4 and its caption to a new location in the document, and after updating the cross-references, the new instance of Figure 4 becomes Figure 1. But what can you say about text references to the figure? Microsoft Word has no way of knowing whether your intent is to reference the initial Figure 4 or the clone Figure 1. Depending on the sequence of your text updating, you may get error messages. It is prudent to search the final version of the document for the text "Error!" to see if any such problems have arisen during the final stages of editing.

Note: Occasionally, formatting is not successful when you update your document. If this happens, try turning on Microsoft Word's "Formatting" view by clicking the paragraph symbol ¶. This view uncovers hidden formatting commands in Microsoft Word. From this view, confirm that you have selected all appropriate formatting elements, including those just before and just after the element you copied.

3.2.4 Tables

Like figures, tables are common and important elements in technical documents, and they need to be easily editable by all contributors. In this section, we describe the *STREAM Tools* method for creating and editing tables.

> ***3.2.4.1 How to Create and Cross-Reference a Table Template.*** The logic behind creating and positioning tables is the same as for figures. Therefore, before beginning your work with tables, it's important to understand that each table actually consists of two independent objects that happen to sit next to each other—the caption and the tabular information (table). Each of these are manipulated separately, but if you use the methods described below, the tabular information and the label will "travel" together in your document as one linked unit.

There are two ways to create tables:

1. Copy the template table (recommended for most cases).
2. Create a new table.

To reuse the existing table by copying the template table its caption, see Section 2.4.2.4. Section 2.4.2.4 also lists the entire procedure for copying and pasting tables so we won't cover that again here. After you have inserted a table, you will want to reference it somewhere in the text.

To cross-reference a table:
1. Click the **References Tab** → **Cross-Reference**.
2. Select *Reference type:* **Table**.
3. Uncheck *Insert as hyperlink*.
4. Select *Insert reference to*: **Only label and number**.
5. Pick the desired table from the list and click **Insert**.

> ***3.2.4.2 How to Alter a Table Template.*** Aside from altering the actual content of the table, writers frequently need to edit the caption style or numbering style to be different from the *STREAM Tools* templates. The steps for altering a template's caption style appear below.

CHANGING THE NUMBERING STYLE. While many different instances of changing a numbering style might occur, one of the most common is switching from a single number ("Table 2") to a dual number ("Table 2.1"). This change occurs most often when writers transition from a shorter document such as a journal article or stand-alone report to a thesis or longer document that has several major sections or chapters. To change between the styles:

1. Select one of the caption numbers that you'd like to update.
2. Click the **References Tab** → **Insert Caption** → **Numbering**.
3. Select your preferences for the appearance of the caption in the dialogue box.
4. Click **OK** in all dialogue boxes and the caption changes to reflect the styles you chose.
5. Press **Ctrl-A**, **F9** to update the cross-references in the entire document.
6. Confirm that your changes have occurred in other parts of the document.

3.2.4.3 Common Typesetting Mistakes.

TABLES RUN ACROSS MULTIPLE PAGES. Obviously, you want your tables to be as concise as possible, and sometimes where you place a table in the text causes it to run across multiple pages. To prevent this from happening:

1. Select the entire table.
2. Click **Page Layout** → **Breaks**.
3. Select **Next Page** under Section Breaks.

Occasionally, your team might need to generate large tables that travel across pages. If this is the case, first ask whether the table can be divided into several, smaller tables to highlight salient features in greater detail. If the table must be large, then be sure to break the table at a new column/row rather than in the middle of a column/row. Likewise, on the new page, retype the headings for the column/row in case the pages of the table are somehow separated or users can't view them as a single larger sheet (as in a bound book).

POOR ALIGNMENT WITHIN THE CELLS. Be judicious when selecting alignment options within the cell (right-justified, left-justified, or centered). The goal should be to make the table as readable as possible.

3.2.4.4 Common Stylistic Mistakes in Tables.

OMITTING UNITS AND VARIABLE NAMES IN THE TABLE HEADINGS. Include the variable name, variable symbol, and the units of that variable in every table so that readers can be certain of the table's meaning.

PLACING UNITS IN EVERY CELL RATHER THAN IN THE ROW OR COLUMN HEADING. While units are necessary, if the units are the same for all entries in the table column, place them in the heading of that column rather than after each entry. It makes the table more concise and easier to read.

USING TOO MANY LINES (RULES) IN A TABLE. Writers typically include far too many lines in the tables they create, thinking that the extra rules will help readers sort among items. In fact, the rules frequently cause the exact opposite reaction as readers get bogged down in searching the boxes. Aspire to design elegant tables where the data can be presented completely, but also with as little intrusion as possible by nondata elements such as rules. Use rules only when absolutely necessary, such as separating heading text from the columns/rows.

TYPE IS TOO SMALL. Be sure that your table can be read when reproduced. Technical tables often contain a great deal of data and consequently writers frequently shrink type to fit more data into the table. This mistake leads readers to become frustrated as they study a table and can present problems when the table is reproduced. For example, after photocopying or shrinking a document, a six (6) might begin to look like an eight (8). Choosing the right font size will help your team as you strive to create smaller, clearer, more focused tables rather than larger, more expansive ones that attempt to cover too much data at once.

"AS SHOWN IN TABLE 1 …". The preferred usage is "Table 1 shows…" or "… *the text of the sentence* … (see Table 1).

MEANINGLESS OR REPETITIVE CAPTIONS. Just as with figures, the caption "*Table 12*. Humidity Levels" is not a good caption if humidity corresponds to the rows or (more likely) the columns already indicated in the table. Captions should be concise and informative rather than simply descriptive whenever possible because the caption should add meaning or interpretation to the text. In the example above, a better caption would be "*Table 12*. The humidity levels changed over time as predicted" because it briefly summarizes the importance of the table.

TABLES LABELED AT THE BOTTOM. General conventions state that table captions should be above the table and not below. Unless your publisher's guidelines suggest otherwise, place the table caption above the table. (Note that figure captions, on the contrary, are normally placed below the figure).

3.2.4.5 Tips and Tricks for Tables.

ORPHAN CONTROL. The table and its caption should stay on the same page. If part of the table or the caption runs over to the next page, it is called an "orphan." The template file is already formatted to prevent that from happening. In order to force the lines to stay together:

1. Select both the graphic and the caption.
2. In the ribbon **Paragraph**.
3. Select **Line and Page Breaks**.
4. Select boxes **Keep with next** and **Keep lines together**.

TABLE POSITIONING. The individual preferences (and publisher requirements) for table positioning vary widely. For a document written in double-column format, it is acceptable to switch to a single-column format if the table is very wide. However, in general, you should avoid mixing single and double column templates, because it will complicate your team's process.

CROSS-REFERENCING A REMOTE TABLE. If the table is located far away in the manuscript, help the reader by using the style "Table 18 on page 132 shows ..." Naturally, the page number should be an auto-text. You can do it by clicking **References**, **Cross-reference**, selecting *Table* in the *Reference Type box*, and selecting *Page number* in the *Insert reference to box*.

3.2.5 Front Matter

Long documents such as theses or books often require so-called front matter, such as a preface, acknowledgments, or table of contents. The headings for these sections are usually treated differently from the main document headings because they are generally numbered in Roman numerals while the main text must be numbered with Arabic numerals. The following two sections discuss how to create a template that does exactly these things so that your team can quickly embark on creating longer documents.

3.2.5.1 Controlling Page Numbers. In order to number the initial portion of your manuscript in Roman numerals, first make sure that your document has page numbers.

To insert page numbers:
1. Click the **Insert** tab in the **Header & Footer** group, click **Page Number**.
2. Pick your preference, for example, Bottom of the Page.
3. Pick your desired appearance.

You now have the entire document numbered sequentially. Next, you need to break it in two sections, so that the first section will have Roman numerals and the second section will have Arabic numerals. To accomplish this, you need to introduce a section break between the section that will be Roman-numbered and the section that will be Arabic-numbered.

To create section breaks:
1. Place the cursor at the end of the portion that is supposed to be Roman-numbered.
2. On the **Page Layout** tab, in the **Page Setup** group, click **Breaks**.
3. In the **Section Breaks** group, select **Next Page**. This inserts a section break between the two pages.
4. Keeping the cursor in the first section, on the **Insert** tab in the **Header & Footer** group, click **Page Number**, and select **Format Page Numbers**. Next to the **Number Format**, select **Roman numerals**.

At this point, everything is set, except your Arabic numerals for the second section need to restart from page 1, currently, the numbering simply continues from the first section. For example, if your last Roman numerals page is numbered vii, the next page is numbered 8, instead of number 1.

To restart numbering after a section break:
1. Place the cursor in the second portion of your manuscript, on any page with Arabic numerals.
2. On the **Insert** tab in the **Header & Footer** group, click **Page Number**, and select **Format Page Numbers**.
3. In the **Page Numbering** box, select **Start at: 1**.

Using the same controls, you may also want to adjust other settings, for example, to make sure that the numbers do not show on the title page.

3.2.5.2 Table of Contents. Sometimes you want to add entries to the table of contents that are not numbered Chapter 1, Chapter 2, etc. For example, the preface, acknowledgments, and abstract should be listed in the table of contents, but wouldn't be sequentially numbered headings. In order to include these entries, you first have to create a new style, and then modify the table of contents to include the new style.

Step 1: Create a new style for Front Matter:
1. Manually change the title of the front matter heading to look the way you want. For example, Arial 20, Bold, centered.
2. Put the cursor on your newly-formatted heading and click **Home → Styles** ribbon and click the down arrow at the right.
3. Choose **Save Selection as a New Quick Style** to open a dialogue box, and type in the style name, for example, Front_Heading.
4. Click *Modify* and then under *Style for the Following Paragraph*, pick **Normal**.
5. Click **OK**.
6. Apply this style formatting to all other front heading entries using the **Styles** ribbon just as you would apply any other heading style.

Step 2: Add the front matter sections to the table of contents:
1. Delete the existing table of contents, if there is one.
2. Click **References, Table of Contents**, select **Insert Table of Contents**.
3. In the pop-up window **Table of Contents**, click the button **Options**.
4. In the pop-up window **Table of Contents Options**, find the *Available styles* dialogue box, and in the dialogue window *TOC level* put 1 for Front_Heading. (Note, if you are using Heading 6 for back matter, at this point, remember to put 1 in the corresponding dialogue window as well. Detailed procedures for the back matter are discussed in the next section.)

You should now have a new table of contents with the headings from your front matter listed with their respective page numbers. If you completed the first part of the process listed in this section, then the numbers would be Roman numerals for the front matter and Arabic numerals for the remaining chapter/section headings.

3.2.6   Back Matter

In addition to front matter, large documents also have back matter, such as appendices, an index, or a glossary. You can use Headings 1 through 5 for your document and Heading 6 for your appendices. The *STREAM Tools* template file BasicThesisOr-BookTemplate.doc already contains appendices preformatted in this manner, but you can use the process below to create new back matter in your document.

3.2.6.1   Appendices.
To create a new appendix template in a new document:

Stage 1: Create the appendix:
1. Type a title of the appendix in a new line where you want it to be.
2. Change the style of that line to **Heading 6** by clicking the style selection window in the menu.
3. Click **Home** → **Styles** and select the down arrow next to Heading 6.
4. Select **Modify**.
5. Change the font and size to look the way you want.
6. Click the button **Format** → **Numbering**.
7. Click the button **Define New Number Format**.
8. In the *Number Format* dialogue box, remove all auto-fields except for the last one, for level 6.
9. In the *Number Style* dialogue box, change style to A, B, C.
10. In the *Number Format* dialogue box, add the word "Appendix" before the letter A.
11. Click the button **Font**, select your desired font size, and click **OK**.
12. In the *Number Position* and *Space Position* dialogue boxes, adjust the spacing as desired. You may have to experiment before you get the spacing you like. Click **OK**.
13. Click **OK**.

Stage 2: Add the appendix to the table of contents:
Most likely, you will need to change the settings in the table of contents so that the appendices show in it. Delete the previous table of contents and make a new one, with the desired settings, by following this sequence:

1. Click **References** → **Table of Contents**.
2. Select *Insert Table of Contents.*
3. In the dialogue box *Show Levels*, select 6.
4. Click **Modify**.
5. In the pop-up window *Style*, notice the settings (such as font size and style for TOC 1).
6. Click on **TOC 6**.
7. Click **Modify**.
8. Adjust font size and font style, to match those for TOC 1 Style.
9. The default line indent for Heading 6 is too deep. To reduce it, click **Format**, **Paragraph**.
10. In the pop-up window *Paragraph*, find the *Indentation* dialogue box and change indentation as desired (use 0 pt for no indentation).
11. Click **OK** in all pop-up windows.
12. Confirm that the table of contents now looks the way you want it to.

3.2.6.2 *Indices.* An index at the end of a book allows the reader to find the pages that mention specific words. An index is most frequently encountered in textbooks or manuals. The Microsoft Word Help files provide a comprehensive description of the process of creating an index, should you need it.

However, we want to describe the process briefly here for those teams that might want to create an index because the process is relatively straightforward. First, it's best to save creating an index until near the very end of your writing project because this step will add inline code to your document on every word that is indexed and this code will make the text difficult to read. However, you can hide these marks by clicking on the **Home** tab and then selecting *Show/Hide Paragraph Markings* (indicated by a paragraph symbol).

Once you are ready to create an index, you need to mark the entries for it, and then build the index at the end of the manuscript much like how you would build a table of contents at the front.

To mark entries for the index:
1. Highlight the word you wish to index.
2. On the **References** tab, in the **Index** group, click **Mark Entry**.
3. In the dialogue box pick options that correspond to your needs.

To insert the index:
1. Place cursor where you want it, typically at the end.
2. On the **References** tab, in the **Index** group, click **Insert Index**.

Just like with any other automatically generated list, it will be updated once you press **Ctrl-A**, **F9**.

3.3   USING MULTIPLE TEMPLATES

Teams that use a great deal of legacy content must understand the importance of changing the basic *STREAM Tools* templates. Let's use an example to demonstrate why. Suppose you conducted an important experiment and described your experimental setup and measurement procedures, followed by the display of experimental results, the discussion of what they mean, and the comparison of these results to those reported in earlier publications. This portion of the manuscript becomes the core of the six-page, double-column, camera-ready conference paper. This portion of the manuscript now contains, let's say, three headings, four figures, eight equations, and seven literature citations, all cross-referenced automatically. How many times will you reuse this portion? How different will the formatting requirements be for these future documents?

Here is a typical roster of documents in a mid-size lab that might reuse this portion:

- *A conference paper.* Formatting requirements: double-column, single-spaced, Times New Roman font size 10, single-numbered headings and captions (e.g., Figure 8 rather than Figure 3.2), letter numbering of sections (e.g., *A. Introduction*)
- *A journal paper.* Formatting requirements: single-column, single-spaced, Courier font size 12, single-numbered headings and captions (e.g., Figure 8 rather than Figure 3.2), Arabic numerals numbering of sections (e.g., *1. Introduction*)
- *A master's thesis.* Formatting requirements: single-column, 1.5 lines spacing, Times New Roman font, size 12, dual-numbered headings (e.g., Figure 3.2 rather than Figure 8), numbered chapters (e.g., *Chapter 1. Introduction*)
- *Intermediate and final reports to a funding agency.* Formatting requirements: single-column, single spaced, Arial font size 10.5, dual-numbered headings and captions, letter numbering of section
- *An annual report to the academic department.* Formatting requirements: blue-colored Helvetica font, etc. etc.—you get the idea)
- *A Ph.D. dissertation*
- *An invention disclosure*
- *A report* of a participating undergraduate student to the agency that funds his or her scholarship
- *Three proposals to federal agencies*, some of which will be resubmitted multiple times
- *Three proposals to state agencies* and private foundations
- *A book chapter*
- *A report* to investors in a collaborating start-up company
- *A project web page* ...

... and then some. While the text and figures will hopefully change slightly as the content is refined through iterations, and while the different aspects of your work that need to be highlighted will change depending on the audience, your team will save huge amounts of time by using *STREAM Tools* to reformat all of these documents instead of formatting manually. This time can now be spent thinking about ideas, conducting other experiments, or playing Frisbee with your dog.

To reduce the overhead time costs of formatting, one needs to pay attention to styles. By properly defining and maintaining the styles throughout your document, you will be able to change the appearance of your documents quickly and completely—nearly at the touch of a button. You can get more or less sophisticated with the methods you use to go between the styles, but your first step, in any scenario, is to keep track of styles in your initial document.

3.3.1 Controlling Styles

As demonstrated above, styles are extremely important for those who write long documents and/or reuse their material in different documents. Rather than simply formatting the text sequentially by clicking the user interface buttons for each element of your manuscript, you should first assign a style to each element, for example, a figure caption, main body text, a quote, or a heading. Then, when you want to change how your document looks, you change the characteristics of that style, and these changes are applied throughout the document.

Here is a simple example: suppose you are in the process of writing a 15-page proposal and at a certain point you decide that, in order to fit all your material, you want to drop the font size from 12 to 11. You cannot simply select the entire text and change it to size 11, because your headings are size 14, 13, and 12 (different sizes for different levels), the figure captions are size 10, and the main text is size 12. All you want to change is the font size for the main text from 12 to 11. You can achieve that a hard way or an easy way.

The hard way is to go to each paragraph, right-click on the paragraph text, select **Paragraph**, and then select options you want. After that, you can use **Format Painter** to transfer the new paragraph format to all paragraphs in the document. For a long document, this would be a dreadful process.

An easier way is to make sure that all paragraphs have the same style, for example, Normal. Then you would right-click on the Normal style window in the *Styles* ribbon under the *Home* tab, select **Modify** → **Format** → **Paragraph**, select your settings, and click **OK** in the open dialogue windows. The appearance of text will change throughout the document.

An alternative path to achieve the same result is to change the appearance of one paragraph first and highlight a section. Then select the **Styles** ribbon, right click on the style you wish to change, and choose *Update [heading name] to Match Selection*. You will probably discover multiple alternative paths of navigating through the menu, using keyboard shortcuts to apply styles faster, and creating your own individually defined styles. If you work in a team, do not get carried away creating too many custom styles—it will increase the amount of knowledge that you need to transfer to your team before you get started. In fact, you may find it more efficient not to teach every contributor about altering styles but instead establish a system of keyboard shortcuts that allows a select group of editors to quickly format documents to which others have contributed.

To create keyboard shortcuts:

1. Right-click on the desired style window in the **Styles** ribbon under the **Home** tab (e.g., **Heading 1**).
2. Select **Modify** → **Format** → **Shortcut Key**.
3. In the dialogue window that opens, under the heading *Press new shortcut key*, select a combination of keys that you can remember.
4. Press **Close** → **OK** to return to editing mode.

Since most **Ctrl**+key combinations are used for various functions in Microsoft Word, it is better to rely on **Alt**+key and **Alt+Ctrl**+key combinations in this dialogue window.

3.3.2 Switching Between Single-Column and Double-Column Formats

Switching between one and two columns on the page is a frequent operation for those who, for example, often write two-column camera-ready conference papers and then need to reuse the same material in single column manuscripts, such as theses or grant proposals. In general, the conversion is straightforward. Simply select the text that you want to use, click on the **Page Layout** tab then **Columns** button in the **Page Setup** ribbon, and select the desired number of columns. Most of the manuscript will reformat itself without any problems, but there are likely clean-up issues, mostly with figures, tables, and equations.

Figures may need to be resized. If all of your figures are different, then it is a manual process. If you have many figures that are the same size and need to be enlarged or reduced to the same proportion, rather than dragging the corner every time, you can perform the resizing operation once and then use the Repeat function (either by clicking the counterclockwise arrow in the upper left corner of the Microsoft Word screen, or by typing **Ctrl+Y**) to resize all other figures to the same ratio. To resize the initial figure, right-click on the figure, select **Size**, and change figure size as desired.

Tables might also need to be resized to fit the column width. Just as with figures, if you have many similar tables, you can resize the column width by clicking on the border and dragging it to a standard position, and then repeating the operation with each table.

Equations usually need to be centered on the line and their number needs to be right-justified. As discussed in Section 3.2.2, the position of the equation and the equation number is defined by the tabs. So, if you use *STREAM Tools* templates and the paragraphs that contain your equations have a dedicated style throughout your manuscript, the positioning of your elements will adjust automatically. If that does not happen, then you should either switch templates or create a dedicated style for equations following the procedures described in Section 3.2.2.

3.3.3   Master Documents

A "master document" is a Microsoft Word feature that, in principle, allows compiling long documents from shorter ones. The idea is that by turning off individual sub-documents, for example, chapters in the book, the word processing will take less computing resources. While a noble idea, in practice master documents are not all that useful because auto-numbering, cross-referencing, and literature citations fail when sub-documents are used. It is conceivable that a certain class of documents that have many graphics and no need for auto-numbering could be better processed using master documents. Most documents developed by scientific and technical writers simply do not fit into this category.

3.4   PRACTICE PROBLEMS

The problems in this section do not provide a comprehensive review of writing and typesetting rules. They contain only the most common mistakes made by inexperienced writers. Experienced technical writers can safely skip this section.

3.4.1   Headings

Find typesetting and stylistic mistakes in the hypothetical table of contents below:

The answers are on the next page.

Answers:
- The capitalization of subheading 1.3 is inconsistent with the rest of the text.
- Subheading 1.3.1 is an orphan.
- The word "Comparison" is misspelled.
- The style of sub heading 2.1 is not consistent with the rest of subheadings. In this case, it is too wordy. Long headings are not prohibited, but the author should maintain a consistent style throughout the manuscript.
- The word "Blitz" might have a negative connotation with some audiences.

3.4.2 Equations

Find typesetting and stylistic mistakes in the hypothetical excerpt from an engineering paper below:

For a round planar spiral coil, L_{ANT} can be approximated by [3] with at least 80% accuracy

$$L_{ANT} \approx 31.33 \mu N^2 \frac{a^2}{8a + 11c} \qquad (1)$$

where N is the number of turns in the loop, the a is the coil radius; and c is the thickness of the winding.

The answers are on the next page.

Answers:
- The in-line symbol "L_{ANT}" is too small; it should be the same size as the symbol "L_{ANT}" in the equation.
- Referenced equation numbers should be enclosed with round parentheses, (3), not with square parentheses, [3].
- Unless specified otherwise by the publisher, the equation should be centered on the line.
- The equation number should be right-justified on the line.
- The word "where" does not start a new paragraph and should not be indented.
- The in-line symbol N should be the same font as the equation symbol N.
- The use of commas and semicolons is inconsistent in the last sentence.
- The word "the" before "a is the coil radius" should be deleted.
- The variable μ is not defined.

3.4.3 Figures

Find typesetting and stylistic mistakes in the hypothetical figure below:

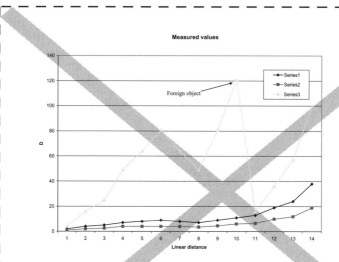

Figure 21. Linear distance vs. D. Response of the new sensor is shown by the red line.

The response of the three sensors is dramatically different, as shown in Fig. 21. The blue line and the red line indicate that the sensors did not detect a foreign object.

The answers are on the next page.

Answers:
- All fonts are too small. A figure should shrink well to a double-column format, and then the font size will be adequate for PowerPoint presentations as well. Since Excel and Matlab default graphs have proportionally small fonts, it is a very common typesetting mistake.
- The x and y axes are not labeled properly. The most common appropriate style is to have variable name, followed by variable symbol, and then by units, usually in square brackets. For example: "Distance, L [cm]"
- The labeling is not descriptive. Series 1, Series 2, and Series 3 are likely to stand for something and should be renamed accordingly.
- The size of the markers is too small, therefore the lines are difficult to distinguish.
- The caption "Measured values" on the top is usually unnecessary. Plotting software puts such captions into figures, but your document will have figure captions underneath for this purpose.
- The graphic should be centered.
- What is shown looks like experimental data, and therefore the markers should not be connected by straight lines. The lines should be used for approximating curves and theoretical values.
- The first sentence of the caption is not informative. The fact that y is plotted against x is obvious from the figure itself. The second sentence of the caption makes an attempt to emphasize important features of the displayed data, but it stops shy of reaching its goal.
- The caption and the text below make references to a "red line" and to a "blue line." Remember that, in most cases, the graphic will be reproduced in black and white, and the lines should be easily distinguishable in this case as well.
- The lines are too thin and the arrow is too small. They are hard to see and will not copy well. Publishers provide different rules, but generally, the line thicknesses vary between 0.2 pt to 2 pt, with the default line thicknesses for the most common elements either 0.5 pt or 1 pt. Check publisher requirements and use your judgment. Do not assume that default lines coming from the graphics software package will be the best.
- The text, "Foreign object" would look much better in a sans-serif font, such as Arial.
- The font of the figure caption and the font of the text below is the same. Generally speaking, it is a good idea to use different font sizes or styles for the caption and the text so that they do not blend in the reader's eyes.
- The text refers to "Fig. 21," whereas the caption is marked "Figure 21." Be consistent about caption marker styles throughout the manuscript.
- The expression "as shown in Fig. 21" is passive voice. Typically, an active voice "Fig. 21 shows" is preferred by publishers.

3.4.4 Tables

Find typesetting and stylistic mistakes in the hypothetical table below:

TABLE 5. RESPONSE AT DIFFERENT FREQUENCIES

Frequency	Capacitance	G	Notes
10	3.8 pF	-	na
60	3.9 pF	-	na
300	4.4 pF	$3.2344 \cdot 10^{-5}$	higher
1000	4.8 pF	$3.555838 \cdot 10^{-6}$	lower

The answers are on the next page.

Answers:
- Centering of entries in inconsistent throughout the table.
- In columns 1 and 3, units are not given, while in column 2, the units are provided. However, they would be better placed at the top line of the table.
- Columns 1 and 2, in the top line, provide variable names, but do not provide their symbols. Column 3 provides the symbol, but does not provide variable name.
- The symbol "G" should probably be "*G*."
- The comments in column 4 are far too cryptic.
- The top line could use bold text to set it apart from the other table entries.
- The precision (number of significant digits) in column 3 is unreasonable.

3.5 ADDITIONAL RESOURCES

A large portion of this chapter discusses the nitty-gritty details of document formatting and we expect that many readers are already familiar with the functions described here. If you are one of those readers, you may think that you need only the occasional reference to Microsoft Word Help in order to accomplish everything you want with your documents. However, even if you are comfortable with the features in Microsoft Word, we encourage you—and every member of your team—to become familiar with the operations in this chapter. Not only does the *STREAM Tools* approach show users how to perform certain tasks, it ensures that each team member approaches tasks in the same manner. When team members use the same functions and processes, a document can flow among numerous implementations (e.g., a conference paper to a journal article) as well as among multiple authors with minimal formatting changes. As a result, your team can spend its time on creative work and research rather than sorting through documents performing minor changes such as manually changing every instance of a heading to bold, 14 point and italics. Time spent on such petty tasks is, pure and simple, time taken away from the more important work of actually generating content, researching, and innovating.

If you feel like you still need a little help with Microsoft Word even after reading this chapter, or if you want more advanced description of Microsoft Word functions, countless online and printed resources are available. You may enjoy some of the following reference books:

- *Word 2007 For Dummies* (For Dummies (Computer/Tech)) by Dan Gookin
- *Microsoft® Office Word 2007 Step by Step* (Step By Step (Microsoft)) by Joyce Cox and Joan Preppernau
- *Teach Yourself VISUALLY Word 2007* (Teach Yourself VISUALLY (Tech)) by Elaine Marmel

Some of the most useful website on the subject include:

http://office.microsoft.com/

http://word.mvps.org/

Even though some readers may desire supplementary materials, we expect that most readers of this book will have enough knowledge of Microsoft Word's primary functions to jump right into the descriptions we explain here. For example, we expect that most readers know how to "copy and paste" or to navigate the menu ribbons or to select choices from a dialogue box, and so we don't treat these basic functions at all. In other words, we generally expect that our readers will have a functioning knowledge of Microsoft Word and the items listed in this chapter represent an upgrade to the skills you already possess. More importantly, we expect that the processes outlined here as part of *STREAM Tools* will generate consistency among all collaborators so that your team members can work efficiently on documents that are mutually compatible. After all, the major objective of *STREAM Tools* is to assist your team with producing quality documents as efficiently as possible.

EXERCISES

Exercise 3.1.
(A) Locate an existing template file for your next conference or journal paper, funding agency proposal, corporate report, or Ph.D. thesis.
(B) Locate the version of this template in Microsoft Word.
(C) Introduce auto-numbering features throughout the document.
(**Note**: Consider sharing the result with your colleagues. If you think this template will be useful for the greater community, consider submitting it to our website, streamtoolsonline.com.)

Exercise 3.2. Download a single-column document template from our website at streamtoolsonline.com and manually convert it to a double-column format.

Exercise 3.3. Create a new custom style for a portion of your document so that you can later convert every first paragraph of every section of the entire document to *italics* and **bold** with less than 10 button clicks.

Exercise 3.4. Go through the list of people in your organization and decide which level of *STREAM Tools* knowledge is appropriate for them.

4

USING BIBLIOGRAPHIC DATABASES

Dr. Meredith: A bit of advice …
Mitch: Oh, uh, thank you …
Dr. Meredith: Always … no, no … never … forget to check your references.

—Real Genius (1985)

4.1 IN THIS CHAPTER

This chapter explains the general issues of using a bibliographic database, including how team members can share and contribute to a bibliographic database as they collaboratively manage the citations and resources associated with a project.

A big difference between references and all the other nontextual elements of a document (mainly headings, figures, and tables) is that managing references requires a steeper learning curve. With other elements, you can download a *STREAM Tools* template, and after a brief instruction on how to "reuse the templates," you are ready to go. Incorporating references, however, requires a separate software package and substantial learning time. If the number of references you are dealing with is small, forget about the specialized software and process them manually. For example, if you are a plant floor

Technical Writing for Teams: The STREAM Tools Handbook, by Alexander Mamishev and Sean Williams
Copyright © 2010 Institute of Electrical and Electronics Engineers

manager and you need to reference a couple of manuals and a newspaper article, just type them in using plain text or footnotes. If, on the other hand, you are a member of a research organization and you need to write a journal paper, a Ph.D. thesis, a large federal agency proposal, or a book, then the time you invest in learning reference management techniques will be returned to you and your colleagues many times over.

4.2   WHY USE A BIBLIOGRAPHIC DATABASE?

There are several reasons for using a bibliographic database.

First is the need for automatic numbering of your literature citations and automatic ordering of the citations at the end of the document. Many journals require that your literature citations be numbered consecutively in the order they appear in the document. In this case, the text would look like this: *"Although bird worms were proven to be affected by zero gravity [22], it has been demonstrated that alien forms are not susceptible to these conditions [23]."*

Second is the need for automatic formatting of the citations list. The expected format is different for each journal. For example, some journals require that the citations appear alphabetically and are referenced by the name of the first author and the year they were published. The previous example would then look like: *"Although bird worms were proven to be affected by zero gravity [Dinkley2003], it has been demonstrated that alien forms are not susceptible to these conditions [Lawrence2004]."*

Third is the opportunity to keep your references organized by your own categories. You may want to be able to generate a quick list of all papers published in your research group in the last five years, or a list of all papers that make new contributions to the body of knowledge on the environmental impact of a certain technology, or a list of all papers by a competing group. Some of these lists will be an ongoing effort, to which several people on your team should contribute. For example, if you want your group to write a review article on research in your field, you could ask every group member to add or mark papers in the database that they consider important in the course of their daily activities in the next six months.

Fourth is the ability to share references. For example, say a graduate student just finished a dissertation, which comprises a 250-page manuscript with 350 references. The next graduate student is continuing the work, starting from scratch. Standing on the shoulders of giants does not mean doing things from scratch.

Managing hundreds or even thousands of references manually in light of all the above issues is an extremely daunting task. It quickly turns into busy work of no practical value. The following section presents additional justifications for using bibliographic databases and the basics of using the most common tool for citation management: EndNote.

4.3   CHOICE OF SOFTWARE

If you adopted Microsoft Word as your flagship writing software, you could, in principle, use the built-in capabilities of the **Citations & Bibliography** ribbon in Microsoft

Word 2007. However, the built-in capabilities of this option are so limited that we cannot recommend it for collaborative writing, partly because authors cannot share these resources among team members since the database of sources resides on a single computer.

Three main database packages exist that are appropriate for collaboration: EndNote, Reference Manager, and ProCite. EndNote is the most popular and easiest to use, and we recommend it as your first choice. Reference Manager comes in at a close second; it has sophisticated office network features, allowing multiple users to access multiple databases at the same time. The problem is that Reference Manager isn't compatible with individual EndNote users, who could be scattered everywhere and do not necessarily belong to your organization. Importing or exporting between EndNote and Reference Manager is not overly difficult, but it is an annoying extra step, so be sure to select your initial software carefully. If you have a powerful IT department and highly streamlined computer support, the network advantages of Reference Manager might outweigh the fact that it is less popular than EndNote. The third option, ProCite, is a close relative to the other two. It does not offer clear advantages over either, however.

If you need to interface to LaTeX, you will also need BiBTeX. EndNote, Reference Manager, and ProCite are bibliography management systems to be used with Microsoft Word, and BiBTeX is the bibliography management system for LaTeX. Since the differences between the first three are almost cosmetic, you may want to make your choice based on what your potential collaborators are already using. After that, you may want to operate them in such a way that you maintain compatibility with LaTeX.

In short, if you are not sure what to pick, use EndNote. You will need to choose between the web-based and the desktop-based modes. The following instructions correspond to the desktop version.

4.4 USING ENDNOTE

This section shows an example of using EndNote database in a research group.

4.4.1 Setting Up the Interface

Install the EndNote software. The website www.endnote.com offers a 30-day software trial, as well as multiple tutorials and webinars teaching the more advanced functions of EndNote. The following example will cover the basics of getting started, as well as a discussion of the applications available for using EndNote in teams. You may need to supplement this info with additional instructions and tutorials selected based on your specific needs.

Once your software is installed, you can either select an existing database (perhaps created by your colleagues) or create a new one.

To open an existing database, click **File → Open → Open Library**, and then select an existing database.

To create a new database, click **File → New File**. Note that when you create a new file, EndNote will generate a *.enl* file and *.Data* file folder. These two, the file and the file folder, should be kept together in order to open attached files from references.

Your next step is to customize the database interface. Specifically, you need to decide which database field entries need to be displayed, which can be omitted, and which custom fields need to be created to meet your needs. Frequently used custom fields are Author, Title, Year, etc. Some groups may want to include classification terms for each paper in their database; some need a custom field for conversion to BiBTeX; some may want to link each entry to a full text .pdf file, and so on. Each user and each group, of course, will have their own preferences for the interface, which will evolve over time and with more collaborative use. To illustrate the importance and the convenience of interface customization, we provide an example of a customized database that can be shared among multiple users.

To see the example, visit the website streamtoolsonline.com and download the file titled "StandardInterface." This is a reference style file; it controls the appearance of the interface in EndNote. In order to add an existing reference style, click **Edit → Preferences**, select "Reference Types," and then select the desired file (in our case, "StandardInterface") from the directory. See the screenshot below for this step.

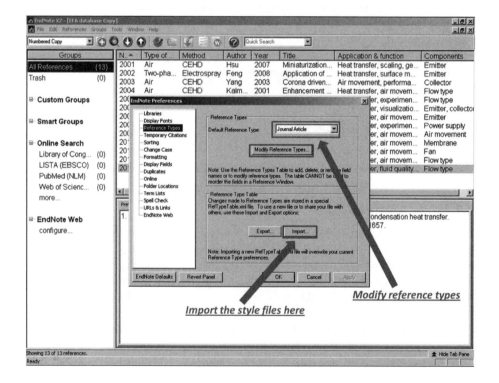

Your next step is to mark "Display Fields" and select fields that you want to display. The screenshot below and the following table show a practical selection of custom-defined columns for a mid-size project.

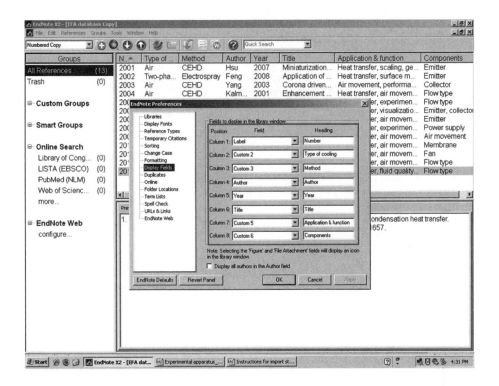

Position	Field	Heading
Column 1	Label	Number
Column 2	Custom 2	Device type
Column 3	Custom 3	Method
Column 4	Author	Author
Column 5	Year	Year
Column 6	Title	Title
Column 7	Custom 5	Application & function
Column 8	Custom 6	Components

Having defined the characteristics that are important to your group, you may choose to develop a detailed taxonomy for your field of work.

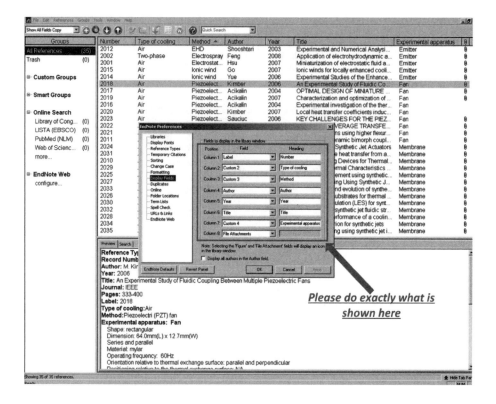

Please do exactly what is
shown here

4.4.2   Adding References

Now you are ready to add references. There are several sources for your references:

a. You can find them online from inside the EndNote software. To achieve that, click **Tools**, **Online Search**, then select the database in your field from the list. This will take you to a classic search interface, where you can search by author's name, words in the title, etc. After completing the search, you can select references of interest to you, and move them to your permanent database.

b. You can find them online by using your web browser with access to online databases, or, for example, Google Scholar and then enter the information manually.

c. You may be able to find references in library databases and then export them to your EndNote software with a few mouse clicks if the database allows this type of function.

d. You may obtain reference collections from your collaborators (and if they use Reference Manager, you can import their files into your EndNote database).

e. You can acquire references previously entered by your group members who are working on the same project. A more detailed discussion of this method comes later.

4.4.3   Citing References

Once you have created the database, citing references is easy. If you use Microsoft Word 2007 and have already installed EndNote, you will see a dedicated EndNote ribbon on your screen, as shown in the screenshot below. After selecting the EndNote ribbon, select the Style for your references (e.g., *IEEE* requires one style, *Nature* requires a different style). It should be noted that, unfortunately, many of the provided styles are placeholders rather than real styles. In other words, their output is quite different from the actual publisher requirements and much work is needed to modify the style files to produce the officially required output. We provide some of the corrected styles at streamtoolsonline.com, and hope that perhaps with time the software makers will update the style files that they provide.

Click **Insert Citation** → **Find Citation**, after which you will be switched to EndNote. Then search and select the citations you want, and click insert. As the last step, click **Update Citations and Bibliography**.

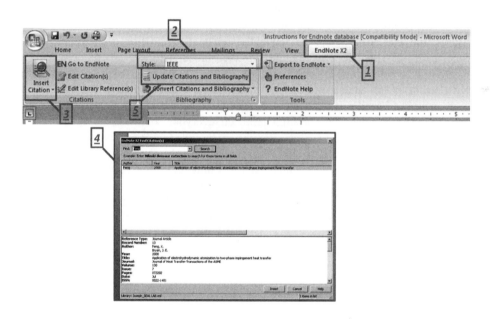

These instructions provide you with a birds-eye view of main functions that you need; we also encourage you to review the free online tutorials available at endnote.com, partly because of the interactive multimedia delivery mode and partly because newer versions of the software may change some of the functions. It is not likely, however, that any major changes will be made, because EndNote is a mature software package.

4.5   SHARING A DATABASE

A research group that works closely in the same field may want to share the same database, so that the references entered by one person can be reused by others in the future. In addition, the group member who entered that reference may choose to add comments, something like *"this is a very important paper for us because it describes the methodology for the numerical modeling of thermal diffusion."* An even more sophisticated approach is to create a classification scheme for relevant papers.

4.5.1   Numbering the Database Entries

To achieve citation numbering, assign each reference in the database a number. If several people want to use the same database in their work, they should be able to enter new references at the same time. To achieve that, the research division is broken into groups or individuals and each group or individual is assigned a block of numbers in the shared reference database. For example, John has the block 201–300, Julie has 301–400, and Jill has 401–500. At the beginning of the project, each user downloads the master database to their computer. Now they have a clone database, which has all entries from earlier dates and the new entries entered by the user in his or her block. Since everyone will enter new references in their block, they will not collide when the database is synchronized later. To synchronize the database, the user downloads the most recent master database to their computer, copies the new entries from the clone to the master, and uploads the new master database to the central location. As an alternative to the periodic synchronization approach, everyone could use the same file that resides on a shared drive, if such a capability is provided by the organization.

There are no special tools in EndNote to assign blocks of numbers for use. This is accomplished simply by maintaining a list at a common location. After all the numbers in the block have been used up, a new block is assigned.

In our experience, even if the system is implemented in the group, many participants choose to ignore these assigned blocks of numbers, starting their database from number 1 because, they believe, it is just easier that way. These participants pay the price later, when they have to synchronize with the master database under the peer pressure of the more efficient group members who have worked within the assigned numbering scheme.

A few simple rules to ask of your group participants:

1. Stay in your block of numbers, even if it means that you have to assign the number to each new reference manually.
2. In order to modify entries outside of your block (e.g., because you found errors) you need to check out the master database—otherwise your changes will be lost during database synchronization.
3. Make sure to check for duplicates—it is likely that someone already found your entry. On the other hand, duplicates do not present any problems, and if a few slip by you, do not worry about it.

4. It often makes sense to put papers generated by the group members into a dedicated block. As team members publish new papers, they add them to this block. This will make it easier to reference prior work.

4.5.2 Compatibility with BiBTeX

Early on, you will want to determine whether you need to maintain compatibility with LaTeX. The software module in LaTeX that manages literature references is called BiBTeX. In BiBTeX, each reference has a field for unique identification. The most common way to identify a paper in the BiBTeX database is to use the first author's name and the year of publication. Once you dedicate one of the custom-defined columns in the database for this field, you will be able to conduct import-export actions between BiBTeX and EndNote or Reference Manager.

The procedures for adding custom fields in EndNote are described above. To display user-defined columns, right-click the **RefID** tablet and select **Reference List Display**. Increase the number of columns viewed and select the columns that you want to be visible.

For example, consider the following paper:

C. P. Hsu, N. E. Jewell-Larsen, I. A. Krichtafovitch, S. W. Montgomery, J. T. Dibene II, and A. V. Mamishev, "Miniaturization of Electrostatic Fluid Accelerators," *Journal of Microelectromechanical Systems*, vol. 16, no. 4, pp. 809–815, Aug. 2007.

The entry in the column "User Def 1" would be *Hsu07*, and if you expect to see more papers for the same author, you can add the first word of the title, so that the entry would look like this: *Hsu07Miniaturization*.

Another facet of compatibility with others is providing readily formatted database entries to others. Some academic authors choose to put readily-formatted BiBTeX and EndNote collections of references to their own work on their websites, thus inviting web page visitors to cite their work. While this practice could be considered slightly aggressive and self-serving, it is entirely within the ethical bounds of the academic community.

4.6 FORMATTING REFERENCES

Maintaining the proper formatting of references according to publisher requirements is a daunting task, as there are literally thousands of formats. Although the style files discussed in Section 4.4.1 reduce the total amount of formatting efforts and the output quality, inexperienced writers tend to make a large number of formatting mistakes when they cite literature, simply because they are completely unaware of the existing conventions. Some of these conventions are quite universal, and some apply only to narrow fields of specialization. Since the number of formatting rules is so large and they vary so much, a writer should develop a certain intuition about formatting requirements.

The following examples intend to provide initial training on this subject for inexperienced writers.

Find typesetting and stylistic mistakes in the hypothetical text below:

A comprehensive overview of interdigital sensors and transducers is provided in [1].

...

One of the earliest examples of using patrolling robots for sensing properties of electric power cables (2) demonstrated technical feasibility of autonomous mobile sensing for maintenance of distributed infrastructures.

...

Computationally intensive algorithms that provide a high rate of automated detection and discrimination of a broad range power quality events [e.g. those described in [3,4] can now be implemented in hand-held diagnostic devices.

References:

[1] A.. V. Mamishev, K. Sundara-Rajan, F. Yang, Y. Q. Du, and M. Zahn, "Interdigital Sensors and Transducers," *Proceedings of the IEEE,* vol. 92, no. 5, pp. 808-845, May 2004.

[2] C. P. Hsu, N. E. Jewell-Larsen, I. A. Krichtafovitch, S. W. Montgomery, J. T. Dibene II, and A. V. Mamishev, "Miniaturization of Electrostatic Fluid Accelerators," *Journal of Microelectromechanical Systems*, vol. 16, no. 4, pp. 809-815, Aug. 2007.

[3]   M. Wang and A. V. Mamishev, "Classification of Power Quality Events Using Optimal Time-Frequency Representations -- Part 1: Theory," IEEE Transactions on Power Delivery, 2003.

[4]   M. Wang, Rowe, G. I., and A. V. Mamishev, "Classification of Power Quality Events Using Optimal Time-Frequency Representations -- Part 2: Application," IEEE Transactions on Power Delivery, 2003.

The answers are on the next page.

Answers:

In text:
- Reference [2] in the second sentence is enclosed in parentheses, whereas the standard is to enclose it in square brackets. Parentheses are used for equation numbers.
- Insertion of reference (2) in the middle of the sentence needlessly interrupts the flow of thought.
- In the third sentence, space is needed between "in" and [3,4].

In the list of references:
- Spacing between the number of the reference and the first initial of the first author is inconsistent.
- The last name "Jewell-Larsen" in reference 2 appears in Arial font. This switching of fonts is a common typesetting mistake when Reference Manager is used. It typically happens when the database line entry is copied from somewhere and the original font setting is preserved. To prevent that from happening, one can strip the font settings from text, for example, by using the command **Paste Special, Unformatted Text**.
- References [3] and [4] lack details, such as volume number and page numbers.
- The italics in the journal titles are inconsistent between references [1] and [2] versus [3] and [4].

EXERCISES

Exercise 4.1.
(A) Create a "master database" for your group using EndNote.
(B) Populate the master database with literature citations, numbered from 1 to 50.
(C) Create a clone database.
(D) Populate the clone database with entries from 101 to 125.
(E) Synchronize the clone and the master databases.

Exercise 4.2.
(A) Create a User-defined field.
(B) Create three categories in this field.
(C) Assign groups of papers to these categories.

5

PLANNING, DRAFTING, AND EDITING DOCUMENTS

Frank Barone: "Luck" is the residue of good planning.
—"Everybody Loves Raymond" (1996)

5.1 IN THIS CHAPTER

Documents, regardless of type, take work to prepare. The actual "writing" of a proposal, report, or journal article represents the product of a great deal of work that occurs prior to touching the keyboard. At the root of this chapter lies the assumption that all writing is "rhetorical," meaning that it has a specific purpose and a specific audience, fits within certain disciplinary conventions, and conforms to quality technical English. This chapter also takes it for granted that writing occurs in a series of interwoven steps, and moves through several phases that cycle back on one another. Figure 5.1 provides a visual representation of how we conceive of this rhetorical, recursive process.

It's important to note that the process outlined in Figure 5.1 represents a synthesis of many different formulations of the writing process. Scores of people have written books, articles, and websites about their approach to an effective writing process and

Technical Writing for Teams: The STREAM Tools Handbook, by Alexander Mamishev and Sean Williams
Copyright © 2010 Institute of Electrical and Electronics Engineers

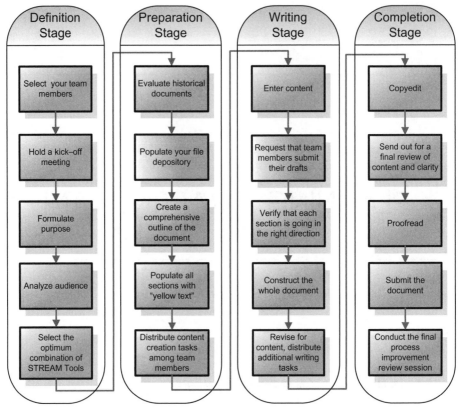

Figure 5.1. The *STREAM Tools* writing process

divided those processes into infinitely complex stages and steps. This chapter takes a more systematic—and somewhat easier to follow—approach by synthesizing these multiple methods into four primary stages that apply across all writing models and textbooks as the best means for communicating your research results, ideas, and arguments. These four major stages are further subdivided into minor steps as a sort of checklist for your writing team. Again, we'd like to emphasize that your team should not view the writing process as completely linear; all experienced writers know that they must cycle back through prior stages as they progress. For example, your first revision in the final step of the "Writing Stage" will quite likely reveal holes in the text that must be addressed. As a consequence of that discovery, your team might need to move back into the "Preparation Stage" so that the team can alter the document outline and assign the new writing tasks that follow. If Figure 5.1 were drawn to represent all possible revision cycles, it would look like a bowl of spaghetti. Accordingly, we've chosen to visually represent an idealized process, knowing that all writing projects cycle and then recycle through multiple stages of the process.

5.2 DEFINITION STAGE

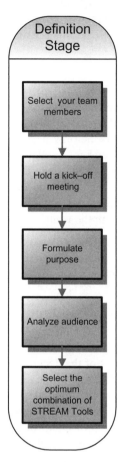

One of the most obvious, yet rarely discussed, components of writing is deciding whether or not a document should be written at all. Is this proposal very likely to be rejected for reasons outside of your control? Is the journal you selected considered the most prestigious in your field? Most likely, this will be a management decision that will be communicated to others who will then execute the actual writing process. Assuming that your organization has decided that it will move forward with composing a certain document, the first stage is to define the scope of the project. Defining the scope, however, first requires compiling the team that will create the document since their participation will be crucial. Once the team is in place, you'll need to hold a formal kick-off meeting to articulate the purpose and audience of your documents and then select which *STREAM Tools* to use. Much like an initial specifications document for any product, the work done in the definition stage determines the overall strategy of the document without specifying the ways that those strategies will be realized in the actual manuscript. The following sections detail each of the steps for establishing document definition.

5.2.1 Select Your Team Members

You need to match knowledge, skills, and availability of your team to the upcoming tasks in creating the document. Do not necessarily limit yourself to the immediate group with which you are working. Perhaps you need to contract the services of a graphic designer for a few key visuals, have a very senior person review the abstract, or enlist the services of the IT department to set up your file management system. Perhaps you need a *STREAM Tools* expert to guide you and make sure that all team members are comfortable with Microsoft Word and your chosen document-sharing plan. Regardless, the team should be constructed of those individuals who are most capable of contributing to the final document, even if those individuals are not necessarily in your immediate group.

As you build your team, beware of constructing representative teams. Often teams fail when individuals are selected for a project based upon their title or position in the organization rather than the skills they can bring. If your management or research leader has mandated that your team must be representative, research the background of individuals in the group and try to select the person most likely to meet your needs *and* represent their area. Sometimes, of course, representative teams work, but most often they fail because, like politicians who represent different states or districts, the representatives end up squabbling over turf rather than moving the writing project forward. If possible, simply try to avoid representative teams.

Obviously, team selection is one of the most important factors in writing successful manuscripts. We have dedicated all of Chapter 6, "Building High Quality Writing Teams," to discussing the particulars of working in teams. We encourage you to familiarize yourself and your team members with Chapter 6 if collaborative writing is a new adventure for your group.

5.2.2   Hold a Kick-off Meeting

Generally speaking, meetings are evil. But avoiding meetings completely is a road to disaster, because a team accomplishes much more than just work at a kick-off meeting. The most important reason to hold a kick-off meeting, even if it is the only meeting you hold for the duration of the project, is to allow your team members to begin to build rapport with one another as they come to learn about their peers and share their unique qualifications for the project. The kick-off meeting should be structured in a way that provides opportunity for socializing so that the team members forge relationships that will—to the greatest extent possible—promote cohesion in the team.

STREAM Tools Commandment #6:
Do not assume that others know what you expect them to know.

Of course, a kick-off meeting cannot be all fun since serious work needs to be accomplished. For example, the remaining steps of the definition stage should be brainstormed and discussed at this kick-off meeting so that all team members are aware of the methods you will be using to author the document, the purposes of the document, the document's audience, and the timeline for producing the manuscript. If the team members share an understanding of the project scope and have had an opportunity to contribute to formulating the scope, then the team is likely to become productive very quickly. The more differences you can work out at the beginning of a project, the better your team will be. Why wait until halfway through to learn that one author has written for experts and one has written for a general audience because each had a different understanding of the document's purpose?

Because the kick-off meeting is so crucial for future productivity, even if your team cannot meet in person, you should still have a "virtual" kick-off meeting that covers roughly the same topics. You might need to hold several shorter meetings since people's attention wanes on conference calls or web-based interactions, but you still want to have all the team members share as much understanding of the project as possible. In Section 6.4 of this book, we discuss in depth many ways that you can build successful virtual teams. If your team will be working virtually—and in today's workplace, it's highly likely at least some team members will work remotely at least some of the time—we encourage you to study Section 6.4 for hints.

5.2.3   Analyze the Audience

At your kick-off meeting, your team should come to an understanding not only about how they'll collaborate, but also about their audience. If your team members share an understanding about the major audience and that audience's characteristics, then deciding on other things such as content and style becomes immensely easier. Additionally, when team members share the same vision of the audience, revision time can be reduced since all authors will have been writing to the same "person."

Generally, documents are written for one of five audience types:

- General readers
- Managers and decision makers
- Technicians
- Operators
- Experts

Each of these audience types has specific knowledge, beliefs, needs, expectations, and ways of acting on documents. To be effective, your document should anticipate—and clearly address—these audience expectations. Often, it's helpful to conceptualize your audience as a "persona," a figure with a name that embodies the general characteristics of your audience: their education levels, their biases, and their reasons for reading the document. Your team creates a "picture" of a person by brainstorming the audience's characteristics, then combining them all under a name—say "Brian." The character "Brian" then comes to represent the audience and all people are working with the same image (and sometimes teams even use a photograph of a person to make it more "real"). Software development teams are very familiar with this concept of creating "personas."

The documents you prepare could, in principle, be written for any number of audiences since most documents have secondary and tertiary audiences. However, of the audiences types referenced in Table 5.1, writers of technical document will most likely be writing for experts and managers/decision makers (or a combination of decision makers who are also experts). Use the characteristics outlined in Table 5.1 to seed your team's conversation about what kind of person Brian really is.

In practice, of course, these audience types bleed across the boundaries, but meeting the needs of one audience type usually takes precedence over the others. This is your PRIMARY AUDIENCE and this group represents the people who can help you achieve the purpose you've established for your document. Additional readers are called the SECONDARY AUDIENCE and might include gatekeepers who transmit the document or those who receive the document as reference material but do not act on the purposes of the document. Another type of audience is the TERTIARY AUDIENCE, and might be people who have a passing interest in the document but have no direct influence on the outcomes it desires. You can imagine this audience as individuals who might simply like to know what's going on.

As a result of articulating the specific nature of your audience, the team should agree on—and probably even memorize—a short statement that follows the suggestions in the *STREAM Tools* Audience Assessment Tool.

TABLE 5.1. Five Audiences and How to Write for Them[1]

General Reader

Definition: Readers outside of their particular field of specialization.

Characteristics: Typically read for enjoyment and have little prior knowledge on the topic so this is NOT a "captive" audience.

Writing Strategies:

<u>Content</u>: Topics that relate to their daily lives; writing must include ample background information, usually in summary form rather than detail; give practical information rather than theory; provide extended definitions; use anecdotes and other human interest information.

<u>Organization</u>: Employs narrative, chronological form; moves from least complex to most complex, from most interesting to least interesting, and from general to specific.

<u>Style</u>: Informal; uses plain language, few technical terms, and no jargon.

<u>Design</u>: Includes lots of white space, color, and eye-catching graphics including simple charts, maps, bar graphs, and photos.

Managers and Decision Makers

Definition: Readers responsible for decisions regarding personnel, production, or profits.

Characteristics: Interested in effects and costs rather than in theory or mechanical applications. These readers may have broad knowledge of the field but are not involved in technical work.

Writing Strategies:

<u>Content</u>: Includes concise background information; makes recommendations based on data and includes non-essential data and information in an appendix.

<u>Organization</u>: Deductive reasoning is used with the most important information at the beginning.

<u>Style</u>: Formal but readable and in plain language; includes verbal explanations of data.

<u>Design</u>: Uses headings and white space for easy access to data; includes graphics such as pie charts, bar graphs, simple line graphs, and tables.

Expert

Definition: Readers trained in the theory and probably the applications of a specific field.

Characteristics: Looking for new information; desire to evaluate the content that is presented in order to apply or expand their knowledge; this is a captive audience.

Writing Strategies:

<u>Content</u>: Includes detailed background information that evolves from theory and leads to practical applications; research methods must be outlined in sufficient detail for replication; authors must draw conclusions from the data.

<u>Organization</u>: Reasoning is inductive with the narrative moving from specific to general content; must include conclusions and recommendations at the end; adheres to typical scientific report form.

<u>Style</u>: Formal and objective with standard terms, abbreviations, and technical formulae or equations; longer, more complex sentences and paragraphs.

<u>Design</u>: There is little need for white space but this reader requires excellent headings and a format that includes more complex tables, line graphs, charts, and illustrations.

TABLE 5.1. *Continued*

Technician

Definition: Readers trained to build and maintain specialized equipment.
Characteristics: Interested in *how* equipment works and not in theoretical experimentation or explanation.

Writing Strategies:

Content: Includes a general description of equipment, parts, operating principles, and maintenance; emphasizes details for troubleshooting rather than theoretical background.
Organization: Ideas are presented sequentially or chronologically.
Style: Uses active voice with standard terms and abbreviations but few definitions; verbal explanations accompany visuals in short sentences and paragraphs.
Design: Includes carefully-labeled drawings and descriptive headings surrounded by plenty of white space; shows numbered steps with colorful charts, graphs and photographs.

Operator

Definition: Readers responsible for actual operation of equipment.
Characteristics: Interested in *how* equipment works and not in explanations of why it works.

Writing Strategies:

Content: Emphasizes mechanical operation; includes detailed operating instructions.
Organization: Ideas are presented sequentially or chronologically.
Style: Uses active voice and imperative mood with no formulas or equations; sentences and paragraphs are short and precise.
Design: Uses lots of white space surrounding numbered steps, illustrations, and photos; employs blow-up diagrams in order to explain operation; includes warnings and cautions set off by lines, boxes, and colors.

[1] This table adapts the work of Carolyn Plumb, Director of Educational Innovation and Strategic Projects at Montana State University.

The STREAM Tools Audience Assessment Tool

Our audience is _____

who know _____,

who believe _____,

who expect_____

and will use this document to_____.

5.2.4 Formulate the Purpose

A third agenda item for your kick-off meeting is to build understanding about the document's purpose: what does your team (or organization) expect to achieve by communicating to a specific audience? What do you *want* from *them?* This is the document's purpose. In technical writing, there can be many purposes—to persuade, to inform, and to instruct—and often those purposes overlap just as audience types overlap. However, just as a team must identify their primary audience to produce effective documents, the primary purpose must be decided prior to constructing the document. *In short, begin with the end in mind.* At the end of the process, if your team had its way, what would happen after the audience read the document? Would the audience fund your project? Would the audience agree with your interpretation of data? Would the audience complete the task? Each of these purposes—persuasion, exposition, and instruction—require different approaches to writing.

5.2.4.1 Persuasion. In its simplest form, *persuasion* is about *change*, changing what others think, what they do, and what they believe. Persuasion is often confused with "argument," but technically speaking, they are not the same. "Argument" refers to the structure of writing and the logic behind the presentation. Persuasion, when presented in a quality argumentative form, drives an audience to see things in a new way. Said another way, persuasion is the goal and argument is the method. Some common examples of persuasive texts in technical contexts are:

- grant proposals (persuading evaluators to fund your project);
- process change proposals (persuading others to alter operations);
- recommendation reports (persuading readers to assume a certain course of action);
- journal articles and technical papers (persuading readers that your interpretation/ application of data is correct or solves the problem posed).

5.2.4.2 Exposition. The primary concern of expository writing is presenting information in such a way that others can draw their own conclusions. Technical writers will be familiar with exposition because it's about painting a picture of what happened: what did you see, hear, and touch? What did the machine do before it broke? How did two chemicals react when combined with a third? Exposition, when done well, enables readers of a document to visualize what the document expresses. Consequently, that audience builds a common understanding with the document's authors about the point under discussion. Quality exposition requires careful descriptions, precise definitions, and thorough coverage of relevant data because the purpose of exposition is to enable readers to feel confident about their understanding of a topic. Common examples of expository texts in technical contexts are:

- manufacturer's safety data sheets
- the "Results" section of a report or journal article
- incident reports

5.2.4.3 Instruction. Documents that instruct are easy to identify by their focus on procedures, stages, steps, and imperative tone. Composing instructions or manuals assumes that the team of writers possesses more knowledge about a process than a target audience does. As a consequence of this level of superior understanding, instructing others requires writers to assess carefully the technicality of their instructions to ensure that they are appropriate for the target audience. Quite often, those who instruct forget that the reason for composing a set of instructions is precisely that others *do not* have the same level of knowledge. While "dumbing down" a process might seem like the logical thing to do, writers who hope to instruct really should begin with the assumption that the audience can learn the material if authors present it well. The burden is on the writers—not the readers—to describe processes or explain details of procedures or outline consequences of actions in a clear manner. This approach is called "reader-based prose" because it assumes that a document has been prepared to lessen the burden on the reader and that, if a reader isn't able to duplicate the process, it is the document's fault— not the reader's. Some common examples of instruction in technical contexts include:

- the methods sections of lab reports or journal articles;
- process descriptions of safety procedures;
- installation manuals;
- usage guides and handbooks.

In reality, nearly all documents contain some element of each of these three purposes, just as most documents are written with multiple audiences in mind. For example, a grant proposal clearly attempts to persuade the reviewers, but its success relies on careful exposition of the problem as well as a precise description of the processes and methods proposed to address the problem. Likewise, journal articles usually include a section that describes a problem, outlines a process used to study the problem, presents precise findings, and attempts to persuade readers that the author's conclusions logically evolve from the findings.

Even though multiple purposes might exist, your team should still settle on one single, primary purpose that all team members understand and agree upon. To help keep the purpose clearly in mind, your team might compose a statement using the *STREAM Tools* Purpose Tool.

The *STREAM Tools* Purpose Tool

Our purpose is to _____

our audience that _____,

so that they will _____

after reviewing our document.

5.2.5 Select the Optimum Combination of *STREAM Tools*

As a final step in your definition, your team should select a combination of *STREAM Tools* that will be most suitable for the project. The goal is to strike a balance between tools that are more efficient but complex and tools that are simple but less efficient. Remember that the components of *STREAM Tools* are modular; you need only learn the processes that are relevant to your particular project, and each tool addresses particular challenges. You can refer to Figure 1.1 to remind yourself of the three main components of *STREAM Tools*—Writing Quality, Document Design, and File Management—and the problems they aim to solve. Additionally, the chapters in this book align with each of the major modules: Chapter 7, for example, addresses Writing Quality, Chapter 3 addresses Document Design, and Chapter 6 addresses File Management among collaborators.

A few examples will help to demonstrate how to select *STREAM Tools* that are appropriate for your team, based upon this modular approach. For example, if the team will only generate a couple of figures for the manuscript, teaching everyone all the complexities of auto-numbering would be excessive when it would be faster to integrate the figures without cross-referencing. Conversely, if multiple authors will submit a sizeable chapter for inclusion in a long report, it makes perfect sense for you to distribute a fully formed *STREAM Tools* template to all co-authors and show them how to use all the features including auto-numbering. It would also be appropriate to determine ahead of time which collaborative technologies your team will use: email, SharePoint, a wiki, or another file exchange system. If you expect only one or two iterations, email may suffice, but if you expect 10–15 iterations, your team will need a shared file space. You will also need to consider who is on your team and what technologies they can access. While it might suffice for your internal team to use SharePoint, authors outside of your organization wouldn't have access. Consequently, you'll need to establish another mechanism such as a wiki like those offered for free by PBWorks.com.

5.3 PREPARATION STAGE

While the definition stage helps you create the scope of the document and build understanding among your team members about the document's audience and purpose, the preparation stage actually moves your team toward authoring the content. As your team prepares to write, a few key questions remain: What do we know about this type of document? What files do we already possess that we could mine for content? How should we organize the document? What content do we already know we will need to create from scratch? Finally, who is going to take accountability for actually composing each part of the document, and on what timeline? In the preparation stage, your team will address these concerns by analyzing documents from the group's past archives, populating your file repository, creating a comprehensive document outline, populating your outline with "yellow text"—a sort of placeholder—and finally by distributing the actual tasks to team members or groups. We will discuss each of these steps in the following section.

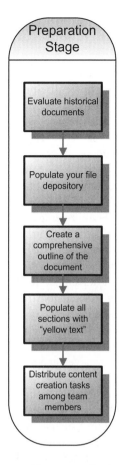

Preparation Stage

Evaluate historical documents

Populate your file depository

Create a comprehensive outline of the document

Populate all sections with "yellow text"

Distribute content creation tasks among team members

5.3.1 Evaluate Historical Documents

To paraphrase the title of an article by Lee Clark Johns, "the file cabinet has a sex life." In other words, documents that live in the file cabinet often reproduce themselves as writers look for models. Just about every company, research group, or individual has a "file cabinet" of sorts that they examine for possible ways to structure their documents. In fact, writers in companies and research groups *should* reference the file cabinet—the way others have "done it before"— prior to undertaking a writing project. These historical documents are usually good models of writing style, typical document length, and layout preferences; as well as examples of the sections and formats expected by a particular publisher or funding agency. Starting your document by following the path paved by others is always a good place to begin. In fact, the *STREAM Tools* method, outlined in Chapter 1 and further developed in Chapter 2 and Chapter 3, relies on a single fundamental principle: *never start from scratch!* Your team should leverage as much existing material and knowledge as possible, including not just the templates for your document, but content, bibliographic sources, and document structure.

> **STREAM Tools Commandment #7:**
> Never start from scratch.

However, digging into the file cabinet should only be the beginning. As outlined above, each situation has a unique audience, context, and set of expectations. To uncritically take a previous document and insert your own text into its existing format limits your thinking instead of expanding it. Historical documents should be used as models only *after* you've determined the audience and purpose of your document. Use historical documents to suggest possible ways to present your content both in terms of style and structure, but avoid using any actual content besides "boilerplate" text. Boilerplate text is text that is not specific to any one document, such as a company's mission and vision. Since it hardly ever changes, boilerplate content can often be inserted wholesale into unique documents and document types, assuming that the document calls for the content. Likewise, items such as biographical descriptions, team qualifications, or standardized processes can be imported as boilerplate, should the document call for them.

However, it is important to remember that historical documents should serve only as *references* as you develop a new document targeted toward a specific audience and context; historical documents should not be merely duplicated with new, revised content. Some types of historical documents that your team might examine include journal articles, conference proceedings, theses and dissertations, proposals, and reports. Each of these has specific considerations that we discuss further.

5.3.1.1 *Journal Articles.*

Journals often require formatting, usage, and citation methods, among other things, which are unique to the journal or to the discipline. For example, *Nature* has a complex website with at least 20 separate pages of guidelines for submitting a manuscript and a four-page summary sheet of those guidelines (see http://www.nature.com/nature/authors/gta/index.html). Likewise, articles submitted to any of the IEEE transactions and journals must adhere to six pages of guidelines (see www.ieee.org/portal/cms_docs/pubs/transactions/TRANS-JOUR. DOC). Assuming that your writing team has clearly articulated the audience and purpose of your document, you may have already determined which journal you plan to target prior to authoring the document. In such cases, the team should reference the submission guidelines (sometimes called "instructions for authors") on the journal's website as well as studying those guidelines in actual practice by examining several sample articles. Even initial submissions to a journal should implement the required guidelines—everything from heading style to citation style—since adherence to the guidelines speaks to the credibility of the authors. In other words, a team demonstrates that they "belong to the conversation" partly by presenting their arguments in the format that journal reviewers expect. If a team chooses to submit an article without using the appropriate guidelines, reviewers immediately start to question the degree of care that the authors used in conducting their study. Simply stated, never underestimate the power of superficial appearance.

Many journals provide style files for their contributors; however, when journals produce Microsoft Word style files they frequently lack usability because the creators don't effectively implement styles in the file or many automatic features such as auto-numbering. In most cases with Microsoft Word style files for journals, the philosophy is something like "use your favorite methods, so long as the final document looks just like we prescribe." Some journals provide style files in TeX and LaTeX and these style files are very useable: all appearance elements are included so the authors just need to paste their text and after a few tweaks, everything will be auto-numbered and paginated optimally. However, as we discussed in Chapter 1, the problem with this approach is the steep learning curve and relatively low acceptance of TeX and LaTeX outside of specialized circles. Because Microsoft Word style files can be as robust and convenient as those for LaTeX/TeX, and are more widely used, the *STREAM Tools* website provides style files for some popular journals and we encourage you to visit streamtoolsonline.com to see whether a file for your favorite journal has been created. If it has not, we encourage you to create one!

5.3.1.2 *Proceedings/Papers.*

Proceedings papers and conference papers often have requirements that mirror those of journals, especially if the conference is tied to an organization that also publishes a journal (as is the case with the IEEE organizations, for example). In this case, the guidelines for proceedings papers will be published prior to the due date for manuscripts, and authors need to adhere to these guidelines just as they would heed instructions for a journal article. In the absence of published guidelines for preparing proceedings or conference papers, authors should reference the main journals in that field or subfield and implement those guidelines. Just as appropriately preparing manuscripts for journals demonstrates membership in the community, meeting the expectations of the community shows readers and reviewers that your team "knows how things are done."

5.3.1.3 Theses and Dissertations.

Theses and dissertations are unique publications that rely on a mixture of disciplinary norms, professional society guidelines, and university rules. In general, theses and dissertations don't look exactly like journal articles, books, or proceedings. Therefore, looking at historical documents recently prepared at your university, in your field, and for your supervisor will help you ascertain the appropriate conventions for these documents. You should also consult with the manuscript review office at the university early in your writing process. They often have specific guidelines that you must follow. *STREAM Tools* makes the process of submitting a properly formatted thesis or dissertation much easier because you can follow the guidelines in Chapter 3 for altering the look of headings (for example) to meet the institution's requirements. Likewise, you can alter things like margins and page number requirements in the *STREAM Tools* template to match the requirements of the institution. The most important thing to remember is that using a template will streamline your process enormously since using auto-text and other features will reduce the time needed to properly format the document and generate a table of contents.

We have seen thesis templates developed by university staff with the user in mind. These actually discuss the Microsoft Word features needed for compiling a long document, but are relatively rare. Most universities provide templates that discuss the appearance of the final document, but pay no attention to the logistics of compiling a complex 200-page manuscript. If the template your university provides is of this type, one way to proceed is to download the generic thesis template from streamtoolsonline. com and to tweak the styles, as discussed in Section 3.3.1.

5.3.1.4 Proposals.

Proposals merit special mention because they all share a specific purpose: persuasion. Every proposal is written to encourage the audience to act, think, feel, or believe differently than they currently do. Consequently, nearly all proposals have similar parts, although specific contexts, such as a grant proposal or a document responding to a government request for proposal (RFP), might have unique requirements. However, since all proposals share a persuasive purpose, the writing team should begin by clearly articulating the final outcome that is desired from the reader. Is it funding? Is it a process change? Is it new equipment? Is it a contract to build a road? Working backward from the desired outcome, quality proposals build a case for action or change by demonstrating why this particular course will address the specific problem. In other words, quality proposals clearly articulate *both* the problem *and* the solution, while carefully showing how the proposed course of action will *solve* the problem. Most proposals include detailed descriptions of the plan of action including timelines, deliverables, and evaluation criteria. They also frequently include statements of the authors' qualifications and end by specifically requesting the action desired. Table 5.2 presents a generic and idealized structure for proposals that authors can use to help guide their process when no specific proposal structure is available.

TABLE 5.2. Generic Structure for Proposals

I. Introduction
   A. Purpose of the document (to propose some action)
      1. Brief statement of problem (~1 sentence).
      2. Brief statement of solution (~1 sentence).
   B. Overview of the document (see parts below)
II. Problem Statement
   A. What is the origin of the problem?
      1. *What is the ideal state?*   In an ideal world, what would happen, what would we
         know, what would we do, etc.?
      2. *What is the current state?*   Comparing and contrasting to the ideal state, what
         characterizes the situation now that calls for action? How is the current state
         inadequate, compared to the ideal state?
      3. *What are the parts of the problem?*   Most problems contain multiple constituents.
         What are the smaller pieces that combine to form the larger problem?
   B. Why is the problem important?
   C. Who is impacted by the problem?
III. Solution
   A. Overview of solution (often a figure called a "theory of action" or a "logic model"
      showing strategies, objectives, and goals).
   B. Detailed solution statement that aligns with "the parts of the problem" showing how
      each constituent piece will be addressed.
   C. Implementation plan
      1. Schedule of deliverables and benchmark dates.
      2. Personnel assignments.
   D. Assessment plan that measures alignment of goals/outcomes with "ideal state"
IV. Conclusions
   A. Summary of problem
   B. Summary of solution
   C. Request for action

As always, check with guidelines that are specific to the proposal context. The guidelines shown above are meant only to be the most general parts of a proposal and we advise proposal writers to always—*always*—consult with the audience or funding agency about specific requirements that might not be clearly articulated in request for proposal documents. The unwritten requirements might include types of data graphics they prefer, specific content areas, questions that need to be answered, or who should be on the team. Often, no matter how pointed your questions are, you cannot get this information from the funding agency. This intangible unwritten knowledge is part of the elusive "grantsmanship" skills, and it resides with successful applicants and those who regularly serve on proposal review panels. Your task in this case is to find a good mentor who can guide you through the process and explain what is happening behind the scenes. However, even though certain proposal contexts will have various specific and sometimes unwritten requirements, the basic logic of a proposal, problem and solution, and the basic purpose—persuasion—remain.

TABLE 5.3. Sample Report Types

Informal	Formal
• Trip reports	• Informational report
• Field and lab reports	• Analytical report
• Progress and status reports	• Feasibility studies
• Meeting minutes	• Recommendation report

5.3.1.5 Reports. Reports generally fall into two categories, informal and formal. Describing the distinction between them can be tricky, but a good operating principle is that "informal" reports usually require less outside research, preparation, and content than "formal" reports do. Formal reports are often longer, more structured, require a team of writers, and carry more weight than informal reports. What both report types share, though, is their purpose: exposition. In most cases, reports record actions or events for others who will use the information contained for guiding actions. Reports usually assume a perspective of "showing the facts."

Technical communication textbooks, for example, John M. Lannon's *Technical Communication*, generally agree on the classification of reports. Table 5.3 synthesizes some of these sources to show samples of report types.

Most writers in technical settings will be familiar with the primary parts of a formal report:

- *Executive summary:* provides a very succinct description of the motivation, problem statement, approach, and results.
- *Introduction:* outlines the context of the report, including which problems, if any, necessitated the report, the purpose of the report, background and state-of-the-art, the topics covered in the report (scope), and outlines the document's contents.
- *Methods:* describes in careful detail what procedures were used during the research process, including materials, and is written clearly enough that another person could reproduce the study exactly.
- *Results:* presents the data and observations that the research methods uncovered. These are simply "the facts" without significant interpretation about what the facts mean.
- *Conclusions:* suggests what the results mean with respect to the topic being researched. Conclusions also synthesize and present trends or important patterns.

Often, formal reports will have additional sections required by that particular type of a report. For example, recommendation reports will recommend a course of action. Similarly, some reports might require abstracts or appendices. However, all formal reports will include the sections above.

Informal reports, by comparison, tend to be less structured and shorter but still contain an introduction that orients readers to the topic, results that present data relevant to the topic, and conclusions that suggest what the results mean. Informal reports can also include a brief section outlining future actions, for example, how a project that has fallen behind schedule will be brought back into alignment with the plan. Similarly, meeting notes might include topics for the next meeting or outline future action that participants must complete.

Regardless of the specific type of document—a formal recommendation report, a memo, a proposal, a conference paper, or a journal article—the key point to remember is that each situation has specific requirements for the writing team. Understanding how others have composed similar documents in the past, including the various purposes and unique structures of each document, will ensure that your team members are operating from the same basic understanding about how your document works within a historical "conversation" of documents. If your team understands this context, you will have an easier time creating your document during Stage 3: The Writing Process.

5.3.2 Populate the File Repository

Populating the file repository and evaluating historical documents are closely linked. After you have evaluated documents that your team thinks will be important to access as they author and compose the document, you should place those files into a shared document repository so that everyone on the team works from the same set of shared documents. These documents can include any number of items and you will probably need quite a few files in the shared space in order to get started. Not only will you need sample documents in your repository, you'll also have "informational" content as well as "legacy" content.

Informational content might include, for example:

- The request for proposals
- A proposal submission guide
- An appropriate *STREAM Tools* template file
- Samples of successful (or not) proposals submitted to this agency
- A manuscript development timeline
- A sample budget template.

Each of these documents contains information that the team needs in order to successfully complete the process, but these documents do not contain the actual content.

By comparison, *legacy content* might include, for example:

- Prior proposals, technical reports, publications, and presentations on this subject from your group
- The most relevant references, including published papers in this field
- Bibliographic citations and sources from prior work
- Image files relevant to the topic

- Written notes from the kick-off meeting
- Boilerplate such as mission/vision or personnel bios.

Each of these documents contains content that you might actually use to help complete the process. Certainly, you'll have to generate some new content; however, as the *STREAM Tools* method teaches, the more that your team can leverage existing content—cut and paste—the more efficient your team will be.

Many ways exist to establish file repositories including: shared network drives, a full collaboration package such as SharePoint, wikis, Google Docs, or even a good old file cabinet. We recommend wikis and SharePoint, and discuss both options in more detail in Chapter 6, under the subsection titled "Selecting Communication Tools to Support Teamwork." Your team might reference this section to determine which method would be most appropriate for your needs.

5.3.3 Create a Comprehensive Outline of the Document

At this point, your team knows the purpose of their document and has established the audience, studied historical documents, and constructed a file repository to begin sharing content and orient the team. The next task is creating a comprehensive outline. At this stage, your team will determine what the document should say in order to achieve the purpose, weighing these considerations against any requirements imposed by an audience such as a specific topics required by a request for proposals. The best way to begin constructing your document is to create a comprehensive outline.

Most team members likely will not have thought much beyond the first-level headings at this point—saying "we need a section on broader impacts, a project description, and an assessment plan," for example. One way to spark a discussion about the best possible outline is to have the team review materials in the file repository. What have others done? Remember that it is your team's job to walk the line between suggesting something innovative and demonstrating your membership in the community of prior authors. One way to do this is to imitate the structure of an earlier, successful document while including new content or new sections that this particular situation might require. Again, *STREAM Tools* teaches that it's most efficient to adapt existing work to new purposes. Consequently, if your team utilizes good models, your process not only become more efficient, its chances of successfully achieving its purpose increase. Of course, you should never uncritically duplicate another document. Even as you draw on the wisdom of the community of documents in the repository, take care to weigh the constraints of your particular situation against the constraints of model documents, adjusting your document to the specific audience and purpose at hand.

Most writers will be familiar with organizing content through outlines. Tables of contents are another way of organizing content that looks much like an outline, and using tables of contents, in fact, is the method recommended in *STREAM Tools*. Examine Figure 5.2, which shows an outline of this chapter's main headings as they appear in the table of contents. Notice how outlines and tables of contents accomplish the same purpose. All levels of headings are shown for each of the first two sections of this chapter (but of course your team should create an outline like this for your entire

I.   In This Chapter

II. Definition Stage

    a. Select your team members

    b. Hold a kick-off meeting

    c. Select the optimum combination of *STREAM Tools*

    d. Analyze the audience

    e. Formulate the purpose

        i.   Persuasion

        ii. Exposition

        iii. Instruction

III. Preparation Stage

    a. Evaluate historical documents

        i.   Journal articles

        ii. Proceedings/papers

        iii. Theses and dissertations

        iv. Proposals

        v.   Reports

    b. Populate the file repository

    c. Create a comprehensive outline of the document

        i.   Using deductive structures

        ii. Using Microsoft Word's outline feature

    d. Populate all sections with "yellow text"

    e. Distribute content creation tasks among team members

        i.   Choose a drafting strategy

        ii. Synchronizing writing styles

    f. Control versions of shared files

Figure 5.2. Outline of the first two major sections of this chapter

document as we did). The outline can go on for many, many pages, if your team does it well.

As part of the *STREAM Tools* method, we recommend creating a comprehensive outline prior to drafting text, and allowing that outline to become your table of contents.

Not only will having an outline/table of contents help the team structure content, it will also help the team determine what content still needs to be developed. Having a good outline also assists the team when it comes to dividing writing responsibilities, assuming your team will be working this way. In other words, outlining is not merely organizing content that already exists; it's a process of discovering what content must be included as well as what content can be omitted.

Once drafted, the outline becomes a container of sorts that enables the team to "fill in the appropriate parts." Sometimes the content will shift as your team writes, but in general, if you spend time planning your document prior to writing, these shifts are minor. As with all *STREAM Tools* approaches, the object is to speed the drafting process. In this spirit, we suggest that having a "container to fill" usually requires less effort than "inventing the container" on the fly as you write.

5.3.3.1 *Using Deductive Structures.* One method of creating your "container" is to implement a deductive structure in your outline. Usually, outlines proceed from large topics to more specific ones, where the elements of the large topic can be disassembled into the smaller topics. If you look back at Figure 5.2, the outline of the beginning of this chapter, you'll see, for example, that "Evaluate Historical Documents" has five major subsections that describe some of the documents teams might examine prior to writing. Regardless of the topics in your document, determining the overall structure of your document is the first step in drafting because it reveals the major groupings that will be addressed.

Fortunately, many technical and scientific documents follow either the standard report format (introduction, methods, results, conclusions) or they follow a format requested by the audience, as in the case of most grant proposals and government RFPs. In this case, your team's task will be to record the major sections as listed in the RFP held in the file repository, then list topics required in each subsection, and then list sub-subsections. Documents structured this way are *deductive*, which means that they tell readers the most important things at first and gradually become more specific. Over the course of a particular document, this flow from general to specific occurs cyclically as each topic gets its own general heading with more specific subheadings and content coming after each subdivision. Visualizing the structure that moves back and forth between general and specific sometimes helps writers as they begin to draft because it demonstrates the relative balance of content treatment. This technique also helps ensure that writers adequately develop a topic by showing the complexity of its subsections, as well as visualizing the relative "weight" of a topic. Figure 5.3 demonstrates this technique with a book chapter on trust in virtual teams by one of this book's authors. Notice how each of the sections moves from a larger topic, for example, "virtual teams" to the differences between virtual and face-to-face teams to the composition of those teams. Each time, the content becomes more specific, but the overall topic is announced in the heading (and in the opening text of each section). Notice also how the "expanded" sections have relative balance, each with an A and a B and two or three subpoints. Together deductive structure and balance provide readers with a structure that is easy to comprehend and retain.

5.3.3.2 *Using Microsoft Word's Outline Feature.* A second way of organizing content within your container is to use the outlining feature of Microsoft Word and then use the outline to create a table of contents. Microsoft Word's outline feature is a robust tool that speeds the outlining process considerably by allowing writers to select topics and move them in the document hierarchy or move them to another part of the document all together. Figure 5.4 shows a screen capture of Microsoft Word's outline feature exactly as it appears on the screen for the document referenced in Figure 5.3.

To see a document such as the *STREAM Tools* basic template in outline view, select "View" from the toolbar on the top of Microsoft Word's interface, then on the left of the view toolbar, select "Outline." This selection changes the view of the current document to an outline view based upon your headings and their heading levels. Since the *STREAM Tools* process requires that you begin with a template document, you should always have a ready-made outline that your team can alter. In other words, your team can change the content of the headings to suit your needs and add subheadings as necessary by clicking *ENTER* after an existing heading and using the *LEVELS* list to indicate which level of heading it should be. Microsoft Word automatically indents or outdents the headings based upon the level you select.

Microsoft Word also uses a series of pluses and minuses to indicate whether or not a topic has subtopics. A plus indicates a complex topic with subtopics and a minus

---

I.　　Introduction and Background

　　A.　　Constituents of a quality team

　　B.　　The role of trust in teams

　　　　1.　　Components of trust in teams

　　　　2.　　Types of trust

II.　　Virtual Teams

　　A.　　Differences between traditional teams and virtual teams

　　　　1.　　Composition

　　　　2.　　Technology and the virtual team

　　　　3.　　Social presence

　　B.　　Trust in virtual teams

　　　　1.　　Social information processing

　　　　2.　　Swift trust

III.　　Building Strong Virtual Teams

IV.　　Implications and Future Research Directions

Figure 5.3. Visualizing "weight" of sections in a document

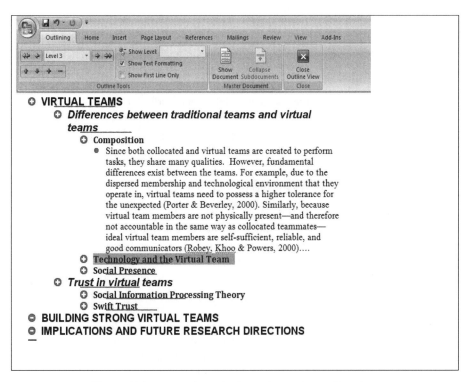

Figure 5.4. Screen shot of Microsoft Word's Outline View

indicates a stand-alone topic. Microsoft Word also uses bullets to indicate content—the body text—that comprises the text related to a particular topic. As you can see in Figure 5.4, there are four main topics to the sample chapter. Topic 1 is fully collapsed, meaning that authors can only see the heading. Topic 2 is partially expanded and shows all of the subheadings within the section and shows the body content within the third level heading of "Composition" (the text has been abbreviated here). The third and fourth major topics have no additional content and so are fully expanded as indicated by the absence of a gray line under the heading and a minus sign before the heading.

As they write, authors can collapse or expand topics by highlighting a line then clicking the plus or minus button in the upper left of the interface. To move topics, subtopics, or body content, authors can simply highlight a topic, then click and drag it to another place in the hierarchy. Alternatively, authors can use the up and down arrows in the upper left of the interface next to the plus and minus buttons. This method of moving topics allows writers to move only one place at a time, while highlighting, clicking and dragging enables writers to position text wherever they prefer in the document.

Microsoft Word's Outline feature is extremely helpful as authors structure their document because it allows expansion, compression, and mobility of topics. It also enables authors to easily insert or delete topics without the cumbersome task of numbering and lettering outlines manually. Finally, the Outline feature easily becomes a container for content as authors simply insert body text—in the form of bullets— under a heading. If there is no body text for a topic, then the topic either needs to be more fully developed or absorbed into another topic. Likewise, if a particular topic begins to develop too many body paragraphs, which are indicated by the bullets in Outline view, the authors might want to think about adding additional subheadings. One great advantage of the Outline feature is that it allows you to visualize your document, much like a table of contents, to see just how adequately and equally each topic has been developed.

5.3.4   Populate All Sections with "Yellow Text"

At this point in the process, your team has both a repository of documents and an outline of the document according to the guidelines indicated by your audience and purpose as well as similar document types. The next task is to determine the generic *type* of content that should populate the outline. This is where *STREAM Tools* introduces the concept of "yellow text." To create yellow text, type into the body of the document, select the highlight tool on the Home Ribbon, and then run your cursor over the text to make it yellow.

In *STREAM Tools*, "yellow text" is shorthand for the description of content, but not the content itself. In other words, yellow text allows your team to decide *what type* of content is needed in a specific section long before the team has actually written that particular content. In addition to helping guide content creation by explicitly articulating what is needed in each section using yellow text, you make it easier for members of your team to re-appropriate applicable legacy content. It is entirely possible that a member of the team will know where a specific type of content already exists in a form that could be adapted to the new situation. How many times have you been part of a writing team where you thought "You know, I wrote a very similar argument in that proposal/report/journal article that I submitted last year. I bet I could adapt that content to fit here"? In short, the yellow text has two purposes:

1. To record in the outline what type of content needs to be included in the final document.
2. To direct the team to files in the repository that might contain content that can be adapted for a new purpose.

In practice, many yellow text entries will combine both sets of information, the generic type of content necessary and a reference to a possible source to adapt. For example, in the Results section of a paper, the project leader could write "make sure to include the results of measurements and compare them to simulations; refer to last year's tests for a model." This steers the writing team in the right direction, but does not include the actual text of the results. Writing content comes later as part of the Writing Stage detailed in Section 5.4.

The point of yellow text is to populate the outline with guides to constructing the text in order to assist in clarifying meaning that headings might leave ambiguous.

Descriptive headings are certainly advantageous, but yellow text clarifies beyond a doubt what needs to be included in a particular section. Think of yellow text as "stage directions" from the director of a play: they contextualize what is happening in the play and what the outcome should be without actually telling the actors how to speak the lines. Yellow text accomplishes the same thing: it tells people what needs to be included without actually specifying the text.

Note: Do not confuse "yellow text" with Microsoft Word's "comment" function. The yellow text is highlighting over the actual text itself and is actually in the document itself, between the lines of the outline. The yellow text is not a comment placed in the margin or indicated by the sometimes yellow mark associated with a comment.

5.3.5   Distribute Writing Tasks Among Team Members

Once a comprehensive outline that is populated with yellow text is completed, writing assignments can be distributed. Of course, there are many ways to divide writing tasks, and project leaders need to decide the most effective way to draft their documents *before* they give assignments. In other words, not only should the team be clear about what they're writing, for whom, and why, they should also share understanding about *how* they will write. In this section we outline a few approaches to constructing writing teams as you consider how to divide work among team members. The most important thing to remember, of course, is that assignments should be given based upon a member's ability to execute the task with efficiency and precision, whether the individual is writing the content alone or as part of group.

5.3.5.1 Choose a Drafting Strategy. The actual act of writing a document

can be daunting. An author might stare at a screen for a while and then grudgingly start typing words on the page. However, if the team has prepared a good outline with yellow text, the process of drafting a document is less like composing from scratch and more like inserting text into existing containers—again, this is the *STREAM Tools* approach of using materials that exist rather than creating everything from scratch. Using existing structures doesn't mean authors won't have difficulty writing or that they won't stall on certain tasks, but using the outline and yellow text as a series of boxes "to fill" definitely makes writing less daunting.

When teams reach a point where they are ready to draft, there are generally three approaches to take: solo drafting, divide and draft, and collective drafting. Each of these approaches has advantages and drawbacks, which are outlined below along with a brief description of each approach.

SOLO DRAFTING. Drafting alone has a long history. Many times when we say "author" we imagine the lone writer sitting a desk letting flashes of genius appear in words on a page. That image is deeply rooted—and deeply problematic in many ways because it contributes to the writing anxiety (sometimes called "writer's block") that so many writers feel as they sit down to draft. Drawing on that lone author/genius model, we hesitate to begin writing because we spend time looking for the right words; we think we have to get it right the first time. Additionally, when we author alone, we have more investment in the texts we write, so critiques often hit us harder. Experienced writers practice several techniques to reduce writer's block including:

- Arranging for time alone. Turn off the phone, quit email, and eliminate the possibility of electronic interruptions.
- Talking over the subject with someone and taping your conversation. Make a rough transcription of the conversation as a starting point.
- Recording your own thoughts aloud as you drive, walk, or exercise and then transcribing your thoughts. Also, consider trying modern speech recognition tools, which have now improved so that they are quite useful. You may choose to carry a digital recorder that can plug into a USB port; there is even speech recognition software that will transcribe text for you. Currently, the leading suite of software tools in this area is called NaturallySpeaking.
- Forcing yourself to write something to fill space on a page even if it's only a meaningful quotation. Explain the quotation and why it's relevant to your thinking to get started.
- Writing frequently for shorter time periods. Plan to write 30 minutes every day rather than 5 hours on a single day so the material stays fresh in your mind and so you know that you "have to write" for only 30 minutes.

For those who are a bit more adventurous, some authors have suggested these more exotic techniques:

- Give yourself little rewards. For example, you cannot have that piece of cake in front of you until you finish this page.
- Divide your tasks into five numbered categories. Throw a die. If you get a number from 1 to 5, work on that task for the next hour. If you get a 6—lucky you—take a break.
- Hang upside down for a while. The new blood circulation pattern will help your brain function better.
- Work outside. There are laptops with bright screens suitable for use outdoors, for example, many Fujitsu laptops have this feature.
- Explain the essence of your manuscript to a complete outsider (your friend or relative) and have them write it up for you.

Usually, a combination of techniques works best (whether traditional or exotic) and a complete range of techniques would fill a large book. If you feel anxiety about writing, you are certainly not alone. Many others around you feel the same way, largely because we hold strongly to our notion of the lone author/genius model. For most

TABLE 5.4. Solo Drafting: Strengths and Weaknesses

Solo Drafting Comparison	
Strengths	*Weaknesses*
• Enables efficient drafting	• Relies on the author to have complete knowledge on the issue
• Produces consistent documents	
• Frees time for other team members	• Restricts opportunity for multiple perspectives and approaches
	• Increases opportunities for tension
	• Presents additional risk for missed deadlines

workplace writing situations, we simply can't wait for genius to descend upon us; we have work to get done—fast.

Even with the challenges sole authorship poses for writers, it does possess many advantages that can help ease the writing burden of the team, especially when one person on the team has demonstrated particularly strong writing abilities. In this case, asking for a single person to author the text might be a good idea because the consistency of style, look, and mechanics that a single author brings might save time in the editing portion of the project. Relying on a single author also increases the accountability for the text since one person is ultimately responsible for it. Finally, solo drafting frees other team members to work on other tasks, such as conducting research for the author, or editing text as the author produces it. Adopting the solo drafting strategy does require a huge amount of trust on the team's part because the team relies on that single person to represent the ideas for the whole group. Additionally, using the solo drafting strategy requires that the non-authoring team members subordinate their role and, in a way, become subject to the needs of the author. In short, the sole author, once the writing begins, has charge of the project.

Although solo drafting can be very efficient, it can also have some downsides. Obviously, the project will suffer if the sole author has a significant knowledge gap. Likewise, the sole author might have a particular viewpoint on the issue that doesn't adequately represent the interests of the whole team. As a result, tension might develop among team members who feel that their inputs are not valued or heard. Finally, and very pragmatically, relying on a sole author means that if that author misses a deadline, or becomes ill, or is drawn away on another project, the entire team will suffer. In most large writing situations, solo drafting is not the ideal strategy because of these weaknesses. Table 5.4 outlines the strengths of solo drafting.

DIVIDE AND DRAFT. The second strategy, divide and draft, is the most common approach and the one in which most writers feel comfortable. In this strategy, different authors are assigned responsibility for different portions of the text, either due to their interests or expertise. Multiple individuals write their pieces of the document separately and periodically check in with one other to make sure that they all still agree on the direction of the document. This strategy works like a computer network, where the parts add together to form a whole greater than any one of the parts and where failure

TABLE 5.5. Divide and Draft: Strengths and Weaknesses

Divide and Draft Comparison

Strengths	Weaknesses
• Employs a familiar paradigm	• Produces inconsistent texts
• Enables efficient drafting	• Adds additional time to the project for extensive editing at the end of the drafting process
• Protects the team from wholesale failure through a networked approach	
• Offers thorough treatment of multiple topics by area experts	• Assumes writers will maintain awareness of other authors' work
• Integrates multiple perspectives on the topic	
• Doesn't overtax any single team member	

by one piece of the system doesn't signal the collapse of the entire project. This strategy brings together the experience, vision, and perspectives of multiple people, and when the final pieces are compiled, usually results in a document that is stronger than any one person could have produced.

However, using the divide and draft strategy leaves a large portion of work for the very end of the writing process. Whenever multiple authors are involved in a project, inconsistencies will invariably arise even though the team might have carefully prepared a style guide. Realistically, one cannot expect different writers to sound completely alike even when working from the same style guide and after working together for a number of years. Additionally, unless writers share drafts in process, individuals might produce text that contradicts, challenges, or leaves out content vital to another section. For example, in the case of outlining dependencies where one point relies on prior points, one author might incorrectly assume that another author has adequately established the context for later discussion, when in fact they had not. Consequently, the efficiency gains of this approach are somewhat mitigated by the overhead necessary at the end of the drafting cycle to make a multi-author document internally consistent, in terms of both content and style. To overcome this difficulty, one single editor should be appointed, preferably someone who has not written in this particular document and therefore can look at it with fresh eyes. The role of the editor is to meld individual contributions into a single, consistent text. Table 5.5 outlines the strengths and weaknesses of the divide and draft strategy.

COLLECTIVE DRAFTING. Collective drafting requires the most time investment from authors, but usually produces the highest quality documents. This strategy requires so much time because authors literally write together, either physically side by side, or by utilizing an Internet-based application such as GoToMeeting or Adobe Connect for sharing files among writers in real time. In web applications such as Adobe Connect or GoToMeeting, one team member initiates the meeting and has the document in question residing on his or her computer. The document-holder member opens the document and then shares his or her screen with other team members, who have accessed the meeting through a web browser. At this point, the team member who initiated the meaning can share keyboard and mouse controls with other team members so

TABLE 5.6. Collective Drafting: Strengths and Weaknesses

Collective Drafting Comparison

Strengths	*Weaknesses*
• Builds strong ties among team members	• Requires extraordinary amounts of time
• Integrates multiple perspectives into the	to be done well
process	• Relies on team members possessing
• Infuses the process with energy	negotiation skills
• Produces consistent final products	• Runs the risk of producing groupthink to
• Produces highly accurate products	the detriment of the product
	• Can induce ill will among team members

that everybody on the team now has the opportunity—one-by-one—to write in the document that resides on the computer of the meeting initiator.

This approach works best in teams of three or less, because having more than three voices becomes chaotic and counterproductive. However, the multiplicity of voices present during the drafting process ensures complete treatment of topics and provides an energetic setting that easily carries the drafting process forward. Multiple writers can talk through their ideas as they write together, and in doing so, no surprises appear in the final versions of the document. This means that: dependencies are addressed more easily and comprehensively, the style is consistent, and content in one place doesn't conflict or challenge content in another place. Finally, having multiple eyes looking at a single document increases the overall quality since different readers will see and hear different mistakes or weaknesses in the document.

STREAM Tools Commandment #8:
Iterate.

However, even though this highly interactive process builds rapport among team members, the amount of time it takes to draft this way can be staggering. Consider that potentially every sentence, every point, every turn of phrase has to be discussed and negotiated. While this generates a great deal of collective ownership in the document, the process takes a long time. A related weakness is the concept of "groupthink" where team members manage to persuade themselves and each other of a particular perspective, even though that approach might not be most productive. In this case, maintaining the close social bonds that form while drafting becomes more important than the quality of the finished project. Another downside of this approach presents itself when team members either do not get along well or begin the process with highly divergent viewpoints. If the team enters the drafting phase while maintaining strong differences of opinion, an extraordinary amount of time will be necessary for negotiating differences prior to and during the drafting process. Even with these significant weaknesses, and assuming that teams have the time to engage in this process without missing deadlines, this approach can be very powerful. In fact, a large portion of this book was written in this very manner. Table 5.6 outlines the strengths and weaknesses of collective drafting.

5.3.5.2 *Synchronize Writing Styles.* Regardless of the way that writing tasks are distributed within your team, differences will always exist among participants. Consequently, the more that your team can completely articulate the final form of the document *prior* to embarking on the writing process, the easier the writing process will be. For example, something as simple as two team members who differ on the spelling of a color might derail the project and significantly damage the synergy among the team. So, before your team begins to write and after the writing assignments have been given, your team needs to decide, for example, if the color just lighter than black is spelled "grey" or is spelled "gray." Both are correct. Another example is that some writers will choose to use dashes for emphasis and some will use commas. Both are correct. Both depend on unique style differences of individuals. Because styles can be so different among individuals we recommend that writing teams construct a *style guide* prior to writing and a *style sheet* that evolves with the project. We discuss each of these below.

DEVELOPING AND MAINTAINING A STYLE GUIDE. When working with a team, each participant's unique style can be very problematic because as different authors weld their pieces together, the resulting document will look exactly like what it is: a patchwork compilation of different styles. Consequently, whenever writing as part of a team or as part of an organization, teams should use a "style guide" to direct their work. Style guides assist with consistency across the document and across authors in multiple areas. Consistency across the team and across the document is not only important for authors, but for the reader as well; stylistic inconsistencies, such as interchanging references or visual cues, can be confusing. This is why the purpose of *STREAM Tools* itself is to ensure that multiple writers produce a consistently formatted document by utilizing the built in style features of Microsoft Word.

Disciplines often have a style guide that they follow like the *Chicago Manual of Style*. Likewise, companies and publications often utilize style manuals specific to that organization, and teams working within the organization must adhere to those guidelines. Frequently, though, these guides are either too complex for easy use, or conversely don't provide coverage of issues relevant to your team (like using alternative spellings for grey/gray). Another complication is that writing teams often don't have one set style that they *must* use, so their style evolves during the composing process which results in a great deal of reverse editing for consistency. If a writing team makes as many decisions as possible *before* writing, authors will know from the beginning how to spell "grey/gray," how to label figures, and whether the document has an informal or formal tone, for example. While *STREAM Tools* reduces the load of much of this work, teams still should develop or adopt style guides prior to composing.

One might think that if a single person has been assigned to compile the final document, then style guides and templates are not important. However, the issue is efficiency. If the materials from numerous contributors arrive in as many formats as there are contributors, then the compiler is stuck with endless hours of mouse clicking to get the document to look right—a step that could have been avoided. In some cases, there is a special administrative assistant hired to compile documents. However, in most cases, the mouse clicking that could have been avoided falls to the group leader and final approver of the document, whose time is usually the most costly. When a group leader is forced to complete these types of small changes, it ultimately costs the organization great amounts of money—not only because the leader is forced to complete unnecessary low-skill tasks, but because he or she is prevented from spending that time performing other strategic activities like locating funding opportunities or resolving personnel issues. Synchronizing writing styles and introducing some of the select features of *STREAM Tools* will help alleviate most of these issues.

The "*STREAM Tools* Style Guide Tool" (adapted from Carolyn Rude's book, *Technical Editing*) represents the minimum topics and decisions that need to be made to ensure consistency.

The *STREAM Tools* Style Guide Tool

Verbal Style

1. Meaning of words and only one term per concept

2. Level of diction, complex or simple sentence patterns, formal or informal style

Visual Style (*STREAM Tools* accounts for much of this)

1. Typefaces for each type of text, such as headings or body text

2. Layout choices, such as the position of headings and figures

3. Elements, such as icons and colors

4. Table and figure labels, typeface, use of callouts and captions

Mechanical Style

1. Spelling

2. Capitalization

3. Numbers

4. Punctuation

5. Documentation style (for references and bibliography)

6. Abbreviations

7. Emphasis devices such as bold, italics, or underlines

Mechanical Style

    I.   Spelling: all words will use the less formal, American usage.

          a. Example: gray

          b. Example: theater

    II.   Capitalization

          a. The initial letter in all lists will be capitalized

          b. *STREAM Tools* will be capitalized and italicized at each use

Figure 5.5. Sample entries in a style guide

A-D	E-H	I-L
CD (for 'compact disc')	Email (not e-mail)	Internet (initial capital)
M-P	Q-T	U-Z
Military Police (initial capital)	Typeface	Under-the-Influence

Figure 5.6. Sample entries in a style sheet

When drafting the style guide, teams should first list the topic and then list an example of that particular topic (Figure 5.5).

Because style guides are comprehensive, they can grow to be lengthy depending upon the complexity of the project. However, articulating each of these decisions prior to writing speeds the editing process, making it easier for multiple authors to integrate their work into a single unit. Again, the main idea of *STREAM Tools* is to fill containers, not to make decisions on the fly, simply because those decisions lead to inconsistencies that impact the document's credibility with readers and create more work for editors.

DEVELOPING AND MAINTAINING STYLE SHEETS. While *style guides* are comprehensive and prepared prior to authoring, *style sheets* evolve with the project as authors make specific decisions about items not covered within the parameters defined by the style guide. A common method for developing a style sheet is to prepare a grid that records decisions alphabetically in a grid as shown in Figure 5.6 (adapted from Carolyn Rude's *Technical Editing*.)

The *STREAM Tools* Style Sheet Tool		
A-D	*E-H*	*I-L*
M-P	*Q-T*	*U-Z*

The challenge of using a style sheet is that authors frequently make decisions unconsciously based upon their experiences and therefore may not record their choices on the sheet. A second challenge is that authors might forget to refer to the style sheet as they write, introducing preventable inconsistencies into the writing. However, if writing teams participate in constructing as much of the style sheet as possible prior to beginning the writing process, they will be more aware of the choices outlined. In addition, as teams become more skilled at collaborative authorship, they will begin to see the utility and efficiency of referring to style sheets as they enter the completion stage of the process outlined in Section 5.5. In short, referring to the style sheet and recording choices on the style sheet while writing significantly reduces the amount of time that team members will spend editing documents.

Once your team has successfully defined the project and adequately completed the groundwork necessary for an efficient writing process by evaluating historical documents, populating a file repository, creating a comprehensive outline, populating the outline with "yellow text," and distributing writing tasks, then writing can actually begin. In all, the first two stages of the *STREAM Tools* Writing Process should compose about 50% of the project time—excellent preparation leads to efficient writing and completion.

5.4   WRITING STAGE

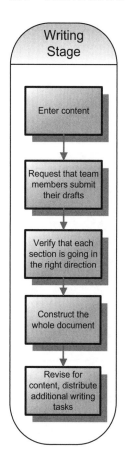

The actual process of writing a document should only occur after a thorough definition and preparation process as outlined in the sections above. Sometimes, of course, your team will need to produce a document quickly without having the necessary planning time, but in most cases, if your team did plan, not only will the actual writing be easier, the end result will be of far higher quality. And just as definition and preparation are both a process, so is the writing stage. In the *STREAM Tools* process, teams move from creating content to collecting drafts to verifying that each team is on target, compiling the document, and finally to revising for content (and moving through the process again, as necessary). We discuss each of these steps below.

5.4.1   Enter Content

Content comes from many sources: from published literature, from new information or original research generated by your team, from presentations, conversations, or other types of content that you might have in your file repository. Regardless of the source, almost every document will combine existing, "legacy" content as well as new content. Legacy content, of course, comes from the files in your repository, while new content is generated by your team to fill holes in the documents that legacy content cannot.

5.4.1.1   Legacy Content. Appropriate reuse of material that you already possess can save huge amounts of time while improving the impact of the document. Usually, only senior team members will have the best picture of what legacy content can be included because they'll have greater experience and a broader range of exposure to various documents. For example, a senior professor is aware of an excellent "Background and Motivation" section in the Ph.D. thesis of a recent graduate from a sister lab, and can direct a new graduate student to that section rather than asking him or her to spend time "reinventing the wheel." When entering legacy content, your team will need to modify the content to suit the novel purpose because it's unlikely that the old material will fit exactly into the new context. Refer back to your audience and purpose to determine which "yellow text" sections the legacy content might fill. Copy the text (or figure or table) into the new document and when the time comes, your team will integrate that content with the new content so that your document sounds fresh.

This leads to an important point: reuse of legacy content needs to be managed carefully to avoid becoming "too efficient" by straying into the area of plagiarism. Plagiarism represents one of the "cardinal sins" of technical and scientific writing for good reason, since the point of this type of writing is often to explore new topics and present new content. If your document looks too much like an earlier piece, then not only does it present information that has already been published, it demonstrates that perhaps your team wasn't willing to do the work necessary to adequately solve the problem your team is writing about. In either case, simply copying and pasting can be very dangerous and needs to be managed carefully.

Some exceptions exist, of course, depending upon the type of document. For example, in a report that goes out to customers, a company's mission and vision might be copied and pasted exactly as they appear in the file repository. Likewise, "standard" content describing a common procedure or method could be imported from the repository; however, in general we recommend that any text that has been *directly imported* from the file repository should be marked in the document by highlighting it as "red text" to show that this information is "hot" and needs to be integrated and/or cited. When your team generates new content to surround the red text and modifies the red text to integrate seamlessly with the new content, you can remove the red highlighting—making sure to retain any appropriate citations, of course.

5.4.1.2 *New Content.*

5.4.1.2 New Content. Every writing situation is unique, even though many situations share similarities. One proposal for the National Science Foundation probably looks just like another in terms of headings and section divisions, yet the content will be largely novel in a new proposal. The same goes for journal articles: each journal has a particular way of structuring articles, but your article will not contain the same content as another even though they might sound alike and look alike. Much of your file repository comprises these sample documents, which your team will use to construct a comprehensive outline of the document. Your team will also enter appropriate legacy content so that you're not creating everything from scratch as you write. Instead, as *STREAM Tools* teaches, your team "fills containers."

But even filling containers takes a lot of work and original thought and your team will need to develop new content to go with the legacy content. To adopt a metaphor, think about the process of painting a wall. The best paint jobs start with a thorough coat of primer, followed by an initial coat of paint. Then the painter sands to remove rough edges, cleans the paint of debris, and applies another coat. The painter might repeat the process of sanding and painting several times, depending on what is being painted, before the job is finished. Writing is similar in that research shows that the best writers never think their first pass is the final one. And, in reality, it almost never is. Most formal documents must go through three, four, or five iterations before they are ready to be viewed publicly. Consequently, writers need to drop the pretense that they'll get it right on the first try. They won't; you won't. And even if your team does think that they nailed the first draft—or piece of a draft—on the first try, odds are that an editor or more senior team member will review the document and find all sorts of problems.

Using the *STREAM Tools* method of re-using as much legacy content as possible eases the process of generating new content, but seasoned writers know several things: that at some point they will be forced to simply sit down and write, that they can't afford to be married to their content, and that they'll almost certainly have to revise what they write. Writing becomes far less daunting when we realize that we don't have to get it right on the first try. Nobody expects us to.

5.4.1.3 *Control Versions of Shared Files.* A final concern as your team writes documents is that shared files require a method of confirming who is working on which pieces of a document. This critical concern relates both within specific teams and across teams so that separate groups working on the same document know who has control of which portion.

While using appropriate naming conventions reduces the opportunity for error in your team, a risk still remains. Therefore, when sharing files among multiple team members (or across teams), each individual should "check out" and "return" documents—much like you would a library book—to indicate that for the present time, that document (where "document" is to be understood as any portion of a writing project) is being used by another person. This "check out" system provides a back-up in the instance that somebody has forgotten to change the name of the document indicating the status.

In *STREAM Tools*, we suggest that you use server technology, such as SharePoint or a wiki to make versions available to multiple users. We discuss these technologies in more detail in Chapter 6, but a brief word here is in order. One powerful product, SharePoint, keeps track of versions and check-in/check-out status, among other things. However, SharePoint has a learning curve and requires the support of IT staff, so it might not be the right choice for your team. Perhaps your team might choose to use a wiki to accomplish the same ends. With wikis, users must record the status of the document, at minimum "checked out" or "available." This status flag alerts other team members that they should not be working on the document at the same time and that they should check back later to continue their work on the document or to review the work that another individual has completed. This process creates a history of the document's developments while simultaneously incorporating quality control, since multiple authors review new work as it develops. Using a wiki, one author writes a new piece of text, another author reviews the contribution, potentially adding revisions to the first round of text and then submits it to other team members who might go through the same process—one at a time. This process creates deeply interwoven documents that possess:

- Consistent writing style
- Thorough coverage of content areas
- Precise development of logic
- Accurate mechanics

If a team implements a process like this and shares files successfully, the team will spend its time writing rather than struggling to figure out which document contains what content or where a certain heading was in one document versus another document. We recommend utilizing this file management system to avoid "leapfrogging." As with all *STREAM Tools* processes, the purpose is to let your writing team be as efficient and effective as possible by using standardized approaches. It also encourages the team to see writing as a collaborative process since no team member will "own" a particular piece of a document. All team members will share, to the extent they want or are able, in creating a document and all team members are equally able to critique and modify another's work. This helps teams past the mental roadblock of believing that they have to get it right the first time because the process simply won't allow that to happen!

5.4.2   Request that Team Members Submit Their Drafts

One important result of viewing writing as a process is that we can ask team members to submit drafts early and often to the team leader. This step might seem unnecessary if we view writing as a process—why would teams submit intermediate drafts?—but the step is key because it builds accountability into the process. Unfortunately, many of us will put off our duties until just before they are due. Writing simply doesn't work that way. If a team puts off beginning their work until just before the deadline, not only does it cause great stress, it also produces a poor document that has not benefited from the process of going through multiple iterations. Therefore, it is important that teams and their subgroups complete their assigned sections as soon as possible.

On the other end of the spectrum from procrastination, a team without intermediate deadlines may continue to iterate endlessly. In this case, a team has taken to heart the idea that writing is truly never finished and as a result continues working on a piece of text until it actually begins to get worse. Think again about the painting metaphor. There's a breakpoint where too many coats of paint begin to obscure architectural details. Too many coats of paint also create the possibility that errors will be introduced: maybe somebody uses the wrong shade of paint on one wall, or creates a drip that dries into a bump, necessitating yet *another* iteration of the sand-and-coat process.

In every writing process, a point of diminishing returns exists for continuing iterations; accordingly, writers need to recognize when they've reached that point and are actually beginning to make their documents worse. Likewise, going through too few iterations will produce a poorly developed or ill-conceived document since enough time has not been spent improving the document. If a team is forced to submit their drafts at staged intervals, both downfalls can be avoided.

5.4.3   Verify that Each Section Is Headed in the Right Direction

A close cousin to intermediate draft submissions is verifying that each submission is headed in the right direction, usually the job of the project leader. The phrase "headed in the right direction" is somewhat ambiguous for the good reason that an experienced project leader has to keep in mind multiple considerations when evaluating intermediate drafts. For example, do all the documents demonstrate the right attention to audience and purpose? How are the writing teams themselves getting along? Are the teams strong enough to continue? What about modifications to the outline which become necessary as the content emerges? Often necessary content doesn't fit within the existing outline, requiring the team to retrofit the outline to the content. Do the separate pieces overlap, and if so do they complement or contradict each other?

These represent only a few possible considerations that confirm that the project is moving in the right direction. However, in all cases, the confirmation progress requires that teams and individuals submit their drafts at planned intervals to somebody charged with a global view of the project. Perhaps that person is a designated leader, or perhaps it is the person chosen as an editor. Regardless, a single point for collecting and commenting on individual contributions will make the process most efficient.

Finally, as a result of this review, teams might be given extra research jobs or additional writing tasks, or might be asked to abandon some content and move in a different direction. As teams are tasked with new objectives, they should cycle back through the stages of locating and entering legacy content and generating new content. Even with this extra work, teams will produce documents more efficiently when asked to re-route their activities in the middle of the writing process simply because changes that "head off" problems will be minor compared to changes or requests made at the end of the process. Again, it is important to remember that writing is never perfect and is always in process. If we become too wedded to our own text, we forget that what we're really doing is achieving some purpose *through* the document. Keeping the purpose—what the document is trying to achieve—in mind can help writers accept feedback and revision suggestions more easily.

5.4.4   Construct the Whole Document

At this point, your team has successfully integrated legacy content with new content and cycled through several iterations with a central reviewer by submitting their documents at scheduled intervals. The time has come to compile the document into one cohesive whole. This particular aspect of the *STREAM Tools* Writing Process is best left to a single individual, perhaps the team leader or the reviewer who has collected the portions of the document throughout the process. This person's job is quite complicated because they must look back to the document's purpose, the document's audience, and to any additional considerations that might exist such as particular content that must be included.

The task of compiling the document is also more complicated than simply pasting together pieces from separate individuals, because the document has to look and sound like it was created by a unified team. If your document looks like or reads like it was stitched together from 10 different sources, it will fail, plain and simple. Very, very few situations will allow for this type of patchwork approach to writing because it appears shoddy and incomplete and speaks to a lack of concern for how the document will be perceived.

So, how does the person compiling the document transform the various contributions they've received into a seamless document? Consider these steps as your team compiles its manuscript:

1. Review the audience and purpose guidelines.
2. Review any formal requirements for content or formatting required in the writing situation.
3. Review the comprehensive outline (even if it was modified) and confirm that you have all the required pieces.
4. Open (or create) a template for your document and change the headings in the template to match the comprehensive outline.
5. Paste the submitted content into the outline at the appropriate positions.
6. Save the entire document.
7. Edit ruthlessly as outlined in below in Section 5.4.5.

This process has proven effective to the *STREAM Tools* authors for over hundreds of documents of all types, and so we encourage you to adopt it. The key point of this process is that the team cannot stop at the compiling stage. A document that has been constructed from multiple voices is never, ever complete and ready for the audience. It will require a great deal more work before the document is even ready to be shared outside of your team.

5.4.5 Revise for Content and Distribute Additional Writing Tasks

After the document has been constructed from the separate parts, it needs to be revised extensively to ensure that it appears seamless to an audience. While your team might be tempted to focus at this stage on small matters of grammar, mechanics, and formatting, these represent only a small part of the whole picture. In fact, many surface issues will be handled in the "Completion Stage" of the *STREAM Tools* writing process and so the focus here should be on what technical writing handbooks (some listed at the end of this chapter) call *"comprehensive editing"* as opposed to "copyediting" and "proofreading." Your team will move through these latter two phases, but only after the comprehensive editing process has woven the document into a seamless whole.

In what follows, we outline the basic knowledge necessary for editing at all levels (including copyediting and proofreading), but we focus on comprehensive editing. For example, we discuss marking up hardcopy and the symbols you should use. We reintroduce the very important *STREAM Tools* Editorial Mark-up Table—a short-hand method of commenting on texts that speeds the editorial process but also systematizes the feedback editors give to writers. We also include a discussion of the robust editing and reviewing tools available in Microsoft Word.

5.4.5.1 Comprehensive Editing. Assuming that your team has employed a quality preparation process, the audience, purpose, content, and style should all be known to team members since they were articulated prior to drafting the document. Now the editor is left with a compiled document that needs to be audited against the standards outlined in the Definition Stage and in the Preparation Stage. Comprehensive editing achieves these goals. When working through documents that have recently been compiled and are in the process of being woven together, editors (or team leaders)

TABLE 5.7. *STREAM Tools* Editorial Questions Tool

STREAM Tools Editorial Questions Tool	
Analyze the Audience, Purpose, and Use	*Evaluate the Document*
• Who will read the document and why?	• Is the *content* complete and appropriate for the audience?
• What do readers already know?	• Does the document employ an *organization* that the audience will easily recognize and will make sense?
• What should users know or do after reading this document?	
• What are the readers' attitudes toward the topic?	• Has the document used *visual design* to support the purpose, ease access to content, and reveal organization?
• What should happen as a result of this document's use?	
• What will readers do with the document after reading it?	• Does the *style* meet accepted standards for this type of document and is it appropriate for this audience?
• Will users read the document straight through, skim, or choose only parts to read?	• Are *illustrations*, figures and tables used to clarify content?

usually make long marginal comments or append queries to the document. These notes and queries might ask authors to clarify their content, or to review particular requirements of the document. The editor might suggest potential revisions that improve the document or bring a particular section into alignment with other sections. The possibilities are quite numerous as the editor performs the job of combining several voices to make one seamless document that meets the needs of the audience and the purpose. Since an editor might have many concerns, we've constructed the *STREAM Tools* Editorial Questions Tool shown in Table 5.7. The tool presents a series of useful questions to help editors focus their commentary among all the possible things that could attract their attention.

Of course, this table does not exhaust the possible options for concerns that editors might have. The point is that editors begin the process by asking questions of the document to ensure that it meets the needs of the audience, appropriately addresses the purpose and use, and has been presented in a way that demonstrates the authors have carefully considered why, how, and by whom the document will be read. Think of this step as a confirmation that the document has met the specifications articulated in the Definition and Preparation Stages and use this time to suggest high-level revisions that bring the document more in line with those specifications while ensuring seamless presentation.

5.4.5.2 STREAM Tools *Editorial Mark-up Table (STEM Table).* A second tool for helping editors as they improve the quality of documents is the *STREAM Tools* Editorial Mark-up Table. The *STREAM Tools* Editorial Mark-up Table (STEM Table) represents one of the most important time savers for managers and leaders who have to review documents. Much like the standard editing and proofreading marks used by editors listed in Section 5.5, the STEM Table (Table 5.8) enables reviewers and authors to note a problem quickly without any elaborate explanation. While the notation symbols in the STEM Table will initially take some time for reviewers and authors to

TABLE 5.8. The Extended *STREAM Tools* Editorial Mark-up Table (STEM Table)

Comment	Abbreviation Deciphered	Meaning	Section in This Book
c:\AA	Analyze the audience	The document does not address the right audience.	5.2.3
c:\AP	Analyze the purpose	The document has not addressed the purpose or has no clear sense of purpose.	5.2.4
c:\awk	Awkward	Sentence is awkward. Possibly word sequence, word selection, or sentence structure need to be changed.	7.2; 7.3; 7.4
c:\bold	Bold font	Toggle bold font.	
c:\casual	Casual wording	The wording is too casual. People may speak like that, but this wording is not suitable for formal writing.	7.2.1.2
c:\colloq	Colloquial	A colloquial expression. People may say it, but it is not appropriate in this context.	7.2.1.2
c:\EOI	End of iteration	The manuscript contains too many errors. The editor stopped at the EOI point and expects the writer to learn from previous mistakes, apply them to the entire body of the manuscript, and bring it back for the next iteration.	5.3.5.1; Chapter 7
c:\glob	Global change	A request to correct this type of a problem throughout the document. This comment is to be used in combination with other comments, when the same type of mistake occurs multiple times and the editor does not want to correct it every time.	Self-explanatory
c:\gram	Grammatical error	A catch-all comment for grammatical errors.	Chapter 7
c:\muw	Misused words	You are using words incorrectly.	7.2.2.1
c:\model	Model document	Please refer to a good model document after which the current manuscript is structured.	5.3.1
c:\purpose	Purpose	The purpose of this part of the document is not clear. Should it be persuasion, exposition, or instruction?	5.2.4

TABLE 5.8. *Continued*

Comment	Abbreviation Deciphered	Meaning	Section in This Book
c:\struc	Structure	The document lacks proper structure.	5.3.3
c:\STH x.x	Writing for Research Teams	Read Section x.x (for example, Section 5.2) from this book, *Technical Writing For Teams: The STREAM Tools Handbook.*	Self-explanatory
Written in pencil	Regular comment	The comment or correction does not need a discussion.	Self-explanatory
Written in red pen	Talk to the reviewer about it	Usually, a complex subject nature that requires a discussion.	Self-explanatory
c:	Comment	This is not a replacement text but rather a comment.	Self-explanatory
c:\it	Italics	Toggle italics font.	Self-explanatory
c:\pw	Poor wording	The sentence is poorly worded.	7.2
c:\pbw	Problems with black and white	There is a possibility that the document would be printed in black and white, making references to color. For example, saying "red line shows" is meaningless and annoying to the reader if the figure is in black and white.	3.2.3.4
c:\pwt	Problems with terminology	Poor selection of terminology, could be confusing, misleading, or just incorrect.	Self-explanatory
c:\rep	Repetition	Repetitive use of the same word or root.	Self-explanatory
c:\rm	Roman	Use Times New Roman font.	Self-explanatory
c:\tog	Together	Let's rewrite this part together.	Self-explanatory
c:\S&W	Strunk and White	An error discussed in Strunk and White, one of the most famous books on grammar. Read the book.	Self-explanatory
c:\sp	Spelling	Incorrect spelling.	Self-explanatory
c:\sp?	Spelling?	Possibly incorrect spelling.	Self-explanatory
c:\WV	Watch the video	Typesetting mistakes, which are described in the video tutorials.	

learn, the payoff is quite substantial because reviewers—those managers and group leaders whose time is most expensive—can make very substantive commentary without typing (or handwriting) long notes.

The system is fairly simple: the initial characters (c:\) indicate that a comment follows (as opposed to actual text that needs to be entered into the document). The characters following the slash (\ ) indicate that nature of the problem. The table also provides references to sections in this book where one will find full discussions of various topics, so that the writing team can refer to specific sections if they are unclear about how to revise. Our experience using the STEM Table indicates that once a group has learned the system, the review process becomes much quicker as does the revision process since all members of the team refer to the same set of common symbols.

While we have included here a set of possible marks, individual teams might have already evolved their own symbols or might wish to create their own. If your team would like to add to the STEM Table, visit the *STREAM Tools* website at streamtoolsonline.com and add your marks. Alternatively, you can also download a version of the STEM Table with blank rows from the website if you choose to create your own version and circulate it among your team members.

5.4.5.3 *Strategies for Editing Electronic Copy Using Microsoft Word— An Overview of Microsoft Word's Commenting, Reviewing, and Proofing Features.* Finally, those who review documents might choose to make their marks electronically rather than on paper. Microsoft Word contains a robust set of tools for commenting on documents, as well as for reviewing and proofreading. For example, most Microsoft Word users are familiar with the squiggles that appear under misspelled words or poorly phrased sentences. Probably fewer people are aware that authors can alter why those squiggles appear, can turn them off entirely, or better yet, use them effectively. But the squiggles are only a part of the suite of tools available for reviewing (and writing!) documents. Microsoft Word enables commenting, change tracking, and side-by-side comparison of documents. As part of *STREAM Tools*, authors should use these functions to enable efficient collaboration among the team members. Below, we provide an overview of these functions, including when to use them and basic instructions on how to use them.

COMMENTING ON DOCUMENTS. In traditional editorial practice, editors provide queries to authors in the margins or on paper sticky notes. But Microsoft Word enables reviewers to comment electronically on the document itself by inserting "balloons" that appear at the point of the comment. These balloons appear on the right side of the document in an expanded "margin" and can be printed if the document authors choose to review the comments in print rather than on the monitor. The primary purposes of the comment function include asking authors questions, clarifying particular points, correcting incorrect information, or suggesting revisions that would strengthen the document.

Figure 5.7 shows a commented page from an early draft of this chapter. Notice that two separate people commented on this chapter, as indicated by the initials. The color assigned to each reviewer will also change, although that color isn't reproduced here.

Commenting on documents requires only a few steps to begin:

1. Save the file as a different name to protect the integrity of the original version (just in case something goes wrong).
2. Click to the **Review** tab on the top of Microsoft Word's interface.

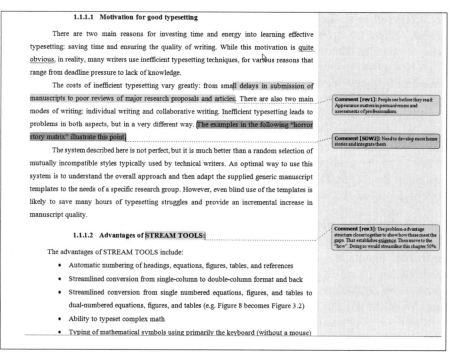

Figure 5.7. Commented page from an early draft of this book

3. Verify reviewer/user information (see below).
4. Turn on change tracking by clicking **Track Changes**.
5. Highlight or insert the cursor or where you'd like to comment.
6. Click **New Comment** and type your note in the box that appears on the right margin.

While most of these steps are straightforward, and most users are probably familiar with commenting, step 3, "Verify reviewer/user information" requires a bit more commentary. When a team has authored a document, it's vital that each individual be accountable for their own work and Microsoft Word allows readers of a document to see who has commented or made changes in a document. Unfortunately, most authors and editors overlook this vital step. In many cases, following the steps below would eliminate confusion over who has made what commentary by establishing a reviewer's "identity":

1. Click the **Review** tab on the top of the Microsoft Word interface.
2. Click the small arrow on the **Track Changes** button.
3. Select *Change User Name*.

4. Select *Popular* on the left side navigation.

5. Type your name and initials under *Personalize your copy of Microsoft Office.*

After you complete this step, every time you leave a comment in a document or make an edit, your identity will appear along with that comment in case an author needs to speak with you about your note.

REVIEWING DOCUMENTS. After the team members responsible for editing the document have commented on the authors' work, authors have the opportunity to review the comments made by the editors and make appropriate changes. To view the commentary, simply open the document and either 1) scroll through it reading the comments as they appear, or 2) click the **Review** tab, and click the **Next** button on the **Comments** ribbon to move to the next comment. Alternatively, for a more global view, authors can select **Reviewing Pane** and all the changes and comments in the document will appear in a separate window on the left side of the screen. Assuming that the editors selected **Track Changes** before they began working on the document, every change they introduced will appear in the reviewing pane, and authors can then sort through all of the comments and changes proposed. This review stage can be repeated as many times as necessary throughout this step.

5.4.6 Distribute Additional Writing Tasks

Once your team has completed the review process, whether on paper or electronically using Microsoft Word, the teams will need to return to the document and make the appropriate revisions. Sometimes this involves substantial rewriting that might include additional research. Sometimes, it's a matter of deleting some words or reorganizing a few paragraphs. Whichever the case—small revisions or large—the project leader will need to assign a priority to the tasks that the teams must complete. Each team can then complete the tasks as required, carefully reviewing the commentary from the reviewer as well as additional instructions from the team leader (who might also be the reviewer).

After the document has been compiled and reviewed in the manner we've described, version control becomes even more imperative. Refer back to Section 5.4.1.3, "Control Versions of Shared Files" as a reminder about controlling file versions. At this stage when your team has a complete document and now is in the process of improving it, "leapfrogging" becomes a real concern because changes that have been implemented might not be included in the file if teams leapfrog over each other. To avoid this common problem, pay very close attention to the "check-in/check-out" procedure so that each team's revisions are included.

Finally, expect that your team will complete the "Writing Stage" more than once; the process is iterative and so it should be viewed as a series of cycles. Each cycle improves the document as a whole under the careful guidance of the editor or project leader. Again, each team and team member must subordinate their ego to the goals of the document. Nobody "owns" the text that they have written; genuinely internalizing the idea that writing is a process will help with this.

5.5 COMPLETION STAGE

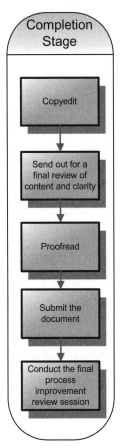

The completion stage represents the final portion of the *STREAM Tools* writing process. At this point in the process, your team has clearly defined the project, prepared to write, completed some writing, and undergone several revision cycles. Your document is almost ready for reviewers outside of your team. We say "almost" because the document still needs to be "copyedited" before it goes to external reviewers for their feedback on content and clarity. After the document has been copyedited and reviewed, the team makes minor mechanical and formatting changes, proofreads the document, and submits it. As the final step in completion, the team conducts a "postmortem" on the project to review the process and discuss ways that it might be improved in the future. We take up each of these steps in the following sections.

5.5.1 Copyedit the Document

In comparison to the formative feedback offered in comprehensive editing as outlined in Section 5.4.5, the purpose of copyediting, as noted in Rude's *Technical Editing*, is to confirm that a document is correct, consistent, accurate, and complete, not to suggest major changes to content, organization, or style. Copyediting, then, is what most people think of as "editing" and probably "proofreading" because it ensures the document's adherence to accepted principles of "good writing" on the surface level rather than addressing deeper issues. However, copyediting is just the second phase in an editing process that stands *between* the type of comprehensive editing we previously discussed and proofreading which we address in Section 5.5.3.

Copyediting, like comprehensive editing, addresses multiple aspects of a document, and accordingly, your team should view copyediting as a series of steps rather than a single review of the document. Your team should review for *correctness*, *consistency*, *accuracy*, and finally *completeness*, addressing the concerns outlined below one a time:

1. *Correctness*: Does the document use standard English in spelling, punctuation, and grammar? Does it follow rules published in dictionaries and grammar guides?
2. *Consistency*: Does the document present terms, numbers, and words consistently throughout? Are there arbitrary variations in usage, terms, or numbers?
3. *Accuracy*: Is the content accurate? Do the tables have accurate numbers? Do equations calculate? Are titles properly used? Does the document tell the truth?

4. *Completeness*: Does the manuscript contain all of the parts required for a document of this type? Have all the questions been answered or the topics been addressed?

The kind of mistakes that your team will be looking for during copyediting—particularly mistakes of correctness—tend to derail readers the most. Errors such as misspelled words or improper subject-verb agreement severely deflate a reader's confidence in your document and damage the document's credibility. Consequently, teams should pay close attention to copyediting and not view it as a perfunctory step.

However, we recognize that in addition to producing the highest quality documents possible, writing teams need to copyedit documents *efficiently*. We have identified the most common errors made in technical documents and developed a system, to speed up the copyediting process. The *STREAM Tools* Editorial Mark-up Table, introduced in Section 5.4.5.2, shows annotation marks, explanations, and examples of the most common errors that technical writing teams make. Even though we recommend using the *STREAM Tools* Editorial Mark-up Table as a basis for both comprehensive review and copyediting, writers should also be familiar with the standard copyediting and proofreading symbols shown in Table 5.9, since editors may also include some of these marks in your documents.

In short, the copyediting process looks for the kinds of superficial errors that tend to detract from a document's credibility. Readers are very likely to dismiss a document with many surface errors or even one error in accuracy, so we encourage your team to copyedit with care. Make no mistake: editing carefully takes time. Your overall project plan should build in sufficient days to complete the process—a process that involves both the marking of the document (either on paper or electronically) as well as correcting it. Finally, we encourage your team to designate a single person to complete the review process and one other person to make the corrections. Involving too many people in this step will only introduce errors. Once the document has gone through careful copyediting and revisions and both the reviewer and the author have made the appropriate changes, the full team should review the complete document one last time before it goes out for external review. Team members may find something that wasn't apparent in early editing stages, so be prepared to make *small* corrections, additions, or deletions at this step. We hardly need to emphasize that this is not the time to introduce large-scale changes. This time should be reserved for the team to look proudly upon the work they've completed and confidently agree that the document is ready for final review.

5.5.2   Send Out for a Final Review of Content and Clarity

Once your document is complete—is in a form that you believe is acceptable for submission to the final audience—your team should get one more level of feedback from a very experienced, senior person, ideally somebody external to your organization but not a member of the final audience. The purpose of this step is to receive words of wisdom about the content and clarity of the document prior to the final submission. Often, these reviewers will provide a different perspective from any of the members of

TABLE 5.9. Common Copyediting and Proofreading Symbols

Instruction	Editing Mark (in the line only)	Proofreading Marks (in the line and in the margin)	
Delete	Seattle summers events	Seattle summers events	
Delete and close up	Seattle summer evvents	Seattle summer evvents	
Replace	Seattle summer calendar (events)	Seattle summer calendar.	events
Insert	Seattle summer events	Seattle events	summer
Transpose	Seattle events summer	Seattle events summer	TR
Insert space	Seattle summerevents	Seattle summerevents	#
Close up extra space	Seattle summer events	Seattle summer events	close (extra #)
Run together/no new paragraph	She reads. He writes.	She reads. He writes.	run in
Line break	She reads He writes.	She reads He writes.	break
Instructions: Don't set what's circled	Seattle summer events (which?)	Seattle summer events	which
Ignore marked changes	Seattle summer events	Seattle summer events	stet
Spell out	(1st) event	(1st) event	sp
use symbol	(eleven) summer events	(eleven) summer events	‖
Center	]Seattle summer events[	]Seattle summer events[	c
Align	‖Seattle summer events	‖Seattle summer events	fl
Make italic	Seattle summer events	Seattle summer events	ital
Make Roman	(rom)(Seattle summer events)	(Seattle summer events)	rom
Wrong typeface	(Seattle summer events)	(Seattle summer events)	wf
Capitals	seattle summer events	seattle summer events	caps
Lower case	Seattle Summer Events	Seattle Summer Events	lc
Superscript	9 8	9 8	supe
Subscript	R	R	sub
Period	Seattle summer events	Seattle summer events	⊙
Comma	Seattle summer events	Seattle summer events	⅋
Colon	Seattle summer events	Seattle summer events	:/
Semicolon	Seattle summer events	Seattle summer events	;/
Quotation marks	Seattle summer events	Seattle summer events	ᶹ/ ᶹ
Apostrophe	Seattle summer events	Seattle summer events	ᶹ
Parentheses	(Seattle summer events)	Seattle summer events	(/)

your team, and as an experienced reviewer—a sort of "in house" external reviewer—he or she can read your document with the same critical eye that your ultimate audience will have. This senior person might find places where the logic could be improved or where you should include another reference or two to cement your case, for example. Perhaps your team overlooked a relevant counterargument or didn't make one of your points confidently enough. A senior reviewer will help improve your document by addressing these sorts of issues.

However, enlisting the help of senior colleagues—either internal or external—must be undertaken with care. Senior people are almost always willing to help others, but your team must clearly articulate the purpose of the review for the senior person and should only submit a final document. Unless your team is completely stuck, submitting a draft to a senior person would be a waste of time because drafts are simply not ready for the level of feedback that you need from an outside reviewer. It's difficult to comment on the quality of something that is still in formation because the devil is in the details, and the details are not there yet. Naturally, senior people are busy, so be careful to build adequate time into your process so that the reviewer has time to thoughtfully comment on the document and your team has time to make any suggested revisions.

Finally, like nearly every other step in the *STREAM Tools* Writing Process, your team should use this review as one more opportunity to cycle through revisions. Hopefully, your document will only require very superficial modification at this point, but it's possible that a senior person will point out a significant flaw. If that is the case, the project leader must assign additional writing tasks to a team or teams, and the document will cycle back to the "Writing Stage," in which each team contributes revisions, the team leader compiles, the whole document is once again reviewed for content and clarity, and then it is copyedited. The external reviewer probably won't want to see the document again, so your team needs to be very clear about the revisions required if they are significant. Your team should also implement those changes with extreme care, keeping in mind that the person who suggested the changes might not be available to review them as they appear in the new document.

5.5.3 Proofread the Document

After carefully incorporating the responses and the final suggestions offered by the senior reviewers, the manuscript should be proofread one more time. Ideally, the proofreaders will not be the same people who wrote the document or contributed to the comprehensive editing. At this point, authors and editors have already had their chance to polish the document and are too likely to miss errors either because they have seen this manuscript too many times or simply because they know what the document says. A person who has only contributed to the copyediting stage would be an acceptable choice, however, to make the final surface changes necessary.

Since the point of proofreading is quality control at the surface level, proofreaders need to be careful not to work to the point of fatigue and must be careful about becoming involved in what the document says. Experienced proofreaders use a variety of techniques not only to reduce fatigue but also to reduce the likelihood that they will be swept into the document's content. Three common strategies that your team might use are listed below, ordered from most effective to least effective; all work best with a printed document instead of one on a computer screen.

1. *Review with a word window.*   Essentially, a word window allows an editor to see only a few words at a time—perhaps half of a line—while concealing the remainder of the page. To use this method, cut a small window about the height of a line of type and about half of a line long into a standard sheet of paper then review each line of the document window by window, beginning with the last page and continuing to the first page. This method produces excellent results, but also requires a great deal of time.

2. *Read one line at a time, backwards.*   Similar to the word window technique, using this approach requires a proofreader to look at a single line of text, moving from the end of a document to the beginning. Sometimes covering the text above the line being reviewed is helpful, although experienced proofreaders can mentally mask the lines not being reviewed.

3. *Read from the end of the document to the beginning.*   At minimum, review the document from the end to the beginning. When reading backwards it is more difficult to become involved in the content, though it is still possible. Attempt to look at each word and punctuation mark alone without reference to the words earlier in the document.

These strategies, of course, are idealized. In practice, your team members will probably have to move between words or lines because ensuring correctness often means knowing a bit of context. For example, should the word be "there," "their," or "they're?" Only the context can tell a proofreader that. Likewise, most punctuation relies on context, so a proofreader might have to look at multiple lines or words to discern, for example, if a comma appears correctly or if a semicolon would be a better choice.

Microsoft Word contains a host of built-in features that proofread for authors on the fly. These most often appear as the squiggles under words or sentences. While writers can choose to alter the specifics of these features, generally, editors (and authors) can work with the default features. The only exception to this might be setting language, especially if your team comes from diverse English-speaking populations because different countries often spell words differently or have slightly different grammatical conventions. For example, the spelling of "color" is American English but the same word is written "colour" in British English. This is just one example, but others exist. To set the language to the dominant audience dialect (if your team is writing for a journal in the UK, for example, use British English settings), select the **Review** tab on the top of the Microsoft Word interface, then click *Set Language* on the **Proofing** ribbon. This opens a list of languages and dialects, from which you can choose the language that is most appropriate for your audience.

Another commonly used feature of Microsoft Word is the spelling and grammar check. This particular function can be very helpful for editors (and writers) to review their document prior to finalizing it. This function, while useful for helping point out potential problem areas, should be used with extreme caution because it quite frequently introduces errors if a user simply allows the grammar check to make changes automatically. Even though the grammar check can introduce errors, it is useful for the times it alerts authors and editors to a problem or two that they might have missed. It is worth the time to run as a final step—assuming the author or editor is willing to invest the time in carefully reviewing the grammar check's suggestions. Once the proofreader has reviewed the changes suggested by any automatic feature, he or she should *always* review the document one last time before submitting it to the audience to confirm that auto-change suggestions have not introduced new errors.

Proofreading can be tedious and time consuming and, because it occurs at the end of the drafting process, writers typically don't devote enough time to doing it well. However, the superficial errors uncovered in proofreading are the most distracting for readers, and more importantly, detract from the document's credibility. If the document contains silly mistakes, the audience might come to believe that the data or conclusions fall victim to an equal amount of carelessness. Again, writers should never underestimate the power of superficial appearance. Doing so jeopardizes not only the document's usability, but more importantly, its credibility.

> *STREAM Tools* **Commandment #9:**
> Never underestimate the power of superficial appearance.

5.5.4   Submit the Document

Finally! Your team has gone through a very thorough process and is now ready to submit the final document to the audience. It seems like an innocent step—just click the button or send a letter. However, a great many projects are ruined at the submission step. As you submit the document, think of potential things that can go wrong on the other side: a Microsoft Word document is complex, sensitive, and vulnerable. Once the file is out of your hands, who knows how much it will change once opened on another person's computer. Automatic references might disappear, figures might move around, fonts might change, and pagination might be ruined.

Because so many things can go wrong with submission, we encourage you to create an Adobe PDF file from your final Microsoft Word document prior to submission. PDF files usually maintain the formatting of the original document, ensuring that the audience sees the document exactly as you wrote it. Yet, even in PDF format, changes can occur, such as color illustrations rendering in black and white. If your document relies on the power of a color illustration, the document will be much less effective in black white. Therefore, after you have produced the PDF, confirm that the document looks exactly as your team intended it to before you submit it to the audience.

As another example to illustrate how carefully your team must guard your document's formatting and presentation, imagine a situation in which a single manuscript must be submitted as a collection of individual files (e.g., introduction, background, etc.). An administrative person might take your single Microsoft Word document and chop it into pieces *before* creating PDFs of each piece. What a nightmare! By chopping up the Microsoft Word document, all of the automatic features of the document will be destroyed, and the PDF versions will replicate all the formatting that was obliterated when the Microsoft Word document was divided. This serves as a lesson *never* to allow an administrative person or someone outside your team to have the final say on how your document looks. To avoid such a scenario, you should create a single PDF file and then use Acrobat's tools to extract the pages into separate files. Be careful to save each extracted section as a unique name so that you don't accidentally overwrite the entire PDF file. Only after you have carefully reviewed each of the separate files for consistency of page numbers, figure references, and other formatting issues should you submit the files or give them to an administrative person to submit.

Thus, beware of the desire of third-party participants to make last-minute changes to the document. Such changes might be necessary, but they need to be strongly justified. At a certain point you have to say "good enough." As the old adage goes, in this case, "better" is the enemy of "good."

> ***STREAM Tools* Commandment #10:**
> "Better" is the enemy of "good."

One final, painful element of manuscript submission is meeting publisher requirements. Most publishers do not care how much busy work you will have to endure to meet the requirements that they specify; they would rather leave it as your problem alone. Publishers worry about reducing their production workload, not yours. You may be asked to submit each figure on a separate page, to remove any auto-numbering features, to change spacing between the lines, and so on. We have to admit that, unlike LaTeX, Microsoft Word does not provide a good set of options for these situations. You may have to move your figures towards the end manually or strip auto-text features. For the latter, you can copy portions or the entire document and then paste them as Paste Special, Unformatted text. Whatever you do to make the final document meet the publisher's needs, *be sure to retain a formatted copy* of your document that preserves all automatic features. Do not chop up your original formatted document. Instead, save the formatted document using a new name and submit the new document. This is important because it is quite likely that the publisher will request additional revisions prior to publication, many of which will be easier to make in a fully automated and formatted document.

The publisher's request for revisions leads to our final note about the submission process: you might need to substantially revise the document yet *again* after it has been submitted. For scholarly publications, it's very common that your team will have to "revise and resubmit" the paper. Sometimes a journal or publisher rejects a paper with reviewer feedback that suggests that major revisions are in order. If this unfortunate situation occurs—and it will at some point for every writing team—the team must regroup and return to the beginning of the *STREAM Tools* writing process in order to assess how, or if, they want to go forward with the document. The team must decide between several options, such as submitting to a new journal, rewriting small sections, or revising extensively and resubmitting to the same publisher. Regardless of the particular review, the team will almost certainly need to cycle back through portions of the writing process to produce a revised document.

Again, we want to emphasize that when writers genuinely internalize that writing is a process as the *STREAM Tools* approach foregrounds, teams will be less devastated when they receive news that they must rewrite the document. It's all just part of the process of producing successful technical writing.

5.5.5 Conduct the Final Process-Improvement Review Session

No process is complete without a final review, sometimes called a "post mortem." Writing projects are no different. In the final review, team members celebrate their success at producing the final product, but they also examine ways that the process could be improved next time. Perhaps team size was too large or the right expertise wasn't in place. Perhaps the editor asked for too many stylistic revisions that slowed the process unnecessarily. Perhaps the writing assignments weren't equitably distributed.

Many people have written about methods and strategies for conducting a post mortem, but most agree on a few key principles that your team should follow:

- *Conduct the review session immediately following the project.* If you wait too long to reflect on the process, then your team will forget crucial elements about the process.
- *Provide a review of the project's details.* Record the project's goals and audience, how long it took, a list of those who were involved, and so on. The purpose is to remind everyone of the project's scope and give everybody recognition for their contributions.
- *Record things that went well, and things that went poorly.* No project is perfect, but all projects have successes if we look for them. Your team should articulate both the positive and negative aspects of the process. Be sure to involve everyone in the process, perhaps drawing out the contributions of junior team members prior to those of senior team members so that the junior contributors do more than just agree with senior members.
- *Create an action plan for the future.* Based on the successes and failures, record both how your team will overcome challenges *and* replicate successes in future projects.
- *Write everything down.* Conducting the post mortem meeting is a great way to bring closure to a project. However, like writing itself, working in project teams should be viewed as a process, and recording the results of the post mortem meeting gives those on your team an action plan for "revising" future team interactions. Share the written report with all the team members and the team's supervisor so that it can be referenced in the future.

EXERCISES

Exercise 5.1. For a document that you are working on at this time but have not yet sent to its audience (a report, a memo, even an email), use the *STREAM Tools* Audience Assessment Tool and the *STREAM Tools* Purpose Tool to assess how well you have written the document for its intended audience and purpose. Revise the document according to your assessment and send to the intended audience.

Exercise 5.2. Locate the manuscript submission guidelines for a journal in your field (excluding those already referenced in this text). Study the guidelines and, using your knowledge about modifying the *STREAM Tools* template, create a new template for that journal that you might use as you author a manuscript. Upload that template to the *STREAM Tools* website.

Exercise 5.3. For the document you used in Exercise 5.1, create a comprehensive style guide for the project using the *STREAM Tools* Style Guide Tool. Then, prepare a style sheet for that same document using the *STREAM Tools* Style Sheet Tool.

Exercise 5.4. Think about a document that you must write but haven't yet written. For the entire document, regardless of length, create an outline using Microsoft Word. After completing the outline, add some dummy text to the sections, and create a table of contents by selecting the **References Ribbon**, and then **Table of Contents.**

Exercise 5.5. Ask a friend or colleague for a manuscript that has been recently drafted but has not yet reached its final form. Using the *STREAM Tools* Editorial Questions Tool and the *STREAM Tools* Editorial Mark-up Table edit the document, providing commentary that your friend or colleague can use to improve the document.

Exercise 5.6. Get together the advisor and advisee in your organization and go together through the STEM table entries. Pick the feedback codes that you find most useful, and discuss which additional codes would be helpful. For example, we often use codes like "c:\MA2," which indicates that the advisee should read Chapter 2 of Michael Alley's book on scientific writing before proceeding).

ADDITIONAL RESOURCES

Alley, Michael (1996). *The Craft of Scientific Writing*. New York: Springer-Verlag.

Dragga, Sam and Gwendolyn Gong (1989). *Editing: The Design of Rhetoric*. Amityville, NY: Baywood Publishing.

Rude, Carolyn (1998). *Technical Editing*. Needham Heights, MA: Allyn and Bacon.

Weber, Jean Hollis (1999). *Electronic Editing: Editing in the Computer Age*. WeberWoman's Wrevenge: Henderson, NV.

6

BUILDING HIGH-QUALITY
WRITING TEAMS

Lenny: We made it. And it's all thanks to teamwork.
Carl: Yeah, *my* teamwork.

—The Simpsons, 1989

6.1 IN THIS CHAPTER

A great deal of technical writing occurs in teams. Much of *STREAM Tools* concerns itself, in fact, with helping your writing team perform efficiently and effectively by automating processes and specifying practices that will help your team write high-quality documents. These processes eliminate much of the ambiguity that can occur when multiple people collaborate to create a document.

However, what do we make of the "human element" of collaborative authorship? How do different people from diverse backgrounds combine their talents into a single high-performing team? Drawing on the vast amount of literature published on teamwork, this chapter explains what it takes to establish and sustain high quality writing teams by:

Technical Writing for Teams: The STREAM Tools Handbook, by Alexander Mamishev and Sean Williams
Copyright © 2010 Institute of Electrical and Electronics Engineers

- Understanding the benefits and challenges of teamwork
- Identifying team goals and assigning member roles
- Managing teamwork at a distance

We also recognize that teams are frequently distributed over the globe and that those teams collaborate through online tools. Therefore, this chapter also offers guidelines for:

- Building trust among team members who will never meet each other face-to-face
- Working across cultural and geographical boundaries with sensitivity
- Selecting communication tools to support virtual teamwork

After reading this chapter, your team should be aware of what it will take to succeed not just in the act of producing a document, but also of the benefits, challenges, and best practices of managing the human element of collaboration.

6.2   UNDERSTANDING THE BENEFITS AND CHALLENGES OF TEAMWORK

Many definitions of teams have appeared in the last three decades, but, in principle, most definitions share a few common elements:

1. Teams consist of at least two people working together.
2. The team members have diverse and complementary skill sets, not the same skill set.
3. The team works toward a common goal.
4. The team must produce something or solve a problem.

A great deal of literature has appeared on teamwork in industry, focusing on explaining and refining these characteristics, particularly since the 1970s. Many companies, particularly those in the United States, maintained a great deal of suspicion about teamwork throughout most of the 20th century, even as other countries, such as Japan, began to demonstrate that teamwork produces higher quality products faster and more cheaply.

As an industry practice, however, teamwork has now become the dominant paradigm—and has probably been so since the late 1980s. In fact, teamwork has become so dominant that the practice of working in teams appears transparent and common sense to most people, whether they work in universities, financial service companies, or in large R&D labs at companies like Proctor and Gamble (which was one of the first large companies to embrace "quality circles," an early form of autonomous work teams).

The reasons for this paradigm shift have been documented well in the substantial literature available on teams. Below we review the most essential benefits of working in teams, but we also note the principal challenges of teamwork, because many challenges do exist. However, knowing the challenges of teamwork prior to beginning a collaborative project—and developing some strategies for overcoming those challenges—improves the likelihood that these challenges won't derail your team's efforts.

6.2.1 The Payoff of Teamwork

Teams have become a dominant aspect of work life for one simple reason: they work. The now-famous book *The Wisdom of Teams* demonstrates that teams "outperform individuals acting alone or in larger organizational settings." Several subsequent studies also demonstrate the noticeable benefits of teamwork, including:

- Increased employee motivation
- Better product quality
- Higher quality of work life
- Increased employee satisfaction
- Enhanced productivity

These benefits evolve directly from the interdependent nature of teams and specifically from a few qualities inherent in the definition of teams:

1. *Diverse membership.* Teams have multiple members who demonstrate a mix of skills, experiences, technical abilities, worldviews, and interpersonal characteristics—this leads to a richer set of possibilities for solving problems. The members of a team become interdependent as they begin to rely on each other to achieve the team's larger goals and the team comes to realize that no one person can solve the problems they face. The creativity generated by their different viewpoints leads to a better solution than any one individual could conceive.

2. *Centralized group goal.* When team members clearly understand the overall vision and assist in developing that purpose or direction, cohesion results. The cooperative goals that result produce a commitment to solving the problem rather than focusing on individual differences. Additionally, teams with shared goals will more easily develop standardized operating procedures, assuming that group processes have not been articulated for them by the organization or by a manager.

3. *Performance-oriented outcomes.* The team's outcomes differ from the team's goal. The goal might be to "win a grant," but the outcome would be the written

grant proposal. The goal might be to influence the way pharmacologists under-stand a drug, but the outcome would be a research report. So, while the team has shared goals, they also must agree on the tangible deliverables of their work—how they'll know when they're done or how they'll judge their success. Different members will participate in the different aspects of producing the outcomes, but the team must share an understanding of what those out-comes are.

4. *Individual and community responsibility.* Assuming that the team has agreed on its desired goals and outcomes, each member then becomes responsible not only for their own personal successes, but also for those of the team. In other words, somebody skilled at editing might contribute only to the editing func-tions of preparing a grant proposal, but their individual success with that piece determines the success of the entire group. Unless that individual succeeds at the assigned individual tasks, the whole team fails. This dual sense of respon-sibility—first for one's own work and second how it dovetails with the entire team's work—also accounts for the sense of interdependence and respect for diversity that characterizes teams.

Viewed as an aggregate, these characteristics of teams create a circle, where participation builds individual ownership of the problem and outcomes but relies on the group to succeed at meeting those goals. This interdependence between individual success and group success largely accounts for the payoff of working in teams.

6.2.2   Some Principle Challenges of Teamwork

Even though teams have many benefits, challenges do exist for establishing successful writing teams. In principle, one could simply hold a mirror to the four characteristics listed above to discern the challenges of teams, as described in Table 6.1.

Each of these challenges requires a bit of commentary both to explain why the challenge might arise as well as how a team—or the manager directing the team—can avoid these pitfalls.

TABLE 6.1.   Some Characteristics and Challenges of Teamwork

Characteristic	Challenge
Diverse membership	Poor match of member skills to task requirements
Centralized group goal	Competing member goals
Performance-oriented outcomes	Too much focus on the social aspects of the team
Individual *and* community responsibility	No accountability to the team; too much reliance on the team

6.2.2.1 Challenge 1: Poor Match of Member Skills to Task Requirements. This challenge arises when teams emerge without foresight into the project's goals. Frequently, for example, we build teams from those around us rather than considering what skills a project requires and who among our associates possesses those skills. Let's call these "Convenience Teams." Convenience Teams will seldom perform with the quality of a more thoughtfully constructed team either because the members lack necessary skills or because the members possess skills or views that are too homogenous. In the first case—lack of necessary skills—the team obviously will not be able to perform the appropriate tasks without some difficulty or learning. In the second case—homogenous views—the team might devolve into "group think" where the members don't challenge each other by demonstrating a healthy portion of creative conflict. In either situation, the project will suffer.

To avoid the challenge of poor match of member skills to task requirements, take time, first, to confirm what the goals and outcomes of the project will be; this way you can foresee what skills and knowledge will be necessary to complete the project efficiently and effectively. Second, take time to match individual people to individual requirements so that you can be confident the team members cover the range of necessary expectations.

Finally, *beware of representative teams.* Project teams constructed to be representative seldom experience as much success as teams constructed according to skills. Exceptions exist, of course, such as in committees with the purpose of representing. However, most often representative groups do not make high-quality project teams.

6.2.2.2 Challenge 2: Competing Member Goals. This challenge encompasses the flip side of group think and homogeneity, and occurs when team members cannot agree on a centralized goal. Often, group members will join a team (or be assigned to one) and not fully understand the scope or purpose of the project. In this situation, conflict might emerge as team members tussle over the central organizing principle of the team rather than discuss how to achieve a shared goal. Creative conflict that evolves from different perspectives on how to achieve a shared goal should be encouraged. However, conflict over the definition of the goal will most often be counterproductive and lead to interpersonal conflict.

To avoid the challenge of competing member goals, the initial meeting of the team should clearly outline the purpose and goals of the team, including the stakes or significance of the centralized goal as outlined in Chapter 5, "Planning, Drafting, and Editing Documents." For example, the team isn't just "writing a grant proposal for studying how to implement the 3-D Internet in educational settings." Instead, the team is writing a grant proposal to help lay a foundation for pedagogical innovations that will drive the success of the next generation of college students. In this case, the goal is not the grant proposal or the study itself, but rather helping college students succeed through pedagogical innovation. In both cases, we can inquire into the larger significance or purpose behind these tasks to discern the real goal. Clearly articulating the goal—either as it is articulated to the team by a manager, or as it evolves from conversations in the team's kickoff meeting—is the best antidote to this challenge.

6.2.2.3 Challenge 3: Too Much Focus on the Social Aspects of the Team.
Make no mistake: teams require a great deal of socializing (and socialization, too). However, this challenge arises when teams forget their purpose of achieving some specific set of outcomes and instead focus too much on member cohesion or personal interactions. Because people generally like to be liked by their peers and most people enjoy quality human interactions, team members become distracted from their goal and spend more meeting time talking about families, friends, pets, or weekend activities than they do talking about the work they need to accomplish. As a result, the team becomes tightly bonded—a good thing—but the primary focus of the team shifts from task-orientation to maintaining the group's shared social identity. While having a strong team identity leads to a feeling of empowerment, it can also lead to group think, squelching the creative conflict or focus that characterizes the best teams.

To avoid the challenge of focusing too much on the social aspects of the team, team members should institute a process where there is a small amount of time allocated in meetings or conversations for social activities, after which the team will focus on the assigned tasks. For example, if a team is scheduled to work for 90 minutes, then perhaps the first 15 minutes can be socializing and restoring personal bonds and the subsequent 75 minutes can be work-oriented. Certainly, teams should socialize; it builds cohesion. However, teams should focus on the outcomes expected and spend the bulk of their time on task while maintaining the camaraderie established by the more social components of the team.

6.2.2.4 Challenge 4: No Accountability to the Team or Too Much Reliance on the Team.
This challenge results when teams have not built a cohesive group or when team members do not share the same understanding of expectations. In the first case, team members who do not feel as though they belong to the group, either because they have a sense of superiority or because they have been alienated, will work in selfish ways that might run counter to the general direction of the team. They feel accountable only to themselves and believe that so long as they do their part, they're done. This challenge might be summarized by the person who says, "I'll just do all the work because I don't trust anybody in my team will do it as well as I can." Clearly, this works against the sense of community responsibility that makes teams successful. Individuals only succeed if the whole team succeeds, and so whenever actions hinder the success of others, those actions should be curtailed.

On the opposite side of this continuum, individuals might rely too heavily on the other team members and feel no individual accountability for their work. This line of reasoning might be summarized by those who say, "Well, I'll do what I can, and if I can't get my work done, somebody else on the team will pick up the slack. Besides, they're better at it than I am, anyway." In this particular case, the team member exploits the cohesion of the team as well as others' sense of accountability. In many ways, this position is as selfish as the first position and should be curtailed.

To avoid the challenge of no accountability or too much reliance on the team, team members should be assigned clear responsibilities according to their knowledge and skills. We outlined a method for this in Section 5.3.5. Further, team members should report frequently on the progress of their individual components and should not immediately assume the responsibilities of others—either because they think they can do it better themselves, or because they think others would do it better for them. In either case, the individual has stepped outside the boundaries of their expertise and in both cases demonstrated a lack of respect for others.

Ultimately, teams will function best if they have a clear set of goals and expectations and show respect for others on the team. This respect will usually evolve from recognizing that the team has been constructed to include diverse perspectives, skills, and knowledge, and that this diversity most often leads to the best outcomes. If team members see others as contributors rather than competitors, the team members will have more open and honest communication. When individuals feel accountable to others on the team for contributing their share, everybody will feel a greater sense of ownership in their own tasks, and ultimately the team will be more successful.

6.3 IDENTIFYING TEAM GOALS AND ASSIGNING MEMBER ROLES

Most of us have been a member of a team at one point or another in our lives, whether we played team sports as kids, served in the military, or conducted research in a large lab. Each of us has also had our share of positive experiences that balance out some of the more well-known negative team experiences. While some of the ideas above present options for how to construct teams and why teams—in the abstract—succeed or fail, we can identify some concrete tactics for helping teams to succeed.

6.3.1 Define Roles and Procedures Clearly

Teams and groups are not the same. Teams assemble for specific outcomes and to accomplish specific goals, and so whenever we assign teams, or whenever we participate in one, the first step is to understand the type of team we are on, and what others expect our team to deliver. Many publications discuss the different types of teams and their associated outcomes. Perhaps one of the most approachable is that published by the National Defense University in their manual *Strategic Leadership and Decision Making*. In this manual, teams are arranged according to their outcomes as shown in Table 6.2.

Writing teams, then, are rather complex; the same team will move through most, or all, of these stages at one point or another in its evolution. For example, a team might be formed as a *project development team* to imagine some new piece of technology for a company, but that team quickly moves to an *organized action team* as they begin to conduct their research, and the cycle repeats itself as they translate their research into a document. The team again becomes a *project development team* as they design the specifications for the document, moves to a *production team* as they author the content,

TABLE 6.2. The Characteristics and Challenges of Teamwork

Type of Team	Expected Outcomes
Production *(assembly teams, maintenance crews, shift workers)*	Repeated cycles of generating material or service goods according to predefined specifications
Advice and Involvement *(advisory boards, panels, representative groups)*	Provide advice to managers; allow opportunity for member involvement in decision making
Project development *(research teams, task forces, consulting services)*	Design specifications for production; actionable guidelines for implementation
Organized action *(sports teams, negotiating teams, surgical crews)*	Specific, short-term deliverables under frequently changing conditions

and ends as an *organized action team* as specific individuals complete cycles of edits and revisions.

A couple of key points emerge here. First, the team members need to understand their primary charge *before* beginning their work together. If the team members know what type of deliverables others expect, that can guide their work. Second, and specifically in the context of writing teams, team members need to share a vision of where they are in the process. Are they currently working on planning a document or are they actually producing it? Once team members share an understanding about the type of team they belong to, and why their organization wants them to accomplish something, member roles and procedures become much easier to define. Each of these features should be an outcome of a team kick-off meeting as discussed in Chapter 5.

6.3.1.1 Define Team Roles. Team members are assigned to a specific team most often because they have some particular skill set or knowledge base that enables them to contribute in a unique way to the team. In their book *The Wisdom of Teams*, Katzenbach and Douglas discuss how to define team roles in the most effective manner:

- *Assign individuals to specific issues.* Specific people have different talents and so a specific person is most often best suited to work on a particular part of the larger problem. Additionally, if the person knows their specific assignment, it's far easier for them to assume ownership of that piece while remaining accountable to the group for that part.
- *Assign membership based on skills or knowledge, not position.* Membership based on skills helps defuse hierarchical concerns that can cause tension in a team. When members all recognize that they have been included for a particular purpose, it not only increases the sense of obligation to perform on that specific

task, but it also increases respect for the expertise of others. Mutual respect is the foundation of high-performing teams.

- *Assign specific tasks to multiple individuals for later integration.* Tasks and issues are not the same; a task is a course of action necessary to overcome a particular issue. When multiple members collaborate to complete a specific task according to their expertise, that task builds cohesion at an individual level rather than at the level of the whole team. This small-scale cohesion increases involvement and a sense of accountability to others.

- *Require members to complete equivalent amounts of work.* If members have been assigned to specific issues and specific tasks, presumably those tasks will be distributed among the team's membership. It also ensures that each team member has a stake in the outcomes since their contribution becomes a key part of the final product.

- *Move beyond hierarchical interaction.* Teams often fail because one or more members forget that each individual has been assigned to the team for a specific reason. In this case, those individuals' opinions come to dominate and squelch the creative tensions present among the team members. Rather than trying to force one viewpoint, move toward shared understandings of the issues, tasks, and outcomes.

These guidelines provide concrete advice not only on constructing teams, but also demonstrate how teams benefit from clearly assigned roles: members will approach each other with respect; assume accountability for their portion of a project; divide the massive amounts of work into manageable pieces; and coordinate their small-scale actions as they move toward a larger deliverable. Each of these ultimately results in a tightly bonded team where members recognize that their individual contributions contribute to the larger team's success. It requires, however, a genuine belief in the capabilities of others.

6.3.1.2 *Define Team Procedures.*
Just as assigning team roles is key to a team's success, defining team procedures is also key because it tells team members *how* to do what they need to do. Sometimes, organizations have standard operating procedures for addressing the procedures teams should undertake. When the organization possesses these types of documents, obviously, the team should follow them.

However, most organizations have not articulated standard team processes and therefore they allow team leaders or managers to specify how a team should operate. In this case, teams should consider recording and clarifying a few key processes to be sure that the team members operate in parallel. These processes are outlined below.

WHEN AND HOW TO COMMUNICATE. Of all the features of teams, the single most important thing is that teams communicate. Without frequent and quality communication, teams will not build trust and cohesion and will therefore not complete their tasks. Team members should articulate when they will communicate and how they will communicate by addressing questions like these:

When to Communicate	How to Communicate
1. At what intervals will the entire team meet (e.g., daily, weekly, monthly)?	1. Will the team meet face-to-face, via conference call, online, or some combination?
2. At what intervals will specific work groups or sub-teams meet (e.g., daily, weekly, monthly)?	2. Will team meetings be structured by agenda and, if so, who suggests agenda items, who collects them, and who circulates the agenda?
3. At what time of day will the team meet (making sure to allow for time zone differences)?	3. Will team meetings require "formal" procedures (e.g., Robert's Rules) or be informal conversations?
4. How long will meetings last?	4. Who will lead meetings?
5. How far in advance of a meeting will an agenda be circulated?	5. How will the team share documents and information (e.g., centralized server system, wiki, email, bulletin board, document sharing website, virtual world)?
6. Under what special circumstances can an unscheduled meeting be called?	6. What types of information are appropriate to share in which way?

How Decisions Will Be Made. Researchers have identified and continue to refine ways for teams to make effective decisions. However, a few methods appear across the literature as outlined below:

Decision Method	Associated Process
Decision by majority vote	Members debate issues and then, at a point when it appears the options have been exhausted, members cast ballots, secret or public, on the topic. Provides clear results in a relatively efficient manner that most members can accept.
Decision by consensus	Members outline all issues and through discussion build a common understanding of the issues. Builds buy-in for decision and enhances cohesion in the group, but is not suitable when quick or small decisions are necessary.
Decision by leader	The team meets to discuss issues (or not) and defers to the leader's decision. Enables quick action but does not build group cohesion and might lead to a weak decision, particularly on complex issues.
Decision by expert	Similar to a decision by leader except the team defers to the expert on an issue. Shares challenges with the decision by leader model where experts might not have all necessary data and there is less team ownership of the solution.
Decision by tool	An automated decision-making tool (frequently electronic) that enables a team to disassemble a complex problem through structured questioning. If members trust the tool, it can build cohesion and produce group ownership of decisions. Good when regular processes fail.

HOW CONFLICTS WILL BE RESOLVED. Conflict resolution, like the prior two topics, has occupied the minds of researchers for many years and produced a great amount of literature. Perhaps one of the most famous models comes from the best-selling book *Getting to Yes*, which remains a classic in negotiation. Some key tenets of this approach appear below:

Principle	Description
Separate the people from the problem	Conflicts are best resolved when members focus on the issue under debate rather than personalities. Making conflict personal seldom (if ever) results in quality resolution. In cases of personality conflicts, members should agree to assignments that utilize their respective strengths and never stoop to destructive behaviors.
Focus on interests, not positions	*Interests* represent underlying reasons that people desire an outcome that might differ from that of another person. A member should keep asking *why* until the root cause for their position is uncovered. *Positions* represent manifestations of interests, or *how* a person wants to realize their interests (e.g., *interest* = reducing the amount of overtime necessary to write a grant proposal; *position* = involving fewer collaborators).
Expand and invent options	Approach the issue with a "both/and" attitude where the primary goal is to meet the needs of both parties. How can both parties' goals be met if we propose a creative option? Relies on brainstorming possible alternatives by asking "what if" and suspending judgment of options until all options are on the table. Select options, or composites of options, that show promise for meeting most of the needs of both parties.
Use objective decision-making criteria	Parties agree on a "third source" for deciding the merit of one position over another and agree to be subject to the decision of those objective criteria. The objective source can be data, mediators, established conventions, or precedent (e.g., co-authors agree to present a grant proposal to a seasoned, highly–funded investigator to determine which of two organizational schemes is better and to go forward with the expert's decision).

Teams have many opportunities to optimize their performance, two of the greatest lie in articulating the team members' complementary roles and defining what procedures the team will employ to complete its work. In both cases, members feel less anxiety, and when an environment reduces anxiety, the opportunity for cohesion increases. When members understand both their roles and the roles of others, conflict decreases and consequently productivity and group ownership increases. When members consistently employ processes that the team has constructed and see the positive outcomes of those procedures, team cohesion increases even more.

6.4 MANAGING TEAMWORK AT A DISTANCE

Many teams now work across time zones, borders, and continents. These types of teams, called "virtual teams," share some features with traditional teams, but they also demonstrate some unique characteristics that make them a special case for consideration. In its simplest form, a virtual team is simply a group of people who work together on a shared purpose but from different locations, using technology to facilitate communication. The types of teams can be the same as those specified earlier, but these teams are qualitatively different from traditional teams. First, the team members must be more self-motivated, and able to handle the challenges that technology sometimes presents. Second, they must be excellent communicators who can articulate needs and expectations very clearly because technology rarely enables the rich interpersonal cues of face-to-face communication. Finally, team members, often from different cultures and locations, need to trust each other without ever meeting or seeing each other. These concerns mirror many of those that "regular" teams face (e.g., clearly defining roles and processes), but the complexity added by distance, technology, and multiple cultures means that these types of teams need to consider a wider array of issues than teams that work in the same location. Three of these complexities, trust in virtual teams, sensitivity to cultural differences, and selecting appropriate communication tools, are discussed in detail below.

6.4.1 Building Trust in Virtual Teams

Trust represents the single most important factor in successful teams. However, due to the geographic and cultural differences present in virtual teams, establishing trust becomes significantly more difficult for those in virtual teams than those working in traditional teams. Challenges of "social presence," as this idea is called, arise from the relative lack of communication channels enabled by technological communication because people cannot see facial expressions or gestures and cannot hear verbal cues. Additionally, trust usually takes time to develop, and traditional teams have the opportunity to meet by chance, for example, and these chance meetings build trust and shared experiences.

However, virtual teams most frequently have no shared past and members come together for a specific purpose for a specific timeframe. Consequently, virtual team members have much less—or no—opportunity to demonstrate what are considered behaviors that build trust, such as personal sharing or making oneself vulnerable to others by disclosing events unrelated to work. In response to this difficulty, researchers have developed some concepts to address how virtual teams build the trust necessary to successfully complete their assignments. The first is called "Swift Trust" and the second is called "Social Information Processing," and each points out a few guidelines for building virtual trust.

6.4.1.1 Swift Trust. *Swift trust* suggests that team members rely on prior team experiences and abstract understandings of teams to guide their actions in new team situations. Specifically, according to swift trust, team members must:

1. Enter a collaboration with a *predisposition to trust others* because trust is established in the very first moments of a virtual interaction. The trust is strengthened or weakened in subsequent interactions.
2. Rely on depersonalized *judgments of team members based upon their organizational roles* because the primary assumption is that each team member has been included for a particular reason.

6.4.1.2 Social Information Processing Theory. *Social information processing theory* suggests that successful virtual teams include both task-based and social-based information in the same messages. In other words, a team member might demonstrate concern about another's personal life in the same message that includes information about how the team is going to collaborate. Additionally, according to this research, virtual teams that perform the best communicate very frequently, provide consistent feedback on others' work, and alert others on the team in advance of unexpected behavior, such as absence from a scheduled meeting. Walther and Bunz propose six "rules" for successful teams:

1. *Get started right away.* Building trust in virtual teams requires time, and so groups must begin working on task-based elements at the same time they negotiate social elements.
2. *Communicate frequently.* Frequent communication helps to build the shared background lacking in virtual teams and helps disperse work among team members.
3. *Multitask, getting organized and doing substantive work simultaneously.* A modification of the first two rules, this point describes the type of communication that must occur from the beginning and claims that it must occur frequently.
4. *Overtly acknowledge that you have read one another's messages.* Because electronic media does not allow for nonverbal cues, teams must "over communicate" their understanding; it's difficult to know if another has read a message or not. Explicit recognition helps others know that you've read and understood their messages.

5. *Be explicit about what you are thinking and doing.* Similar to point four, explicitly articulating your ideas or thoughts eliminates the ambiguity of the medium. In face-to-face collaborations, we present our opinions in many non-verbal ways that others can read effectively. In electronic communication this is more difficult, so it requires explicitly verbalizing thoughts or proposed actions.

6. *Set deadlines and stick to them.* One of the best ways to demonstrate that you can be trusted is by sticking to deadlines. In an environment rife with ambiguity, performing as others expect makes individuals more credible. Further, when individuals demonstrate their reliability, others are more likely to demonstrate trust by coming to rely on others. This, in turn, builds more trust in the team.

These principles from the concept of swift trust and social information processing reveal complementary concerns. In the first case, people begin a collaboration with expectations and hopes about how others will perform and interact. The second case articulates some guidelines for acting in ways that build the trust necessary for successful teams.

6.4.2   Demonstrating Sensitivity to Cultural Differences

In our increasingly globalized world, team members often come from different cultures, races, religions, and ethnicities, and so success in a team requires understanding the varied backgrounds of those we work with. One of the challenges in discussing "cultural differences" is that *culture* can mean many things and represents a complex network of multiple factors that comprise an individual's cultural identity. It's helpful to think of culture using an iceberg metaphor, where we only see the most superficial aspects, or tip, of a person's identity: we don't know their history, education, beliefs, political preferences, or life experiences. All of these—and many more—contribute to what we call *culture*.

That said, there are some principles we can adopt to help us think about culture in its broadest sense. One of the most commonly used set of principles is presented by Hofstede in his book *Cultures and Organizations: Software of the Mind*. He includes these six "layers" of culture, which are admittedly only just the beginning of very complex distinctions:

1. *National level.* This concerns one's country of origin, whether one currently lives there, recently immigrated to another country, or feels historical ties to a particular country.

2. *Regional/ethnic and religious/linguistic.* Most countries include multiple regional, ethnic, religious, and linguistic groups. For example, in the United States, one could live in the Southeast, be African-American, a Muslim, and speak "standard edited English" (the purported "correct" dialect of American English).

3. *Gender.* People usually identify with one sex or the other, male or female, regardless of sexual orientation, though sexual orientation is often thought to be a subset of gender.

4. *Generation.* When a person was born contributes to their outlook on life, largely because of experiences they share. For example, in the United States, people might identify as "Baby Boomers," "Generation X," or "Millenials" and each has certain shared values and concerns.

5. *Social Class.* Class most often concerns a person's profession, education level, and income as well their prospects and opportunities to which they have access.

6. *Organizational/corporate.* People identify with groups they belong to, whether companies or other organizations, and each of those affiliations contributes to a person's outlook on the world and what they value.

In addition to thinking about culture as a layered set of concerns that make every individual unique, another approach is applying accepted frameworks that help people make useful generalizations about others. It's important to note that generalizations are only that—general—and should never be mistaken as encompassing the entire complexity of any individual. These useful generalizations offer only a starting point for thinking about interacting with others.

The most common of these frameworks is "High Context/Low Context." High context cultures typically foreground the importance of existing relationships and maintaining connections with a group. China and Japan are often cited as high context because of their historical belief in the value of collective action and group harmony. Low context cultures tend to rely more on individual action and demonstrate belief in written laws, regulations, and processes. The United States and Germany are typically cited as a low context cultures. While this concept of "high/low" most often refers to national origin, it can also be adapted in many ways—to ethnicities, religions, genders, organizations, or professions themselves—to discern how people might value relationships and explicit communications.

Finally, in their book *Intercultural Communication in the Global Workplace*, Linda Beamer and Iris Varner offer a series of questions that can help us understand cultures:

1. *In what ways do people learn about information and in what ways do they think?* For example, does a culture value experience more than reading? Does a culture think there are limits to knowledge?

2. *How do people understand the relationship between "doing" and "achievement?"* For example, does a culture focus more on the current moment or future-oriented activities? Are relationships or results more important? How does a group handle ambiguity?

3. *What is our place in the universe?* For example, are humans a part of nature or is our role to dominate it? What is the relationship of divinity (divinities) to human action? How is time understood, and is death a part of life or its end?

4. *What is the importance of the "self"?* For example, is the basic unit of society the individual or the group? Does equality exist and for whom? What role does age play?

5. *What are the ways groups are organized?* For example, can individuals move between groups, and are organizations hierarchical or horizontal? Are personal activities public or private?

These five topics represent just the surface of complexity necessary to understand another culture. However, they do point out that cultures that are different from our own have a coherent set of characteristics that we can identify if we ask the right questions. Most importantly, they demonstrate both the complexity of cultures and the individuals in them, and also that the only way to learn about others is to ask good questions. If we assume we know a group based on our prior knowledge of them, that's a stereotype, and stereotypes never withstand even the most superficial scrutiny. Using these questions to help form a useful generalization can act as a starting point for further questioning that recognizes the distinct diversity that individuals bring to our teams.

6.5 SELECTING COMMUNICATION TOOLS TO SUPPORT TEAMWORK

Because team members are often dispersed and yet work on the same documents, having a site where all team members can upload and modify documents in a streamlined manner is very important for a productive group. Many tools exist for enabling group collaboration, and new technologies for collaboration emerge all the time. Below, we provide an overview of two technologies that have a bit of history, wikis and SharePoint, and are often utilized in team settings (readers interested in full-length guides can find those readily available on the Internet).

6.5.1 Wikis

At the time of writing this manuscript, one of the fastest ways to establish an organized system for file storage is a wiki from the company *PBworks*, available at the website www.pbworks.com.

PBworks allows teams to create and maintain their own collaborative website—a wiki—thereby offering a centralized and up-to-date place for coordinating group work. The wiki is a series of interlinked pages for which editing and viewing privileges are entirely controlled by (but not restricted to) administrators. By tracking all changes made to the wiki and reserving final editorial privileges for the specified administrators, PBworks facilitates moderating and safeguarding an ever-evolving information exchange. Moreover, it gives up to 2 GB of file-sharing/storing capacity for free, and has additional features such as automatic edit notification, page template construction, and both point-and-click and direct source editing for individual pages.

6.5.1.1 Creating a Wiki. To construct your own wiki, simply go to pbworks. com, click "create a wiki," invite users with the "Share this wiki" feature, and begin editing/uploading files. When creating a page, you are given the option of using a prefabricated template. Most of these are quite simple and are not likely to be of much use. However, after you have constructed a page of your own, you can save it as a new template for future page creation. To do this, use the "edit tags" feature to mark the page as "template" (case sensitive).

6.5.1.2 Editing. Editing is, for the most part, self-explanatory. Text can be copied and pasted from programs such as Microsoft Word while retaining most formatting such as italics, font size, and headings (e.g., Heading 1 will remain Heading 1 and will appear as such in a table of contents on the wiki, should you create one). However, other features of Microsoft Word (such as automatic numbering) are non-transferrable.

You can insert links, images, and plugins (e.g., YouTube video, table of contents, etc.) by using the appropriate feature in the editor. Links from one page of the wiki to another are also easy to create. Simply highlight some text and click on the appropriate page name in the "Insert Links" box. Finally, PBworks allows users to comment on pages, and so members of your team might leave explanations or suggestions for other team members.

There is also a comment feature that allows users to comment on a page, perhaps suggesting or explaining an edition.

6.5.1.3 Organizing. Your wiki will be searchable and one can view a complete list of pages at any time by clicking "view all pages." Nevertheless, it would be a good idea to utilize some of PBwork's organizing features. For example, folders can be created in which to store certain sets of pages. Creating a list of folders (with links) on the front page and putting a directory page in each folder will also simplify site navigation immensely. Aside from this, pages can be "tagged" and thereby associated with other pages, even when they are not in the same folder, without the need for creating individual, direct links.

6.5.1.4 Monitoring Edits. There is a link on each page to its edit history and users can subscribe to email notifications and/or RSS feeds to receive information about page updates. Aside from this, one can also go to "view all pages" and see a page listing the number of revisions for each page (click the number to see revision details). The page history gives a list of links to past revisions (noting, in particular, the time of each) with the additional option of comparing any two. It is worth noting, however, that this compare function only lists changes made to the content of a page, not the formatting. Administrators (and only administrators) can delete past revisions.

This leads to another point about privacy, user settings, and edit-control. Wiki users can be granted access to the wiki at any of five levels of control: Administrator, Editor, Writer, Reader, and Page-Level Only (each one receiving fewer privileges than the former). For details on each, see the "user settings" page on your wiki. There the administrators can also, at any time, view and change the permission level of any given user.

6.5.1.5 *Other Suggestions for Wiki Use.* You can use your wiki simply to coordinate a project so that everyone has access to an up-to-date version of group efforts. However, you are not limited to this. You can also use your wiki to schedule meetings, provide links to pertinent outside information, share files, discuss/track progress, and/or assign tasks to individual group members.

Most answers to questions about PBworks can easily be found in the searchable user's manual at http://usermanual.pbworks.com/.

6.5.2 SharePoint

SharePoint is a Microsoft product that provides a collaborative workspace. The term "SharePoint" actually refers to two products, Microsoft Office SharePoint Server and Windows SharePoint Services. Other tools, including email, might also be a part of your system.

There are two primary parts to SharePoint: lists and pages. Much like a wiki, these two functions enable you to create a collaborative website on which you can store and share documents, schedule events, conduct surveys, and more. You can then manage this site and control the editing/viewing privileges of all users. Moreover, SharePoint allows users to stay updated with alerts (whether on-site or by email).

6.5.2.1 *Lists.* A list, as its name implies, is information arranged in list format. However, lists incorporate more functions than might be expected. For example, by means of lists, one can create file-sharing libraries, calendars, discussion boards, etc. Unfortunately, SharePoint complicates matters with its terminology. Although SharePoint only directly refers to a select few things as "lists" (e.g., task and issues lists), it is important to note that *all* SharePoint content is arranged in lists. Document libraries, surveys, and discussion boards, although nominally different, are still essentially lists. Keeping this in mind is essential, because all SharePoint lists are managed and edited in the same way, whether officially deemed "list" or not. Regardless of nomenclature, lists are the organizing structures of SharePoint.

Each list can be edited by whomever an administrator chooses. For example, a document library may be available for addition to any site user, while a discussion board is available to only certain, specified individuals. Moreover, for each particular list, an administrator may specify in detail what each user is able to do when editing. For example, you may wish to create an announcement page to which all users have the ability to add content, but from which only select users have the ability to remove it. Content approval by administrators may also be required, if so desired. To change these and all other list settings, go to "Site Settings" at the top of your page and select "Modify Site Content" under "Customization."

To create a new list, you have three options: go to "Create List" in the "Actions" menu, "Create" on the "Documents and Lists" page, or "Create New Content" on the

"Modify Site Content" page. Regardless, you will end up on the "Create Page," where you will find a series of options from which to choose in creating your list. Below is an overview of each:

A *Document Library* is a space for sharing or storing files (e.g., photos, Microsoft Word documents, or Excel spreadsheets). By default, your SharePoint site should have three document libraries: My Pages, Private Documents, and Shared Documents. However, you can create as many new libraries as you like. A unique feature of SharePoint document libraries is the "check-out" function. If your group is collaborating on a single document, you can store it and make it available for group editing in a SharePoint document library. However, to prevent multiple people from editing a document at the same time, SharePoint allows you to "check out" a file from the library. When a file is checked out, other users will be notified that it is being edited and will have access to a read-only copy of the file. To check a file out, place your cursor over the document title, click the box that appears, and find the option, "Check Out." Once you have checked it out, you can open the file for editing and it will remain checked out until you check it back in (via the same process by which you checked it out). If you are using Microsoft Word, Excel, or other Microsoft Office Suite programs to edit your file, you will be reminded to check it in when you try to exit the program.

Announcement Lists, as their name suggests, allow you to list announcements. The list consists of simple announcement titles on which a user can click to see the full announcement.

Contacts Lists allow you to maintain a current list of phone numbers, email addresses, etc. for those associated with your project. There are default settings for the kinds of information kept in the list, but you can modify them by clicking "Modify settings and columns" in the Actions menu. To change or delete a category (i.e., column) in the list, click where it is listed in the columns section of the page. From this page you can also add or change the order of columns (by clicking the relevant link under "Columns") or change what columns are shown on the default list page (by clicking "All Contacts" under "Views"). Any information not shown on the default list page will be shown in detail when one clicks a particular name.

Events Lists are calendars. They can be viewed in either list view ("All Events" in the "Select a View" menu) or in the more familiar calendar format. As with the Contacts Lists above (and all other lists, for that matter) you can change the kinds of information recorded for events by adding/editing the columns of the list. A particularly useful feature of SharePoint calendars is the ability to have regularly recurring events. When you create an event, you will be asked to specify the recurrence rate. This way, you avoid having to manually enter weekly meetings, etc.

Task Lists allow you to list, prioritize, and assign tasks to individual group members, as well as keep track of the progress of each.

Issues Lists are quite similar to task lists. Differentiate between the two as you see fit.

A *Custom List* is really just a blank list, without any preset columns. By going to "Modify Columns and Settings," though, you can modify the settings to accommodate whatever kind of list you might envision.

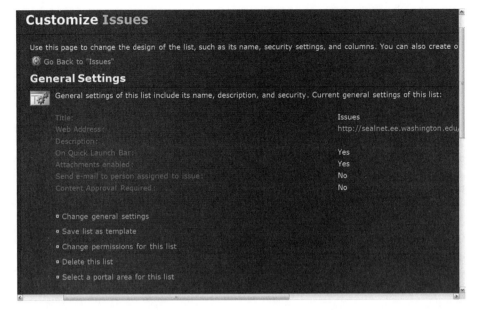

Figure 6.1. Screen shot of SharePoint

Custom Lists created in Datasheet View are exactly the same as ordinary custom lists. However, after creating it you will be taken to a "datasheet" view of the list modeled after Microsoft Access. In fact, you can switch between ordinary, "standard" view and "datasheet" view at any time with any list; it does not have to be created in the Datasheet view. The link to do so will be at the top of the list, next to "New Item," "Filter," etc.

The *Import Spreadsheet* function, as its name indicates, allows you to import a spreadsheet when you want to create a list that has the same columns and contents as an existing spreadsheet. Importing a spreadsheet requires a spreadsheet application compatible with Windows SharePoint Services.

Discussion Boards allow you to create a forum (in either threaded or flat view) for group discussion.

Finally, *Surveys* are lists that allow you to easily poll the members of your group. You can then view the results graphically or individually. The surveys can be multi-questioned and are optionally anonymous.

As a general example for lists, Figure 6.1 shows the customization page of a list made from the "Issues" template. To get to this page, follow the "Modify Columns and Settings" link on the particular list you wish to edit. Note that deleting a list must be done from this page. As you can see, from this page one can change the settings and permissions for the list. If you wished to limit the editing capabilities of users to only those list items created by them, for example, you would go to "Change general settings" and change the "Item level permissions." You would do likewise to require content approval by an administrator. On the other hand, if you wished to specify the

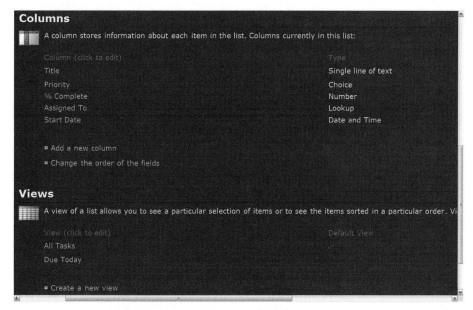

Figure 6.2. Continuing screen shot of SharePoint

reading and editing permissions of individuals or groups of individuals you would go to the "Change permissions for this list" page.

Figure 6.2 continues the page and we see where the list format itself can be edited.

The list consists of columns, which are the categories in which information is stored. There are several types of categories, depending on what kind of information is being stored. As seen above, this list utilizes five types of information storage: single line of text, (multiple) choice, number, lookup (i.e., find/select information already on the site), and date and time. However, you are in no way limited to these. For example, if you wished to associate a particular website with each issue in the list, you could add another column, formatted as a "hyperlink" column.

Views determine how a given list is displayed. In Figure 6.2, there are two: one view displays all issues while the other displays only issues that need addressing today (this view actually requires a "due date" column, which has been deleted in this example). As with the columns above, new views can be created so that your information can be sorted and displayed in any way you like. For example, if you had an issue list of such length that finding your own issues became a hassle, you could create a new view with a filter that only shows issues assigned and/or created by you.

6.5.2.2 Web Pages. Web pages can be created in SharePoint to increase accessibility to your lists or for adding content that does not fit neatly into a list. To create a web page, go to the same "Create" page described above under "Lists." At the bottom of this page you will find three options:

- *Basic Pages* are ordinary web pages to which you can add text, pictures, and tables using your browser.
- *Web Part Pages* are pages in which there are multiple, embedded web pages, or "Web Parts." These allow you to have multiple boxes, each independent of the others, on a single page. In these boxes (parts) you can display any lists you have created as well as non-list content. With regard to the latter, SharePoint gives you several options: you may add photos; create your own content (with either a Rich Text or Source Editor); even embed other, outside websites. These web parts can be easily added, moved around the page, or edited by selecting the appropriate link in the drop-down menu when you click "Modify Shared Page" in the upper-right corner of your Web Part Page.
- *Sites and Workspaces* are additional SharePoint sites, independent of the parent site, which function much like the Web Part Pages above, although the templates are different.

6.5.2.3   Alerts and Site Management.   To keep up to date, you may wish to create alerts for specific parts of your SharePoint site. To do this, go to the Documents and Lists page and navigate to the appropriate aspect of your site you wish to monitor. There are essentially two types of alerts: List Alerts and List Item Alerts. The former notifies you when an entire list is altered, while the latter allows you to monitor a particular aspect of the list (e.g., a particular discussion in the discussion board list). Note that web pages are also list items (in the "My Pages" list).

Managing the site is really a matter of managing the site lists. To do this, go to the Modify Site Content page and select the appropriate list. This will take you to a page from which you can change list properties: for example, add/change "columns," add/change "views" (ways in which the list is displayed), change editing permissions, save list as template, delete list, etc.

SharePoint is a great program for collaborative authoring, and experienced users find it very effective. The prior description provides only the skeleton of the program, and so readers who are interested in learning more about SharePoint can consult any of the following links:

- A fairly extensive, 75-page SharePoint tutorial:
  http://www.sharepointcustomization.com/resources/tutorials/
- Links to websites provided by Microsoft to assist SharePoint users:
  http://office.microsoft.com/en-us/sharepointtechnology/CH011424561033.aspx
- Training. This page gives you access to various training tutorials on such topics as working with lists, managing user permissions, working with picture libraries, etc.:
  http://office.microsoft.com/en-us/sharepointtechnology/CH011424521033.aspx
- User Documentation and Resources. This page is essentially an online help page. On it, you can find details about particular list templates, customizing sites, etc.:
  http://office.microsoft.com/en-us/sharepointtechnology/CH011593601033.aspx

EXERCISES

Exercise 6.1. Reflect on your experience with team work and list your strengths as well as your areas for improvement. Now consult with a co-worker/team mate and ask that person to rate you in the same way. Compare your lists and discuss ways that you can become a better team member.

Exercise 6.2. Conduct an Internet search on the two terms 1) "groupthink" and 2) "conflict resolution." Outline the principles of each term and present those to your manager/team leader and discuss ways that you can avoid the first and improve the second in your own team(s).

Exercise 6.3. For a current team of which you are a member, craft a communication plan that outlines when to communicate, how you'll communicate, and methods for making decisions. Share this with your team leader first, and ask that you be allowed to pilot the plan with your teammates. After using the articulated structures for two weeks, discuss with your team leader the improvements (and challenges) made to your team.

Exercise 6.4. Implement the six rules of Social Information Processing in a virtual team. After two weeks of using these processes, discuss with your team leader the improvements (and challenges) to your team that SIP provided.

ADDITIONAL RESOURCES

Beamer, Linda and Varner, Iris (2001). *Intercultural Communication in the Global Workplace.* New York: McGraw-Hill.

Fisher, Roger and Ury, William (1981). *Getting to Yes: Negotiating Agreement without Giving In.* New York: Penguin Books.

Hofstede, Geert (2005). *Cultures and Organizations: Software of the Mind.* New York: McGraw Hill.

Jarvenpaa, S. L. and Leidner, D. E. (1999). Communication and trust in global virtual teams. *Organization Science*, 10(6), 791–815.

Katzenbach, J. R. and Smith, D. K. (1993). *The Wisdom of Teams.* Boston, MA: Harvard Business School Press.

Walther, Joseph B. and Bunz, Ulla (2005). The rules of virtual groups: trust, liking and performance in computer mediated communication. *Journal of Communication* (55.4): 828–846.

7

ASSURING QUALITY WRITING

I swear that there are more exceptions than rules in the English grammar.
—Gautam Rao, American Desi (2001)

7.1 IN THIS CHAPTER

The title of this section is somewhat misleading. If you find yourself in the position to need this book, odds are pretty good that you've already learned everything in this chapter. Most of this chapter's contents should be a review of basic grammar and mechanics, things that you would have studied in English classes year after year.

However, do not take grammar and mechanics lightly. You've probably heard something similar to this at one point or another: "If you can't communicate your ideas, then you might as well not have them." Of course this overstates the point, but if your team writes well using some of the strategies outlined in this chapter, your proposals will be more persuasive, your journal articles will require fewer revisions, and your readers will understand your ideas better. Think about grammar and mechanics as the final demonstration of your team's attention to detail and precise thinking.

Technical Writing for Teams: The STREAM Tools Handbook, by Alexander Mamishev and Sean Williams
Copyright © 2010 Institute of Electrical and Electronics Engineers

Your team has worked very hard to plan and execute a document, and quality grammar and mechanics help strengthen the credibility of your points because it shows readers that your team has paid careful attention even to superficial items like proper grammar. In fact, studies show that an audience will rate proper grammatical writing as "smarter" than poor writing—even if the ideas in the proper document are not as sophisticated. By contrast, why would readers believe the claims your documents make if those documents are plagued by small mistakes? If your document has errors and weak presentation, it's an easy step for a reader to assume that the reasoning behind the claims presented is also weak. So, rather than thinking about proper grammar as a burdensome set of rules to follow, think about proper writing as establishing your credibility.

Don't let poor grammar and mechanics undermine your team's hard work. Instead, utilize the topics in this chapter to help your team put the competitive edge on its documents by:

- Choosing the most appropriate words
- Writing sentences that clearly communicate your ideas to your audience
- Punctuating for clarity

7.2   CHOOSING THE BEST WORDS

Technical writing aims to convey ideas as clearly and concisely as possible. When your team chooses strong words, the ideas appear vividly and without confusion. If, however, your document contains vague language or words that force a reader to work hard to understand your points, then the document will not have a strong impact. Technical writing teams should strive to choose strong words and to avoid weak words.

7.2.1   Choose Strong Words

Strong words convey meaning precisely and compactly. One writing researcher, Richard Lanham, argues that most writers can eliminate up to one third of their document's length while significantly increasing the document's clarity by choosing good words and eliminating unnecessary ones. The key principles for technical writing teams appear below with examples of each concept.

7.2.1.1   Use Strong Nouns and Verbs.   First, let's quickly review nouns and verbs. *Nouns refer* to a specific person, place, or thing and most often indicate something completing an action. Nouns have many functions, like subjects in sentences, or objects of prepositions. *Verbs express* action or a state of being, so they tell readers what is happening or what something is. Of course it's more complicated than this, but if your team can remember just these two things—*nouns refer and verbs express*—choosing strong nouns and verbs becomes easier. As you write, ask "Who is doing what to whom," and clearly refer to a specific person, place, or thing and clearly indicate what action or state of being occurred.

In other words, *a strong noun refers to one—and only one—thing and can therefore be distinguished from all other things in its class.* Strong nouns can refer to a single concrete object that can be identified by the senses, or they can refer to nonmaterial things such as ideas or values. In both cases, material and immaterial, a strong noun enables readers to exclude other possible references or meanings.

Similarly, *strong verbs vividly describe actions or states in a way that others could visualize the action or state.* Usually, writers find it more difficult to compose with strong verbs than to compose with strong nouns. However, as every good writer will attest, verbs express the core meaning of a sentence. Therefore, as your team revises, attempt to include verbs that clearly describe the action or state of being. Finally, writers should try to avoid passive voice as much as possible because the "to be" forms of verbs do not clearly show who completes what action and, therefore, passive verbs usually require more explanatory words, which results in longer sentences, increasing the likelihood of misunderstanding.

Below, we show two simple examples of weak noun and verb choices followed by a sample revision. The nouns are in **bold italics** and the verbs are underlined.

The ***machine*** <u>was running</u> the samples. The ***centrifuge*** <u>rotated</u> the samples.	"Machine" is a vague noun while "centrifuge" refers to a particular piece of equipment. "Was running" does not indicate the actual action.
It <u>is</u> because of rising fuel ***costs*** that this research <u>is</u> necessary. Rising fuel ***costs*** <u>provide</u> the reason for this research.	"It"—a pronoun—has no referent and therefore requires the strings of "to be" verbs that follow. Asking "who kicks whom" provides an easy revision since the fuel costs provide the reason for the research.

7.2.1.2 *Choose Words with the Right Level of Formality.* In documents composed by technical writing teams the diction, or level of formality, will be relatively serious. Face-to-face communication styles usually possess lower levels of formality than written forms of communication; for this reason, many writers make the mistake of "writing like they speak" and degrade their credibility in doing so. Very few readers of technical documents expect colloquial style and so writing with a "conversational" style will upset the expectations that readers have about technical documents. Finally, slang should never be used in formal written documents unless it demonstrates a particular point.

However, choosing a formal style doesn't mean that documents have to be "stuffy." Take this book's style, for example. We have written in a relatively formal style, yet have retained a level of informality to enhance interest and improve clarity. Had we chosen to write in a more formal manner, we wouldn't use contractions, for example, and we would have chosen to use technical terms—like "diction"—in place of more commonly accepted ones, like "level of formality." Choosing the right level of formality can be difficult, so when in doubt, choose the more formal style for technical documents since readers expect technical documents to be more serious. If, however, your audience analysis indicates that your audience would respond well to a less formal document, don't be afraid of writing in a more friendly way, so long as you retain your seriousness toward the subject.

7.2.2 Avoid Weak Words

Anytime a reader asks, "What do you mean by that?", you have used a weak word. Weak words create problems because they require readers to interpret what authors mean, and in doing so, readers might arrive at a different meaning than that intended. When your team writes with weak words, then, audiences find your documents far less persuasive, and unpersuasive documents seldom achieve the goals that authors intend. Below, we illustrate several different ways that weak words can enter your technical documents.

7.2.2.1 Check for Confusing or Frequently Misused Words. Obviously, you don't want to use the wrong word: noting that a measurement was in millimeters rather than centimeters would simply be wrong. Similarly, using incorrect words that sound alike (e.g., "it's" and "its" or "their" and "there") is simply wrong. Pay special attention to the groups of words below, and when in doubt about any proper word choice, consult a grammar handbook or online resource like those listed at the end of the chapter.

Accept/Except. Accept means to receive something; *except* means to exclude.

I <u>accept</u> the award.

All of the assays are complete <u>except</u> the final one.

Affect/Effect. Affect is usually a verb that means to influence (although it can be a noun that means superficial appearance but would be much less common in technical prose); *effect* is usually a noun that refers to results, although it can mean to cause something or to bring about a result.

How did changing the temperature <u>affect</u> the microbe?

<u>Effects</u> of the temperature change appear in the surface structure.

Amount/Number. Amount refers to things that cannot be counted or are considered as a collective unit; *number* refers to things that can be counted individually.

We have a large <u>amount</u> of work to do on this proposal.

We have a large <u>number</u> of samples to process.

Between/Among. Between indicates a relationship between only two items; *among* indicates relationships among three or more items.

Significant difference exists <u>between</u> the two populations.

We observed 15 instances <u>among</u> all the assays.

Discover/Invent. *Discover* means to find something that exists already; *invent* means to bring something into existence.

We <u>discovered</u> that heat changes the surface structure of the microbes.

Our team <u>invented</u> a new method for testing module inter-compatibility.

Fewer/Less. *Fewer* is used with singular nouns, or things that can be individually counted; *less* refers to collective nouns or things that cannot be individually counted.

We have <u>fewer</u> opportunities for funding this year than last year.

This proposal required <u>less</u> attention than the prior one.

Good/Well. *Good* is always an adjective that modifies nouns; *well* can be either an adverb or adjective, but more often is an adverb modifying a verb.

The results were <u>good</u> for demonstrating our hypothesis (modifies "results").

The test went <u>well</u> (modifies "went").

Its/It's. *Its* expresses ownership or possession; *it's* is the contraction form of *it is*.

<u>Its</u> characteristics include increased conductivity and luminescence.

<u>It's</u> well known that gold conducts well in this application.

There/Their/They're. *There* usually refers to a place unless it's used to refer to a nonspecific noun; *their* represents possession by a group of people; *they're* is the contraction form of *they are*.

<u>There</u> are many people over <u>there</u> (the first is nonspecific and the second refers to a place).

<u>Their</u> work proved invaluable for helping us predict the outcomes.

<u>They're</u> attempting to replicate the phenomenon in different materials.

Your/You're. *Your* expresses possession; *you're* is the contraction form of *you are*.

<u>Your</u> lab has demonstrated outstanding success with that method.

<u>You're</u> going to be required to submit results by the end of the month.

7.2.2.2 Avoid Double Negatives, and Change Negatives to Affirmatives.

A double negative occurs when two negative words appear together, creating significant confusion about the meaning. Any word that expresses a negative might cause writers problems, but some of the more common negative words include:

- Can't
- Didn't
- No
- Nothing
- None

Here are some examples:

Incorrect: We *didn't* have *no* time to run all the samples.

Correct: We *didn't* have time to run all the samples.

Incorrect: The temperature change *didn't* have *nothing* to do with the result.

Correct: The temperature change *didn't* have anything to do with the result.

In general, if your team phrases their sentences positively, double negatives won't be a problem. For example, to rephrase the sentences above in the positive:

Because we had limited time, we ran only a few samples.

The result was unrelated to the temperature change.

7.2.2.3 *Avoid Changing Verbs to Nouns.* Technically called "nominalization," this problem occurs when writers turn verbs into nouns, which results in nouns becoming the focus of the sentence rather than the verb. Nominalization represents perhaps one of the most significant problems for clarity in documents so we encourage your team to pay special attention to it. Study the sentences that follow to see how much confusion nominalizations introduce into a document.

It is our conclusion that the surface deformation was caused by the heat change.

can be revised to

We conclude that the heat change caused the surface to deform.

The second sentence presents the same information far more clearly and with fewer words.

Often in English, nominalizations end in *–tion*, so every word that ends this way should be a suspect. In fact, the word "nominalization" is itself a nominalization since it comes from the verb "nominalize." Some other common examples include:

Conclusion—from conclude

Decision—from decide

Destruction—from destroy

Examination—from examine

Investigation—from investigate

Participation—from participate

Reaction—from react

Suggestion—from suggest

The words above represent only a few possible nominalized words, and the *–tion* form is just one of many ways to nominalize. However, just about any time a noun can be changed to a verb and the sentence made shorter, a nominalization has appeared.

7.2.2.4 Delete Meaningless Words and Modifiers. Technical writers should seek to express ideas as clearly, concisely, and completely as possible. However, all writers occasionally include meaningless words, modifiers, and colloquial phrases that inhibit the clarity of what we write. In general, any word that can be eliminated should be eliminated, including most adjectives. For example, the last sentence originally ended "… including a great many adjectives." The phrase "a great many" became "most." As your team writes and edits, pay attention to these general concepts:

- Check all adjectives and adverbs to confirm their necessity; for example, must it read "really fast" or will "fast" do by itself?
- Avoid superlatives like "most" or "least" because these words are seldom specific.
- Transform verb phrases into solid verbs; for example, "ran into" becomes "hit."
- Eliminate redundant word pairs; for example, "past history" becomes simply "history" since all history is past.
- Eliminate colloquial phrases that add extra words. For example:

Colloquial Phrase	**becomes**	**Revision**
The reason is because		Since (or because)
Due to the fact that		Because (or since)
For the most part		Usually
With regard to		About
In the event that		If (or when)

7.2.2.5 Avoid Jargon. Technical writers must often include technical terms: engineers writing to other engineers will use very specific language for specialists that nonspecialists will not necessarily understand. This specialized language is often called "jargon." But jargon becomes a problem when writers rely too heavily on specialized terms, since all the jargon in the world won't cover sloppy reasoning. Most readers can see through the tactic of using jargon to cover poor thinking and, in fact, will find an overly jargon-filled document less persuasive than one that simply "says what it means." Whenever possible, steer clear of jargon because it makes documents difficult to read; trying to "sound smart" causes writers to produce text that uses far too many words and confounds readers. For example:

> *In spite of the fact that Homeland Security agency heads were not in agreement with respect to central causes of the security breech at the Canadian border, officials determined that immediate interventions were required and the foreign nationals were expelled.*

can be revised as:

> *Even though representatives of Homeland Security couldn't identify the causes of the security breech at the Canadian border, they decided to deport the foreign nationals immediately.*

In the revision, not only has the word count been reduced from 40 words to 26, the meaning is far clearer because the second sentence simply "says what it means." Revising your own sentences to eliminate unnecessary jargon can be difficult because the very problem is that the jargon *does* make sense to you. The best way to revise for jargon is to imagine that a general reader is constantly asking "What do you mean by that?" A careful audience analysis will tell you what your audience will or will not understand and when in doubt, err on the side of clarity for a nonspecialist audience.

7.2.2.6 *Avoid Sexist or Discriminatory Language.* Sexist and discriminatory language enters documents quite innocently. In fact, many writers learned that masculine forms of pronouns should be used when the gender of the subject is unknown or when the pronoun refers to a group that contains both men and women. For example, many writers were trained that this sentence is correct:

Whenever an engineer writes, he attempts to use precise language.

The problem with this sentence is quite clear: there are plenty of female engineers and using the masculine pronoun "he" presents an assumption that engineers are all male. Note that if writers simply make the sentence plural, the problem disappears:

Whenever engineers write, they attempt to use precise language.

In the prior case, the meaning stays the same and yet the sexist overtones have been erased.
The opposite case can be true as well:

When a nurse charts patient progress, she must carefully document all vitals.

While nursing is historically a female occupation, men certainly choose the profession, too. Again, simply making the sentence plural solves the problem:

When nurses chart patient progress, they must carefully document all vitals.

There are countless other ways that writers can unconsciously introduce sexist language into their documents, but the most important concept is that writers need to be aware when they include gender, nationality, religious, race, etc., references in their writing. Unless the sentence refers to a particular group for a specific reason, each time writers include something that refers to an entire group of people, that sentence should be revised or at least carefully reviewed for sexist or discriminatory language.

7.3 WRITING STRONG SENTENCES

In writing, our sentences carry the thoughts and concerns we hope that others will understand, and writing strong sentences increases the impact of the documents we publish. As your team writes, consider three main concepts:

- Write economically
- Include a variety of sentence types
- Avoid common pitfalls that lead to weak sentences

7.3.1 Write Economically

In his much-cited book *Revising Prose*, Richard Lanham proposes a revision method, called the "Paramedic Method," which equips writers with techniques to craft economical—and powerful—sentences. Rather than repeat the entire method here, we want to focus on a few key points that will enable your team to write economically:

1. *Circle the prepositions.* Prepositions require readers to connect actions to nouns, which means that readers must hold much of the sentence in their mind for long periods of reading. Confusion often results. Instead, eliminate prepositions and include active verbs.

   Original: In this test is an example of the use of the method of heating samples in the test device. (20 words)

   Revised: This test shows how samples can be heated with the test device. (12 words)

2. *Circle the "is" forms.* As discussed earlier, "is" verbs generally do not show the real meaning of a sentence and require authors to write far more words to explain the real meaning. Replace as many "to be" verbs (*am, is, are, were, was, be*) as possible with action verbs.

   Original: The most significant point is that the test device heats more evenly than other equipment. (15 words)

   Revised: The test device heats more evenly than other equipment. (9 words).

3. *Ask, "Where's the action?" and "Who's kicking whom?"* Technical writers sometimes use passive voice to disguise who completes actions. The quintessential form of the passive voice is the famous sentence "Mistakes were made." Passive voice obscures who completes the action and in doing so forces readers to interpret more of the sentence. Whenever a search for the "is" forms reveal a passive sentence, ask "Who is doing what to whom?" and rephrase with an active verb.

   Original: John was kicked by Mary. (5 words)

   Revised: Mary kicked John. (3 words)

   Original: The first assays were completed by a technician. (8 words)

   Revised: The technician completed the first assays. (6 words)

   Quite often readers of scientific prose have no problem when writers don't clearly state who is completing what actions; however, "active" sentences present content more clearly most of the time. Whenever possible, use active voice for its precision and efficiency.

4. *Start fast—no slow windups.* As noted before, colloquial phrases detract from clarity and introduce unnecessary words into a document. Eliminate all phrases that don't express meaning in the sentences.

Original: It is my opinion that using a new frequency will have great impact. (13 words)

Revised: Using a new frequency will have great impact. (8 words).

While writers cannot always use these techniques, the concepts of eliminating prepositional phrases, using active verbs, appropriately assigning action, and eliminating start-up phrases should generally be practiced by technical writing teams who wish to produce strong, concise sentences.

7.3.2 Include a Variety of Sentence Types

You probably remember lessons about sentence types called "simple," "compound," "complex," and "compound-complex" from your English classes. Technically, these titles represent different ways of presenting ideas that involve how complicated a sentence is, and style manuals often suggest that writers move among the different sentence types. However, instead of worrying about the types of sentences, your team might choose to think about sentence variety in terms of length of sentences.

Let's examine the sentences in the paragraph above as an example of varying sentence length. The first sentence (a "simple" sentence) contains 17 words. The second sentence ("a compound-complex" sentence) contains 30 words. The third sentence (a "complex" sentence) contains 24 words.

Now, compare the sentence variety in the opening paragraph (which contains variety) to the sentences of the second paragraph just above. In the opening paragraph, we have good sentence variety while in the second paragraph three simple sentences appear, one following the other, in rapid succession. The first paragraph reads much more easily and maintains readers' interest because it contains variety. The second paragraph, however, reads more like a bulleted list because each of the three simple sentences contains exactly nine words.

Writing with a variety of sentence types has its perils, like writing run-on sentences; but in general, writing that demonstrates variety sounds more sophisticated than the staccato form of repeated short sentences. Likewise, consistently writing long sentences might also have a negative impact as readers lose track of their place (at best) or become lulled to sleep (at worst). Write with a variety of sentence lengths and your team will avoid the traps of "machine gun" writing on one hand, and "long river" writing on the other.

7.4 AVOIDING WEAK SENTENCE CONSTRUCTION

Commonly referred to as "awkward sentences," weak sentence construction can result from any number of things ranging from poor verbs to nominalizations to incorrect grammar. Writers do make some common mistakes, though, that result in awkward-sounding sentences and most of these can easily be corrected to make the sentence more precise and less confusing. Below, we present a number of common mistakes, complete with the technical rule and an example both of the error and of a potential correction for each mistake. Hopefully, by seeing these common mistakes and comparing your own team's writing to them, your documents will avoid the traps of weak sentences.

7.4.1.1 Comma Splices. When writers join two complete sentences with a comma, this error is called a "comma splice." Comma splices are one of the most common errors and usually result from careless punctuation rather than a lack of understanding. To correct the error, writers can simply add punctuation between the two sentences or subordinate one to the other.

Comma Splice Sentence:
The choice of materials was easy, only two demonstrate proper conductivity.

Corrected Sentence Choices:
1. *Written as two sentences:* The choice of materials was easy. Only two demonstrate proper conductivity.
2. *Joined by a conjunction:* The choice of materials was easy <u>and</u> only two demonstrate proper conductivity.
3. *Joined by subordination:* The choice of materials was easy <u>because</u> only two demonstrate proper conductivity.
4. *Separated by a semicolon:* The choice of materials was easy<u>;</u> only two demonstrate proper conductivity.

7.4.1.2 Fragments. Fragments occur when writers do not include both a subject and a verb in a sentence. Consequently, the group of words cannot be considered a complete thought because the fragment requires something else to complete the action. To correct the error, confirm that your sentence has both a subject and a verb (something/somebody doing something or describing something/somebody in a specific way). Endless ways exist to create fragments, but one example demonstrates the idea where the second "sentence" is the fragment:

Fragment:
We observed the reaction. Watching from across the room.

Corrected Sentence Choices:
We observed the reaction, watching from across the room.
We observed the reaction from across the room.

7.4.1.3 Fused or Run-on Sentences. Fused or run-on sentences occur when writers chain two complete sentences—or more—together without proper punctuation or separation. Comma splices represent the most common type of run-on sentence, but any sentence with multiple "ands" or "buts" might be a fused sentence. To correct this error, writers can divide the single sentence into multiple, shorter sentences, or follow the recommendations above for comma splices.

Fused Sentence:
We tested the materials and we observed how they conducted heat but we were
    not able to repeat the reaction after the initial attempt.

Corrected Sentence Choices:
We tested the materials <u>and</u> we observed how they conducted heat. <u>However,</u> we
    were not able to repeat the reaction after the initial attempt.

We tested the materials <u>and</u> observed how they conducted heat<u>;</u> we were not able
    to repeat the reaction after the initial attempt.

7.4.1.4 Misplaced, Dangling, or Two-way Modifiers.

Sometimes sentences are unclear because writers have placed modifiers too far from the words they modify. Readers become confused as they try to understand which modifiers go with which words and might misinterpret your sentences. To correct this error, simply place the modifiers as close as possible to the words they modify:

Misplaced Modifier:
The technician decided to initiate the fire alarm when he saw the smoke leaving
    the lab and entering the stairwell. (*Is the smoke in the lab or in the stairwell?*
    Where is the technician?)

Corrected Sentence Choices:
Leaving the lab and entering the stairwell, the technician decided to initiate the
    fire alarm when he saw the smoke. (*The technician saw the smoke outside of*
    the lab.)

By comparison, dangling modifiers occur when a sentence includes a phrase that cannot modify something in the sentence. To correct this error, confirm that the descriptions in the sentence can sensibly occur.

Dangling Modifier:
Carrying the tray of samples, John's jacket caught the door handle. (*Jackets cannot*
    carry trays.)

Corrected Sentence Choices:
While carrying the tray of samples, John caught his jacket on the door handle.
John caught his jacket on the door handle while carrying the tray of samples.

Finally, two-way modifiers can modify multiple words in the sentence and confuse readers because they don't know which words the phrase modifies. To correct this error, place the modifier either at the end or the beginning of the sentence, depending upon which makes the meaning clearer.

Two-Way Modifier:
The technician said during the meeting John was unable to make a sound argument for his approach. (*Did the technician speak during the meeting or is the technician recounting John's inability during another meeting?*)

Corrected Sentence Choices:
During the meeting, the technician said that John was unable to make a sound argument for his approach. (*The technician reporting at the **current** meeting about John's **prior** actions.*)

The technician said that John was unable to make a sound argument for his approach during the meeting. (*The technician reporting on a **prior** meeting that John attended.*)

7.4.1.5 Faulty Parallelism. Two classes of faulty parallelism are most common. The first refers to errors where ideas of the same importance are not expressed in the same grammatical form. To correct this error, simply repeat the structure.

Faulty Expression:
The grant reviewer praised the proposal more for how it was written than what it actually said.

Corrected Sentence Choices:
The grant reviewer praised the proposal more <u>for</u> how it was written than <u>for</u> what it actually said.

The second refers to errors where items are not successfully compared. These comparisons are formed with "correlative conjunctions" such as *both...and, either...or, not only...but also.*

Faulty Comparison:
To generate the reaction, they tried both heat and to combine the materials in different ratios.

Corrected Sentence Choices:
To generate the reaction, they tried <u>not only applying</u> heat <u>but also combining</u> the materials in different ratios.

7.5 PUNCTUATING FOR CLARITY

Many writers think of punctuation as a nicety, something that doesn't really have much impact on a document. In reality, nothing could be further from the truth! Punctuation not only tells readers *how* to read a document, it also expresses *meaning*. Take something as apparently insignificant as a period. It tells readers to stop; it tells them that they have reached the end of an idea; it tells readers that *this* is not *that*. A little dot does all that, and can do more. In fact, there's an approach to grammar known as "rhetorical grammar" that differentiates, for example, between the meanings that evolve from using a semicolon between closely related sentences rather than periods (as we did just two sentences before this one). Punctuation can greatly assist your readers by making a document more clear and precise because it reveals, in a way, the patterns of spoken speech that convey as much meaning as the words themselves. Without these cues, our sentences would either confuse readers or carry much less meaning. Finally, even though punctuation holds great value for precise writing, do not over-punctuate. Too much punctuation is just as bad as none at all. Generally, your team should add punctuation only if the meaning or conventional usage requires it.

To help your team as it revises and proofreads, we have outlined below some of the major concerns facing technical writers.

7.5.1 End Punctuation

We all know that sentences need punctuation at the end. But all marks are not the same, and so it pays to know the differences.

7.5.1.1 Periods. Periods generally have two uses: they end a sentence that makes a statement and they form abbreviations:

1. I wrote the grant.
2. Mr.; St.; etc.

Periods can also have other specialized uses such as in table or figure titles (e.g., Figure 1. Corona Electrode Voltage), but this use represents a style choice more than a grammatical choice.

7.5.1.2 Question Marks. Question marks have just one use: to end a question. For example:

1. Have you separated the materials?
2. Can you separate the materials?

Different types of questions exist, such as indirect questions and polite requests/ commands, but each type of a question ends with a question mark.

7.5.1.3 Exclamation Points. An exclamation point also has only one function: to express strong emotion or emphasis in a sentence. For example:

1. The test was a success!
2. Ah! I cannot believe it!
3. Separate the materials!

While these examples technically show different types of exclamation (interjection vs. imperative), they all express a strong emotion that emphasizes the content. Technical writing doesn't often contain exclamation points, so be careful if you chose to insert one because in a technical document, the exclamation will stand out!

7.5.2 Commas

Commas cause many writers distress because commas are so common, yet they are the most frequently misunderstood punctuation marks. Commas generally separate items that are not related (as in a list) or separate a subordinate clause from the independent clause. Commas also operate in many conventional ways, like separating items in dates, for example. Some specific times when writers should use commas appear below.

1. *Commas separate items in a series.* The material was dry, brittle, warm, and green.
2. *Commas separate two adjectives preceding a noun.* We utilized a long, tedious set of procedures.
3. *Commas separate complete thoughts when used with* and, but, or, not, for, *or* yet. We utilized a difficult procedure, but the process is very thorough.
4. *Commas set apart nonessential clauses and phrases.* The test, which utilizes high acid levels, is the most thorough test known. *(The reference to acid levels could be removed without changing the sentence's meaning.)*
5. *Commas follow introductory elements like* well *or* yes *and follow introductory phrases like* in the meantime *or any introductory prepositional phrase.* After we completed the test, we cleaned the equipment.
6. *Commas set apart interrupting elements.* The material was dry and warm, which indicated that, despite the difficult instructions, we had done the test correctly.

Commas can give writers trouble because they are used in many situations for many purposes, both stylistic and grammatical. However, when in doubt, stick with the "pause rule." If you would have paused while reading the sentence aloud, odds are that inserting a comma would be acceptable (exceptions to this guideline would be run-on sentences or comma splices).

7.5.3 Semicolons

Semicolons confound writers more than commas and, therefore, most writers tend to avoid them. However, semicolons are predictable and when used correctly, they add sophistication to a document. Readers often interpret that sophistication with language into sophisticated thoughts. Below we present some common uses of semicolons with examples to help your team write documents that sound just a little smarter.

1. *Semicolons separate clauses without conjunctions like* and, but, or, nor, for, *or* yet. We tested the materials according to the established procedure; the results were inconclusive.

2. *Semicolons separate items in a list if individual items within the list contain commas.* We tested gold, which was the best conductor; aluminum, which conducted second best; and nickel, which finished a distant third as we had predicted.

7.5.4 Colons

Colons signal to readers that they should pay close attention to what follows. Colons also appear when the second part of a sentence explains, restates, or describes the first part of the sentence. An example of each of these appears below.

1. *Colons signal the importance of what follows.* In your test you must address these concerns: long-term impacts, short-term costs, and time-to-market.
2. *Colons introduce a second part of a sentence that explains the first.* These drugs proved the best: they showed low long-term side effects and had low cost of production.

One special thing to note about colons is that writers frequently—and incorrectly—place a colon after a verb or preposition and just before a list even though the list items follow grammatically. Study these sentences:

Incorrect: We were able to isolate the microbe by: heat, color and activity level.
Correct: We were able to isolate the microbe by heat, color, and activity level.

In this example, the elements following "by" should not be preceded by a colon because the list fits grammatically with the remainder of the sentence. Notice, though, that there is a colon above following "study these sentences." In that case, the items that follow provide demonstrations of the concept in the paragraph.

7.5.5 Apostrophes

In principle, the rules about apostrophes are straightforward. Apostrophes signal possession and contractions. That's all. However, in spite of these simple rules, writers chronically and erroneously place apostrophes at the end of just about any word that ends in "s." Three correct examples appear below, with the first two demonstrating the same rule in singular and plural.

1. *Possession-singular.* The *technician's* coat caught on the door. (The coat belongs to the technician.)
2. *Possession-plural.* The technicians' coats fell when the rack broke. (Multiple coats that belong to multiple people fell off the rack.)
3. *Contraction.* We weren't able to retest the sample. (Were not becomes weren't.)

It's really that easy. Unless the word expresses ownership of something or unless the word omits letters to form a contraction, there is no need for an apostrophe. Finally, be aware that apostrophes *never* appear in a simple pluralization. For example:

Incorrect	The sample's were tainted.
Correct	The samples were tainted.

This mistake appears *very* commonly so be sure to ask yourself whether the word with an apostrophe expresses ownership or whether it is a contraction; if it does neither of those things, remove the apostrophe.

7.5.6 Dashes and Hyphens

Dashes and hyphens are not interchangeable; each has specific functions. Dashes generally have two functions, one to indicate an interruption or break in thought and the other to indicate an explanation, much like a colon. For example:

1. The test—if we could call it that—was negative.
2. The method we used represented the latest technology—a substitute for all older procedures.

In the first case, the words between the dashes represent an interruption in thought while the second case shows how the words following the dash modify what comes before. (To form a dash in Microsoft Word, type two hyphens, which are on the key next to the zero on the keyboard, and the two hyphens will automatically become a dash after completing the next word.)

Hyphens, on the other hand, have several specific uses:

1. *Hyphens divide words at the end of a line.* With today's word processing software, this is seldom a problem because Microsoft Word automatically moves words around to avoid hyphenation or automatically hyphenates, depending upon your settings.
2. *Hyphens form compound numbers.* Eighty-one subjects; twenty-seven examples.
3. *Hyphens form compound adjectives.* Dark-colored residue; gold-plated watch.
4. *Hyphens clarify awkward formations.* Re-examine; semi-intense.

While the subtlety of dashes and hyphens might appear to be fussy, remember that readers judge your document both by the ideas it contains and by the container. If the container—the grammar and mechanics—shows close attention to detail, readers are more likely to believe the ideas represented in the document were developed with attention to detail too.

7.6 FINAL CONSIDERATIONS

In this last section, we present some selected issues that writers frequently encounter. The list is not exhaustive; these issues simply represent those that are most common. Below we present the issues, using examples when appropriate.

7.6.1   Abbreviations and Acronyms

In general, writers should avoid abbreviations in technical writing unless the abbreviation is generally accepted, such as in the case of *Mr.*, *Dr.*, or *Ph.D.* Units of measure are also often abbreviated: mL., mcg., cm., etc. Note that abbreviations are almost always followed by a period, although it's quite common for units of measure to omit the period.

Acronyms represent a slightly different case where the first letters of multiple words are combined to form another word or shortened form of the word. For example:

NSF (National Science Foundation)
DoD (Department of Defense)
SME (Subject Matter Expert)

Sometimes, acronyms become generally acceptable words, as in SCUBA, which are technically called "acrostics." Your organization almost certainly has its own set of internal acronyms and/or acrostics with their own conventions, in addition to internal abbreviations that mean little outside of your organization. As with all writing, consider who will be reading the document and whether or not the audience will understand the abbreviation, acronym, or acrostic. If there is a chance they won't understand, simply don't use them; even if they will be understood, use them sparingly. In any case, it's best to spell out each term completely the first time it appears, unless it is universally known and commonly used like "*Dr.*"

7.6.2   Capitalization

Capitalization gives writers few problems with one exception: inconsistent use. Most writers in English know the general rules, but writers often randomly capitalize words simply because they appear to be important. Avoid over-capitalizing, but do follow these common rules:

1. *Capitalize the beginning of sentences.* We completed the test.
2. *Capitalize proper nouns and their derivative adjectives.* Proper nouns name a specific person, place, or thing and usually represent one-of-a-kind items such as organizations, places, published works, deities, and people: National Science Foundation, Spain, Pearson's, The Great Gatsby, Alfred Nobel are all nouns, while French, Lutheran, and Dickensian are adjectives derived from proper nouns.
3. *Capitalize titles.* Titles used with a person's name should be capitalized, particularly if the title precedes the name: Professor Mamishev, Doctor Williams, President Lincoln.

7.6.3   Numbers

Technical documents usually include a lot of numbers, and following a few key rules will make your document more clear:

1. *Do not begin a sentence with a numeral.* *Eighty-one* subjects completed the experiment. (not "81 subjects....")
2. *Numbers with more than two words should be written as numerals* (unless they appear at the beginning of a sentence). The sample had 1,000,567 parts per liter.
3. *Use numbers for all specific measurements in scientific and mathematical contexts.* We measured 1.7 g of solution.

When in doubt with numbers, use the construction that will most precisely and clearly state the purpose of the number within accepted conventions.

7.6.4 Dates

Different countries present dates in different ways, so knowing your target audience is important for determining how to present dates correctly. For example, in the United States, both *June 25, 2008*, and *6/25/08* are correct. However, in most European countries, the preferred format is *25 June 2008* and *2008.06.25*. Since almost all date schemes present day, month, and year in a particular order, be sure that your dates contain all three parts in the order acceptable to your audience.

7.6.5 Fractions and Percentages

Technical and scientific writers most often present fractions in numerical form because they represent specific data. However, just as with numbers, fractions at the beginning of a sentence should be spelled out. For example:

The new processors consume 1/6 less energy than the previous generation.
One-fourth of all chips processed by the company were flawed.

Fractions and percentages are interchangeable and the rules for percentages are the same as for fractions:

The new processors consume 16.7% less energy than the previous generation.
Twenty-five percent of all chips processed by the company were flawed.

7.6.6 Units of Measure

Globally, at least three measurement systems are used: the International System of Units (also called the metric system and abbreviated SI), the United States Customary System, and the British Imperial System. Most scientific and technical writing will utilize SI and its associated abbreviations for specific units of measure including length, mass, time, temperature, and power. The metric system has a sophisticated set of units based upon its system of deriving new measurement units from the fundamental ones; accordingly, your team should be very familiar with the units specific to the type of work you write about. For example, the fundamental unit of mass, *kilogram (kg)* can become *grams* (*g*) or *micrograms* (*µg*, sometimes spelled *mcg* in clinical settings). There are at least 20 other derivations using specific prefixes such as *deca-, deci-, giga-, or nano-.*

7.7   A FINAL NOTE ON GRAMMAR

Because grammar and mechanics in English—like all languages—are complicated and take years to learn, the full range of grammar issues is really beyond the scope of this book. In any case, so many good grammar books exist that we couldn't hope to cover all of the issues as deeply as those sources do. However, the issues we've addressed in this chapter seem to be those that concern writing teams most frequently. Focusing on just the things we present here will improve your documents immensely.

ADDITIONAL RESOURCES

Lanham, Richard. (1999). *Revising Prose*. 4th Edition. New York: Longman.

Purdue Online Writing Lab (n.d.). Retrieved May 2009, from OWL: The Purdue Online Writing Lab: http://owl.english.purdue.edu.

Warriner, John E. (1988). *English Composition and Grammar: Complete Course*. San Diego: Harcourt Brace Jovanovich.

8

CONCLUDING REMARKS

Tom Smykowski: It was a "Jump to Conclusions" mat. You see, it would be
this mat that you would put on the floor ... and would have different
CONCLUSIONS written on it that you could JUMP TO.
Michael Bolton: That is the worst idea I've ever heard in my life, Tom.

—Office Space, 1999

8.1 IN THIS CHAPTER

This book wouldn't be complete without some concluding thoughts about *STREAM Tools*. We've introduced a number of ideas throughout the book, some simple and some complex; it remains for us to present our final case regarding the benefits that will come to your writing team after choosing to adopt *STREAM Tools*. As a consequence, the chapter begins with a business case, adapted from a real scenario, for implementing *STREAM Tools*. This chapter also includes some frequently asked questions that might arise as you discuss the *STREAM Tools* method with your colleagues. Finally, since Chapter 1 opened with a few "horror stories," we want to close the book with some

Technical Writing for Teams: The STREAM Tools Handbook, by Alexander Mamishev and Sean Williams
Copyright © 2010 Institute of Electrical and Electronics Engineers

"success stories" shared by *STREAM Tools* users, followed by a multitude of resources on writing. Combined, we hope the sections of this chapter present you with a final, strong incentive for adopting *STREAM Tools* and realizing the gains in efficiency and effectiveness that result.

8.2   BUSINESS CASE

If you are in charge of an organization that produces technical documents, how much does your organization stand to benefit from using *STREAM Tools*? Below we present a business case in order to demonstrate exactly how much an organization can save by adopting *STREAM Tools*. This case uses fictional names but includes real numbers taken from field interviews and from our own experience.

Consider a research group of a mid-size start-up company that has 10 permanent members: a division director, three engineering and science Ph.D.s, one MBA, two MS engineers, and three technicians. The group also uses the part-time contract services of a graphic designer and a grant writer, and regularly works with professionals outside the organization, including an MD, a patent agent, a public relations company representative, and a Washington, D.C., lobbyist. Combined, the team can consist of as many as 16 members working on a project at one time.

Each year, the organization submits about 10 proposals, 5 journal papers, 5 conference papers, 4 patents, 12 internal reports, 5 external reports to sponsors and investors, and 6 press-releases. We will not count emails, memos, or presentations here, but the documents we are counting amount to about 800 pages of written text. The most frequently used figure appears in these documents 15 times, the most frequently used paragraph appears in these documents 20 times.

Each team member spends a certain amount of their time writing these documents. Let's say *STREAM Tools* allows them to speed up the overall process by 20 percent (an average number based on interviewing experienced writers who have already adopted *STREAM Tools*). Table 8.1 shows the distribution of efforts for all team members in this business case and the resulting cost savings of $91,800.

In addition to these cost savings, there will be intangible savings, which, in fact, may even exceed the direct financial benefits. Because the writing and organization are higher quality, more proposals are likely to be funded, more journal papers accepted, and more external reports are likely to be viewed favorably by sponsors and investors. The company's public image will improve. Job satisfaction will also be higher since team members have shifted time from mundane tasks to creative and critical activities.

The largest initial investment involves increased personnel hours as the group members learn to implement *STREAM Tools*; the initial investment might also include attending seminars or inviting speakers to talk about *STREAM Tools*, if the company prefers to pay for explicit instruction rather than relying on self-learning. Table 8.2 presents an estimate of the required time and other costs for each team member to learn *STREAM Tools*. The amount of time varies, because different team members will

Table 8.1. Annual Company Savings Due to Productivity Improvement

	Hourly rate, $	Benefits and Overhead Multiplier	Personnel cost to the company per hour, $	Writing time, %	Hours working for the company, per year	Writing time, hrs	Productivity increase, %	Annual hours saved	Annual savings, $
Director	100	2	200	10	2,000	200	20	40	$4,000
Ph.D. #1	75	2	150	25	2,000	500	20	100	$7,500
Ph.D. #2	75	2	150	30	2,000	600	20	120	$9,000
Ph.D. #3	75	2	150	20	2,000	400	20	80	$6,000
MBA	60	2	120	15	2,000	300	20	60	$3,600
MS #1	50	2	100	20	2,000	400	20	80	$4,000
MS #2	50	2	100	20	2,000	400	20	80	$4,000
Technician #1	30	2	60	15	2,000	300	20	60	$1,800
Technician #2	25	2	50	10	2,000	200	20	40	$1,000
Technician #3	20	2	40	10	2,000	200	20	40	$800
Graphics designer	75	2	150	0	2,000	0	20	0	$0
Grant writer	30	2	60	90	2,000	1,800	20	360	$10,800
MD	150	2	300	3	2,000	60	20	12	$1,800
Patent agent	50	2	100	90	2,000	1,800	20	360	$18,000
PR Rep	60	2	120	50	2,000	1,000	20	200	$12,000
Lobbyist	75	2	150	25	2,000	500	20	100	$7,500
Total savings due to productivity increase:								1,732	$91,800

Table 8.2. Company Costs of Introducing *STREAM Tools*

	Hourly rate, $	Benefits and Overhead Multiplier	Personnel cost to the company, $ per hour	Hours needed to learn *STREAM Tools*	Cost of teaching supplies and software, $	Cost of seminar attendance, $	One-time cost, $
Director	100	2	200	5	$50	$0	$1,050
Ph.D. #1	75	2	150	10	$200	$500	$2,200
Ph.D. #2	75	2	150	10	$300	$500	$2,300
Ph.D. #3	75	2	150	10	$400	$500	$2,400
MBA	60	2	120	10	$200	$500	$1,900
MS #1	50	2	100	10	$200	$500	$1,700
MS #2	50	2	100	10	$200	$500	$1,700
Technician #1	30	2	60	5	$200	$0	$500
Technician #2	25	2	50	5	$200	$0	$450
Technician #3	20	2	40	5	$200	$0	$400
Graphics designer	75	2	150	0	$200	$0	$200
Grant writer	30	2	60	10	$400	$500	$1,500
MD	150	2	300	0	$0	$0	$0
Patent agent	50	2	100	0	$0	$0	$0
PR Rep	60	2	120	5	$50	$0	$650
Lobbyist	75	2	150	5	$50	$0	$800
Total costs of introducing *STREAM Tools*:				100			**$17,750**

learn different aspects of *STREAM Tools*. The lead Ph.D., for example, will attend a workshop on the subject, read the entire book, and memorize keyboard shortcuts for MathType and the editing shorthand. The director, on the other hand, will focus only on the effective editing methods and will learn how to reuse file templates. The exact return on the company's investment is hard to pinpoint. This rough example shows that *STREAM Tools* can begin to "pay for itself" in a matter of weeks, with an annual return on the investment approaching $75,000. And these figures are only for one project team.

How does this logic apply to academic teams, especially in technical fields? If anything, the savings are even larger since so many academics live by the saying "a career in the academy is a career in writing." Consequently, if you operate a large research lab with postdocs, graduate students, and perhaps even undergraduate students, the financial benefits of using *STREAM Tools* will, in terms of percentages, be much greater, simply because so much time is spent on writing in academic settings.

STREAM Tools is a young system, so as the number of users grows, more rigorous case studies will appear in press, and we would be happy to hear about them! Please share them with us at our website, streamtoolsonline.com.

8.3 FREQUENTLY ASKED QUESTIONS

Q. Where can I receive additional help implementing STREAM Tools in my organization?

A. The first resource we suggest is the *STREAM Tools* network of users, which is available through the website at streamtoolsonline.com. New users can also contact a trainer certified to instruct your team members in the system by accessing the list of trainers available at the *STREAM Tools* website.

Q. I am writing a paper for a journal that has a Microsoft Word template for submissions online. Their template does not have any useful automatic features of STREAM Tools, but this is the format that they require. What should I do?

A. Publishers rarely try to make *your* life easy. The goal of their template is only to simplify their own jobs. You should use *STREAM Tools* until the moment of submission. At the last moment, save your document with the *STREAM Tools* features and then save the document again as a new name. After re-saving the document, strip the formatting and adapt it to the publisher's required template. This way, the publisher will have their preferred format to work with, and you will have a document that you can use efficiently in your future work.

Q. I am sending a document formatted with STREAM Tools features to a colleague and it does not look the same on the other side. What should I do?

A. If your goal is to share a document with a colleague who does not use *STREAM Tools*, but you want the document to retain its features and appearance, then you should generate an Adobe Acrobat .pdf file and send the .pdf file to your colleague. If the colleague needs to make changes, they can comment on the .pdf file and return it to you for implementation.

Q. What about WordPerfect?

A. It is possible to develop a similar system for WordPerfect as that described here for Microsoft Word. However, the pervasiveness of Microsoft Word persuades us that dedicating time to WordPerfect would be time wasted. If you are working with a colleague who only uses WordPerfect, share the document with him or her as a .pdf file.

Q. After my document got to 50 pages long, it became impossible to work with because the computer would freeze. What should I do?

A. There are many possible reasons for freezing and crashing when working with large documents.

- If the problem is caused by viruses, improper installations, or system configuration issues, it is time to perform some routine maintenance on your computer.
- If your computer is obsolete (meaning four or more years old), it is probably time to upgrade.
- If the document file size is disproportionally large compared to its length, the most likely problem is with your figures. If you use reasonable resolutions (150–300 DPI) for photos and bitmaps, and use line art instead of bitmaps whenever possible, you should be able to handle several hundred objects per document without much trouble.

Q. I think I found a better way to implement a certain feature.

A. Please share it with the community! Record your suggestions at the *STREAM Tools* website, streamtoolsonline.com, or email it to the authors at streamtools@gmail.com. If this is indeed a better way, it could be integrated in the next edition of this manuscript (with proper acknowledgment, of course).

Q. My question is not in this list. What should I do?

A. Consult the *STREAM Tools* website for possible answers posted by the user community. If your questions aren't answered there (or in this book), please contact the authors at streamtools@gmail.com.

8.4 SUCCESS STORIES

Having opened the book with "horror stories," we'd like to conclude with a couple of "success stories." So far, these stories represent the successes in our research groups, where *STREAM Tools* originated. As *STREAM Tools* becomes more popular, we look forward to hearing about your successes and challenges.

Nels-Jewell Larsen, technology innovation company:
We received so many kudos after introducing the full taxonomy of electrostatic pumps in the shared EndNote database. Although most people already had the software, and some used it in their individual writing, creating a group-wide database was a big step forward. In highly interdisciplinary fields, keyword searches tend to miss many critical papers. Finding the most relevant papers in the sea of literature became much easier and faster when everyone started contributing to the common database. The funny thing, this is just a little productivity technique, a trivial task in comparison with the scientific output of a team consisting of many Ph.D.s, yet so much attention was paid to it in the company.

Professor Mamishev, University of Washington:
In 2006 I was part of a team of 12 professors who spent their summer at Boeing, studying Boeing's engineering and business practices. At the end, we were expected to write a report for upper management. At a certain point, the question came up of who should be appointed to integrate all of the report's content. Many folks were apprehensive about taking on the thankless task of "herding the cats." I volunteered with the condition that everyone on the project agree to use the same template for their input. Everyone agreed, I explained how the templates worked and sent a sample to everyone. Since everyone used my template, it took hardly any time to integrate their output. After just a few iterations, we had a cohesive multi-page document ready for submission.

Professor Williams, Clemson University:
In spring of 2009, a colleague and I were asked to write a book chapter on evaluating the effectiveness of teaching and learning in 3D virtual worlds. After brainstorming with the colleague and using the "divide and draft" approach, we each prepared sepa-rate pieces of the manuscript. I integrated the parts of the manuscript into a single document with STREAM Tools features and we each reviewed the document separately. We then collaborated on a large table that synthesized the theoretical discussion into a rubric that pointed back to section headings earlier in the document to explain the evolution behind specific rubric points. The real payoff from STREAM Tools came when we revised the organization of our original theoretical discussion. As we shifted our theoretical discussion around, the auto-text feature automatically updated the section headings in the rubric, saving us vast amounts of time in scanning through the text to figure out where each point was referenced. We planned, prepared, wrote, edited, and submitted the entire manuscript of nearly 30 pages in just under three weeks.

8.5   ADDITIONAL READING

STREAM Tools is a system that relies on a host of others who have come before us. We have cited some of these sources in specific chapters, but below we'd like to refer our readers to some additional resources that have impacted our thinking and which may be of help as your own team adopts *STREAM Tools*.

8.5.1   Useful Books and Articles

A classic book on English grammar:

> W. Strunk Jr., E.B. White, R. Angell, *The Elements of Style*, Fourth Edition. Longman, 2000.

Excellent books on technical writing:

> Michael Alley, *The Craft of Scientific Writing*, Third Edition. Springer, 1997.
> Joseph M. Williams, *Ten Lessons in Clarity and Grace*, Seventh Edition. Longman, 2002.
> Mike Markel, *Technical Communication*, Seventh Edition. Bedford St. Martin's, 2003.

An excellent article of advice to journal paper writers:

> • S.D. Senturia, "How to Avoid the Reviewer's Axe: One Editor's View," *Journal of Electromechanical Systems*, vol. 12, no. 3, pp. 229–232, June 2003.

8.5.2   Useful Weblinks

A comprehensive list of Microsoft Word 2002 shortcuts:

> http://support.microsoft.com/default.aspx?scid=kb;en-us;290938

Microsoft websites that focus on field codes:

> http://office.microsoft.com/en-us/assistance/HP051861901033.aspx
> http://office.microsoft.com/en-us/assistance/HP051862221033.aspx

A helpful site on Microsoft Word techniques:

> http://www.shaunakelly.com/word/index.html

The conversion tools between Microsoft Word and LaTeX change all the time, and none of them are effective for complex documents. One website that keeps track of various software packages is:

> http://www.tug.org/utilities/texconv/textopc.html

EXERCISES

Exercise 8.1.

(A) Assuming that you have learned at least some aspects of *STREAM Tools*, estimate how much time you will save by using this system. State your thought process.

(B) Analyze the business case of introducing *STREAM Tools* in your organization, class project, research group, etc. Consider the following aspects: what the benefits are, what time and resource investments would be required, how long it would take to implement, who would have to participate, what the division of expertise would look like, which features would be used and skiped, and how long would it take to get going.

Appendix A

FILE TEMPLATE FOR A SHORT SINGLE-COLUMN REPORT OR PAPER

Filename: BasicTemplate.doc

Description: This template designed for simple manuscripts (up to 20 pages or so), written in single-column format, with one-level numbering of figures and tables.

BasicTemplate.doc

Technical Writing for Teams: The *STREAM Tools* Handbook

Copyright by Alexander V. Mamishev and Sean D. Williams

Version 1.0.0
May 2009

Abstract

This template document is designed for generating uniform reports and papers using principles of effective document formatting described in the book *Writing for Research Teams: STREAM Tools* by Alexander V. Mamishev and Sean D. Williams. The main purpose of this template is to enable multiple co-authors to write documents using the automatic formatting features of Microsoft Word. When each co-author uses the same formatting for each element of their manuscript, features such as numbering and cross-referencing of headings, figures, equations, and references becomes much easier. In addition, this approach allows easy reuse of portions of material in different documents.

Table of Contents:

You can update the Table of Contents at any time by pressing **Ctrl-A** (this selects the entire document), then releasing it, and then pressing **F9**. In short: **Ctrl-A, F9**. The Table of Contents is self-generated. The appearance of the Table of Contents can be changed by clicking **Insert, Index and Tables**.

If you need more lists, for example, the List of Figures or the List of Tables, you can insert them and then use similar steps. Better yet, switch to the ThesisOrBook.doc template to have more features needed that you might need for long documents.

1. Introduction

This template contains preformatted elements of a typical report: table of contents, headings, figures, tables, equations, and literature citations. In order to guarantee seamless integration of all documents generated by a group of writers, each writer should be careful in preserving format settings for all basic elements.

There is one main principle of this approach: in order to create a new entry, the writer should copy and paste an existing entry into a new location, and then overwrite the content at the new location.

2. Implementation (Heading level 1)

2.1 Heading level 2

2.1.1 Heading level 3

2.1.1.1 Heading level 4

Four levels of headings are provided as an initial template. In order to update numbering of all automated entries, click **Ctrl-A, F9**. All figures and tables should be numbered.

To create a new figure, copy the existing figure template (with the attached caption) and paste it to a new location. The figure template is designed in such a way that the caption stays with the image.

In order to cross-reference a figure click **Insert, Reference, Cross-Reference, Figure, Only label and number**, then select the figure you want to cross-reference from the list.

An example of auto-formatted text:

Figure 1 shows the conceptual representation of the Electrostatic Air Pump (EAP) technology.

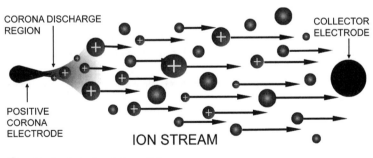

Figure 1. Schematic diagram of ion stream generating from a DC electrohydrodynamic ionic wind pump, where a high voltage is applied between the corona and the collector electrodes [1].

Table 1. This is the template for a table.

a	b	cde
1	2	34

In order to create or cross-reference a table, use the same command sequences as those for figures.

New equations should be created by copying the equation line template below and altering it in a new location. MathType software is recommended for editing equations. MathType is superior to Microsoft Word's built-in equation editor because it has more features and allows exporting to LaTeX.

Example. According to (1), Coulomb's force $\mathbf{f}_C$ acting on an unpaired charge q in electric field $\mathbf{E}$ is equal to

$$\mathbf{f}_C = q \cdot \mathbf{E} \tag{1}$$

To cross-reference an equation, you first have to create a bookmark by highlighting the equation number, clicking **Insert, Bookmark**, and giving that a unique identifier. For consistency, all equation identifiers should start with "eq". For example, equation (1) is bookmarked as "eqColoumbForce".

Several software packages are available for managing literature citations in Microsoft Word. This template relies on software called EndNote. The citations should conform to the requirements of your field or the specific publication source. For example, in the IEEE style, citations should be enclosed in square brackets and look like this [2]. Citations should also be numbered in the order readers encounter them in the text.

References:

[1]   C. P. Hsu, N. E. Jewell-Larsen, I. A. Krichtafovitch, S. W. Montgomery, J. T. Dibene II, and A. V. Mamishev, "Miniaturization of Electrostatic Fluid Accelerators," *IEEE/ASME Journal of MEMS*, 2007.

[2]   J. H. Jeans, *Electricity and Magnetism*, 5th ed., New York, Cambridge University Press, 1927.

Appendix B

FILE TEMPLATE FOR A DOUBLE-COLUMN PAPER

Filename: BasicTemplateDoubleColumn.doc

Description: This template designed for double-column camera-ready papers (up to 10 pages or so), with one-level numbering of headings, figures and tables.

> REPLACE THIS LINE WITH YOUR PAPER IDENTIFICATION NUMBER (DOUBLE-CLICK HERE TO EDIT) <

IEEE-Auto Template, Double-Column Format

First A. Author, Second B. Author, Jr., and Third C. Author, *Member, IEEE*

Abstract—**This template for a double-column paper was created for** *Technical Writing for Teams: The STREAM Tools Handbook* **according to the instructions for authors contributing papers to the disciplines of the Institute of Electrical and Electronics Engineers (IEEE). The original template provided by the IEEE does not have automated typesetting functions. This IEEE-Auto template file is preformatted for automatic numbering of manuscript elements. It should be easy to adjust appearance settings (for example, column width), to meet the requirements of other publishers.**

Index Terms—**About four key words or phrases in alphabetical order, separated by commas. For a list of suggested keywords, send a blank e-mail to** keywords@ieee.org **or visit the IEEE web site at** http://www.ieee.org/organizations/pubs/ani_prod/keywrd98.txt

I. Introduction

THIS document is a template for Microsoft *Word* versions 6.0 or later, designed according to the IEEE template TRANS-JOUR.DOC, available from the IEEE website http://www.ieee.org/organizations/pubs/transactions/stylesheets.htm so you can use it to prepare your manuscript.

When you open BasicTemplateDoubleColumn.doc, select "Page Layout" from the "View" menu in the menu bar (View | Page Layout), which allows you to see the footnotes. Then type over the section of the manuscript and copy the templates of individual manuscript elements to create new elements, such as figures or equations.

The pull-down style menu is at the left of the Formatting Toolbar at the top of your *Word* window (for example, the style at this point in the document is "Text"). Highlight a section that you want to designate with a certain style, then select the appropriate name on the style menu. The style will adjust your fonts and line spacing. **Do not change the font sizes or line spacing to squeeze more text into a limited number of pages.** Use italics for emphasis; do not underline.

To insert images into *Word,* position the cursor at the insertion point and either use Insert | Picture | From File or copy the image to the Windows clipboard and then Edit | Paste Special | Picture (with "Float over text" unchecked).

IEEE will do the final formatting of your paper. If your paper is intended for a conference, please observe the conference page limits.

II. Procedure for Paper Submission

A. Review Stage

Please check with your editor on whether to submit your manuscript by hard copy or electronically for review. If hard copy, submit photocopies such that only one column appears per page. This will give your referees plenty of room to write comments. Send the number of copies specified by your editor (typically four). If submitted electronically, find out if your editor prefers submissions on disk or as e-mail attachments.

If you want to submit your file with one column electronically, please do the following:

--First, click on the View menu and choose Print Layout.

--Second, place your cursor in the first paragraph. Go to the Format menu, choose Columns, choose one column Layout, and choose "apply to whole document" from the dropdown menu.

--Third, click and drag the right margin bar to just over 4 inches in width.

The graphics will stay in the "second" column, but you can drag them to the first column. Make the graphic wider to push out any text that may try to fill in next to the graphic.

B. Final Stage

When you submit your final version, after your paper has been accepted, print it in two-column format, including figures and tables. Send three prints of the paper; two will go to IEEE and one will be retained by the Editor-in-Chief or conference publications chair.

You must also send your final manuscript on a disk, which IEEE will use to prepare your paper for publication. Write the authors' names on the disk label. If you are using a Macintosh, please save your file on a PC formatted disk, if possible. You may use *Zip* or CD-ROM disks for large files, or compress files using *Compress, Pkzip, Stuffit,* or *Gzip.*

Manuscript received October 9, 2001. (Write the date on which you submitted your paper for review.) This work was supported in part by the U.S. Department of Commerce under Grant BS123456 (sponsor and financial support acknowledgment goes here). Paper titles should be written in uppercase and lowercase letters, not all uppercase. Avoid writing long formulas with subscripts in the title; short formulas that identify the elements are fine (e.g., "Nd–Fe–B"). Do not write "(Invited)" in the title. Full names of authors are preferred in the author field, but are not required. Put a space between authors' initials.

F. A. Author is with the National Institute of Standards and Technology, Boulder, CO 80305 USA (corresponding author to provide phone: 303-555-5555; fax: 303-555-5555; e-mail: author@boulder.nist.gov).

S. B. Author, Jr., was with Rice University, Houston, TX 77005 USA. He is now with the Department of Physics, Colorado State University, Fort Collins, CO 80523 USA (e-mail: author@lamar.colostate.edu).

T. C. Author is with the Electrical Engineering Department, University of Colorado, Boulder, CO 80309 USA, on leave from the National Research Institute for Metals, Tsukuba, Japan (e-mail: author@nrim.go.jp).

Also send a sheet of paper with complete contact information for all authors. Include full mailing addresses, telephone numbers, fax numbers, and e-mail addresses. This information will be used to send each author a complimentary copy of the journal in which the paper appears. In addition, designate one author as the "corresponding author." This is the author to whom proofs of the paper will be sent. Proofs are sent to the corresponding author only.

C. Figures

All tables and figures will be processed as images. **However, IEEE cannot extract the tables and figures embedded in your document.** (The figures and tables you insert in your document are only to help you gauge the size of your paper, for the convenience of the referees, and to make it easy for you to distribute preprints.) Therefore, **submit, on separate sheets of paper, enlarged versions of the tables and figures that appear in your document.** These are the images IEEE will scan and publish with your paper.

D. Electronic Image Files (Optional)

You will have the greatest control over the appearance of your figures if you are able to prepare electronic image files. If you do not have the required computer skills, just submit paper prints as described above and skip this section.

1)The Easiest Way: If you have a scanner, the best and quickest way to prepare non-color figure files is to print your tables and figures on paper exactly as you want them to appear, scan them, and then save them to a file in PostScript (PS) or Encapsulated PostScript (EPS) formats. Use a separate file for each image. File names should be of the form "fig1.ps" or "fig2.eps."

2) The Slightly Harder Way: Using a scanner as above, save the images in TIFF format. High-contrast line figures and tables should be prepared with 600 dpi resolution and saved with no compression, 1 bit per pixel (monochrome), with file names as of the form "fig3.tif" or "table1.tif." To obtain a 3.45-in figure (one-column width) at 600 dpi, the figure requires a horizontal size of 2070 pixels. Typical file sizes will be on the order of 0.5 MB.

Photographs and grayscale figures should be prepared with 220 dpi resolution and saved with no compression, 8 bits per pixel (grayscale). To obtain a 3.45-in figure (one-column width) at 220 dpi, the figure should have a horizontal size of 759 pixels.

Color figures should be prepared with 400 dpi resolution and saved with no compression, 8 bits per pixel (palette or 256 color). To obtain a 3.45-in figure (one column width) at 400 dpi, the figure should have a horizontal size of 1380 pixels.

For more information on TIFF files, please go to http://www.ieee.org/organizations/pubs/transactions/informatio n.htm and click on the link "Guidelines for Author Supplied Electronic Text and Graphics."

3) The Somewhat Harder Way: If you do not have a scanner, you may create noncolor PostScript figures by "printing" them to files. First, download a PostScript printer driver from http://www.adobe.com/support/downloads/pdrvwin. htm (for Windows) or from http://www.adobe.com/support/ downloads/pdrvmac.htm (for Macintosh) and install the "Generic PostScript Printer" definition. In *Word,* paste your figure into a new document. Print to a file using the PostScript printer driver. File names should be of the form "fig5.ps." Use Adobe Type 1 fonts when creating your figures, if possible.

4) Other Ways: Experienced computer users can convert figures and tables from their original format to TIFF. Some useful image converters are Adobe *Photoshop,* Corel *Draw,* and Microsoft *Photo Editor,* an application that is part of Microsoft *Office* (look for C:\Program Files\Common Files \Microsoft Shared\ PhotoEd\ PHOTOED.EXE. (You may have to custom-install *Photo Editor* from your original *Office* disk.)

Here is a way to make TIFF image files of tables. First, create your table in *Word.* Use horizontal lines but no vertical lines. Hide gridlines (Table | Hide Gridlines). Spell check the table to remove any red underlines that indicate spelling errors. Adjust magnification (View | Zoom) such that you can view the entire table *at maximum area* when you select View | Full Screen. Move the cursor so that it is out of the way. Press "Print Screen" on your keyboard; this copies the screen image to the Windows clipboard. Open Microsoft *Photo Editor* and click Edit | Paste as New Image. Crop the table image (click Select button; select the part you want, then Image | Crop). Adjust the properties of the image (File | Properties) to monochrome (1 bit) and 600 pixels per inch. Resize the image (Image | Resize) to a width of 3.45 inches. Save the file (File | Save As) in TIFF with no compression (click "More" button).

Most graphing programs allow you to save graphs in TIFF; however, you often have no control over compression or number of bits per pixel. You should open these image files in a program such as Microsoft *Photo Editor* and re-save them using no compression, either 1 or 8 bits, and either 600 or 220 dpi resolution (File | Properties; Image | Resize). See Section II-D2 for an explanation of number of bits and resolution. If your graphing program cannot export to TIFF, you can use the same technique described for tables in the previous paragraph.

A way to convert a figure from Windows Metafile (WMF) to TIFF is to paste it into Microsoft *PowerPoint,* save it in JPG format, open it with Microsoft *Photo Editor* or similar converter, and re-save it as TIFF.

Microsoft *Excel* allows you to save spreadsheet charts in Graphics Interchange Format (GIF). To get good resolution, make the *Excel* charts *very* large. Then use "Save as

> REPLACE THIS LINE WITH YOUR PAPER IDENTIFICATION NUMBER (DOUBLE-CLICK HERE TO EDIT) <

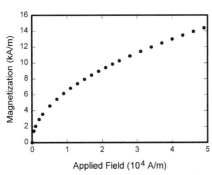

Fig. 1. Magnetization as a function of applied field. Note that "Fig." is abbreviated. There is a period after the figure number, followed by two spaces. It is good practice to explain the significance of the figure in the caption.

HTML" feature (see http://support.microsoft.com/support/kb/articles/q158/0/79.asp). You can then convert from GIF to TIFF using Microsoft *Photo Editor,* for example.

No matter how you convert your images, it is a good idea to print the TIFF files to make sure nothing was lost in the conversion.

If you modify this document for use with other IEEE journals or conferences, you should save it as type "Word 97-2000 & 6.0/95 - RTF (*.doc)" so that it can be opened by any version of *Word.*

E. Copyright Form

An IEEE copyright form should accompany your final submission. You can get a .pdf, .html, or .doc version at http://www.ieee.org/copyright or from the first issues in each volume of the IEEE TRANSACTIONS and JOURNALS. Authors are responsible for obtaining any security clearances.

III. MATH

If you are using *Word,* use either the Microsoft Equation Editor or the *MathType* add-on (http://www.mathtype.com) for equations in your paper (Insert | Object | Create New | Microsoft Equation *or* MathType Equation). "Float over text" should *not* be selected.

IV. UNITS

Use either SI (MKS) or CGS as primary units. (SI units are strongly encouraged.) English units may be used as secondary units (in parentheses). **This applies to papers in data storage.** For example, write "15 Gb/cm^2 (100 Gb/in^2)." An exception is when English units are used as identifiers in trade, such as "3½ in disk drive." Avoid combining SI and CGS units, such as current in amperes and magnetic field in oersteds. This often leads to confusion because equations do not balance

TABLE I
UNITS FOR MAGNETIC PROPERTIES

Symbol	Quantity	Conversion from Gaussian and CGS EMU to SI [a]
Φ	magnetic flux	1 Mx $\rightarrow 10^{-8}$ Wb = 10^{-8} V·s
B	magnetic flux density, magnetic induction	1 G $\rightarrow 10^{-4}$ T = 10^{-4} Wb/m^2
H	magnetic field strength	1 Oe $\rightarrow 10^{3}/(4\pi)$ A/m
m	magnetic moment	1 erg/G = 1 emu $\rightarrow 10^{-3}$ A·m^2 = 10^{-3} J/T
M	magnetization	1 erg/(G·cm^3) = 1 emu/cm^3 $\rightarrow 10^{3}$ A/m
$4\pi M$	magnetization	1 G $\rightarrow 10^{3}/(4\pi)$ A/m
σ	specific magnetization	1 erg/(G·g) = 1 emu/g $\rightarrow$ 1 A·m^2/kg
j	magnetic dipole moment	1 erg/G = 1 emu $\rightarrow 4\pi \times 10^{-10}$ Wb·m
J	magnetic polarization	1 erg/(G·cm^3) = 1 emu/cm^3 $\rightarrow 4\pi \times 10^{-4}$ T
χ, κ	susceptibility	$1 \rightarrow 4\pi$
χ_ρ	mass susceptibility	1 cm^3/g $\rightarrow 4\pi \times 10^{-3}$ m^3/kg
μ	permeability	$1 \rightarrow 4\pi \times 10^{-7}$ H/m = $4\pi \times 10^{-7}$ Wb/(A·m)
μ_r	relative permeability	$\mu \rightarrow \mu_r$
w, W	energy density	1 erg/cm^3 $\rightarrow 10^{-1}$ J/m^3
N, D	demagnetizing factor	$1 \rightarrow 1/(4\pi)$

No vertical lines in table. Statements that serve as captions for the entire table do not need footnote letters.

[a]Gaussian units are the same as cgs emu for magnetostatics; Mx = maxwell, G = gauss, Oe = oersted; Wb = weber, V = volt, s = second, T = tesla, m = meter, A = ampere, J = joule, kg = kilogram, H = henry.

dimensionally. If you must use mixed units, clearly state the units for each quantity in an equation.

The SI unit for magnetic field strength H is A/m. However, if you wish to use units of T, either refer to magnetic flux density B or magnetic field strength symbolized as $\mu_0 H$. Use the center dot to separate compound units, e.g., "A·m^2."

V. HELPFUL HINTS

A. Figures and Tables

Because IEEE will do the final formatting of your paper, you do not need to position figures and tables at the top and bottom of each column. In fact, all figures, figure captions, and tables can be at the end of the paper. Large figures and tables may span both columns. Place figure captions below the figures; place table titles above the tables. If your figure has two parts, include the labels "(a)" and "(b)" as part of the artwork. Please verify that the figures and tables you mention in the text actually exist. **Please do not include captions as part of the figures. Do not put captions in "text boxes" linked to the figures. Do not put borders around the outside of your figures.** Use the abbreviation "Fig." even at the beginning of a sentence. Do not abbreviate "Table." Tables are numbered with Roman numerals.

Color printing of figures is available, but is billed to the authors (approximately $1300, depending on the number of figures and number of pages containing color). Include a note with your final paper indicating that you request color printing. **Do not use color unless it is necessary for the proper**

interpretation of your figures. If you want reprints of your color article, the reprint order should be submitted promptly. There is an additional charge of $81 per 100 for color reprints.

Figure axis labels are often a source of confusion. Use words rather than symbols. As an example, write the quantity "Magnetization," or "Magnetization M," not just "M." Put units in parentheses. Do not label axes only with units. As in Fig. 1, for example, write "Magnetization (A/m)" or "Magnetization (A·m^{-1})," not just "A/m." Do not label axes with a ratio of quantities and units. For example, write "Temperature (K)," not "Temperature/K."

Multipliers can be especially confusing. Write "Magnetization (kA/m)" or "Magnetization (10^3 A/m)." Do not write "Magnetization (A/m) × 1000" because the reader would not know whether the top axis label in Fig. 1 meant 16000 A/m or 0.016 A/m. Figure labels should be legible, approximately 8 to 12 point type.

B. References

Number citations consecutively in square brackets [1]. The sentence punctuation follows the brackets [2]. Multiple references [2], [3] are each numbered with separate brackets [1]–[3]. When citing a section in a book, please give the relevant page numbers [2]. In sentences, refer simply to the reference number, as in [3]. Do not use "Ref. [3]" or "reference [3]" except at the beginning of a sentence: "Reference [3] shows ... ." Unfortunately the IEEE document translator cannot handle automatic endnotes in *Word*; therefore, type the reference list at the end of the paper using the "References" style.

Number footnotes separately in superscripts (Insert | Footnote).[1] Place the actual footnote at the bottom of the column in which it is cited; do not put footnotes in the reference list (endnotes). Use letters for table footnotes (see Table I).

Please note that the references at the end of this document are in the preferred referencing style. Give all authors' names; do not use "*et al.*" unless there are six authors or more. Use a space after authors' initials. Papers that have not been published should be cited as "unpublished" [4]. Papers that have been submitted for publication should be cited as "submitted for publication" [5]. Papers that have been accepted for publication, but not yet specified for an issue should be cited as "to be published" [6]. Please give affiliations and addresses for private communications [7].

Capitalize only the first word in a paper title, except for proper nouns and element symbols. For papers published in translation journals, please give the English citation first, followed by the original foreign-language citation [8].

C. Abbreviations and Acronyms

Define abbreviations and acronyms the first time they are used in the text, even after they have already been defined in the abstract. Abbreviations such as IEEE, SI, ac, and dc do not have to be defined. Abbreviations that incorporate periods should not have spaces: write "C.N.R.S.," not "C. N. R. S." Do not use abbreviations in the title unless they are unavoidable (for example, "IEEE" in the title of this article).

D. Equations

Number equations consecutively with equation numbers in parentheses flush with the right margin, as in (1). First use the equation editor to create the equation. Then select the "Equation" markup style. Press the tab key and write the equation number in parentheses. To make your equations more compact, you may use the solidus (/), the exp function, and appropriate exponents. Use parentheses to avoid ambiguities in denominators. Punctuate equations when they are part of a sentence, as in

$$\int_0^{r_2} F(r,\varphi)\, dr\, d\varphi = [\sigma\, r_2 / (2\mu_0)]$$
$$\cdot \int_0^\infty \exp(-\lambda\,|\,z_j - z_i\,|)\,\lambda^{-1} J_1(\lambda\, r_2)\, J_0(\lambda\, r_i)\, d\lambda\,. \tag{1}$$

Be sure that the symbols in your equation have been defined before the equation appears or immediately following. Italicize symbols (T might refer to temperature, but T is the unit tesla). Refer to "(1)," not "Eq. (1)" or "equation (1)," except at the beginning of a sentence: "Equation (1) is ... ."

E. Other Recommendations

Use one space after periods and colons. Hyphenate complex modifiers: "zero-field-cooled magnetization." Avoid dangling participles, such as, "Using (1), the potential was calculated." [It is not clear who or what used (1).] Write instead, "The potential was calculated by using (1)," or "Using (1), we calculated the potential."

Use a zero before decimal points: "0.25," not ".25." Use "cm^3," not "cc." Indicate sample dimensions as "0.1 cm × 0.2 cm," not "0.1 × 0.2 cm^2." The abbreviation for "seconds" is "s," not "sec." Do not mix complete spellings and abbreviations of units: use "Wb/m^2" or "webers per square meter," not "webers/m^2." When expressing a range of values, write "7 to 9" or "7-9," not "7~9."

A parenthetical statement at the end of a sentence is punctuated outside of the closing parenthesis (like this). (A parenthetical sentence is punctuated within the parentheses.) In American English, periods and commas are within quotation marks, like "this period." Other punctuation is "outside"! Avoid contractions; for example, write "do not" instead of "don't." The serial comma is preferred: "A, B, and C" instead of "A, B and C."

If you wish, you may write in the first person singular or plural and use the active voice ("I observed that ..." or "We observed that ..." instead of "It was observed that ..."). Remember to check spelling. If your native language is not English, please get a native English-speaking colleague to proofread your paper.

---

[1] It is recommended that footnotes be avoided (except for the unnumbered footnote with the receipt date on the first page). Instead, try to integrate the footnote information into the text.

VI. SOME COMMON MISTAKES

The word "data" is plural, not singular. The subscript for the permeability of vacuum μ_0 is zero, not a lowercase letter "o." The term for residual magnetization is "remanence"; the adjective is "remanent"; do not write "remnance" or "remnant." Use the word "micrometer" instead of "micron." A graph within a graph is an "inset," not an "insert." The word "alternatively" is preferred to the word "alternately" (unless you really mean something that alternates). Use the word "whereas" instead of "while" (unless you are referring to simultaneous events). Do not use the word "essentially" to mean "approximately" or "effectively." Do not use the word "issue" as a euphemism for "problem." When compositions are not specified, separate chemical symbols by en-dashes; for example, "NiMn" indicates the intermetallic compound $Ni_{0.5}Mn_{0.5}$ whereas "Ni–Mn" indicates an alloy of some composition Ni_xMn_{1-x}.

Be aware of the different meanings of the homophones "affect" (usually a verb) and "effect" (usually a noun), "complement" and "compliment," "discreet" and "discrete," "principal" (e.g., "principal investigator") and "principle" (e.g., "principle of measurement"). Do not confuse "imply" and "infer."

Prefixes such as "non," "sub," "micro," "multi," and ""ultra" are not independent words; they should be joined to the words they modify, usually without a hyphen. There is no period after the "et" in the Latin abbreviation "*et al.*" (it is also italicized). The abbreviation "i.e.," means "that is," and the abbreviation "e.g.," means "for example" (these abbreviations are not italicized).

An excellent style manual and source of information for science writers is [9]. A general IEEE style guide, *Information for Authors,* is available at http://www.ieee.org/organizations/pubs/transactions/informatio n.htm

VII. EDITORIAL POLICY

Submission of a manuscript is not required for participation in a conference. Do not submit a reworked version of a paper you have submitted or published elsewhere. Do not publish "preliminary" data or results. The submitting author is responsible for obtaining agreement of all coauthors and any consent required from sponsors before submitting a paper. IEEE TRANSACTIONS and JOURNALS strongly discourage courtesy authorship. It is the obligation of the authors to cite relevant prior work.

The Transactions and Journals Department does not publish conference records or proceedings. The TRANSACTIONS does publish papers related to conferences that have been recommended for publication on the basis of peer review. As a matter of convenience and service to the technical community, these topical papers are collected and published in one issue of the TRANSACTIONS.

At least two reviews are required for every paper submitted. For conference-related papers, the decision to accept or reject a paper is made by the conference editors and publications committee; the recommendations of the referees are advisory only. Undecipherable English is a valid reason for rejection. Authors of rejected papers may revise and resubmit them to the TRANSACTIONS as regular papers, whereupon they will be reviewed by two new referees.

VIII. PUBLICATION PRINCIPLES

The contents of IEEE TRANSACTIONS and JOURNALS are peer-reviewed and archival. The TRANSACTIONS publishes scholarly articles of archival value as well as tutorial expositions and critical reviews of classical subjects and topics of current interest.

Authors should consider the following points:

1) Technical papers submitted for publication must advance the state of knowledge and must cite relevant prior work.
2) The length of a submitted paper should be commensurate with the importance, or appropriate to the complexity, of the work. For example, an obvious extension of previously published work might not be appropriate for publication or might be adequately treated in just a few pages.
3) Authors must convince both peer reviewers and the editors of the scientific and technical merit of a paper; the standards of proof are higher when extraordinary or unexpected results are reported.
4) Because replication is required for scientific progress, papers submitted for publication must provide sufficient information to allow readers to perform similar experiments or calculations and use the reported results. Although not everything need be disclosed, a paper must contain new, useable, and fully described information. For example, a specimen's chemical composition need not be reported if the main purpose of a paper is to introduce a new measurement technique. Authors should expect to be challenged by reviewers if the results are not supported by adequate data and critical details.
5) Papers that describe ongoing work or announce the latest technical achievement, which are suitable for presentation at a professional conference, may not be appropriate for publication in a TRANSACTIONS or JOURNAL.

IX. CONCLUSION

A conclusion section is not required. Although a conclusion may review the main points of the paper, do not replicate the abstract as the conclusion. A conclusion might elaborate on the importance of the work or suggest applications and extensions.

APPENDIX

Appendixes, if needed, appear before the acknowledgment.

ACKNOWLEDGMENT

The preferred spelling of the word "acknowledgment" in American English is without an "e" after the "g." Use the singular heading even if you have many acknowledgments. Avoid expressions such as "One of us (S.B.A.) would like to thank ... ." Instead, write "F. A. Author thanks ... ." **Sponsor and financial support acknowledgments are placed in the unnumbered footnote on the first page.**

REFERENCES

[1] G. O. Young, "Synthetic structure of industrial plastics (Book style with paper title and editor)," in *Plastics*, 2nd ed. vol. 3, J. Peters, Ed. New York: McGraw-Hill, 1964, pp. 15–64.

[2] W.-K. Chen, *Linear Networks and Systems* (Book style). Belmont, CA: Wadsworth, 1993, pp. 123–135.

[3] H. Poor, *An Introduction to Signal Detection and Estimation*. New York: Springer-Verlag, 1985, ch. 4.

[4] B. Smith, "An approach to graphs of linear forms (Unpublished work style)," unpublished.

[5] E. H. Miller, "A note on reflector arrays (Periodical style—Accepted for publication)," *IEEE Trans. Antennas Propagat.*, to be published.

[6] J. Wang, "Fundamentals of erbium-doped fiber amplifiers arrays (Periodical style—Submitted for publication)," *IEEE J. Quantum Electron.*, submitted for publication.

[7] C. J. Kaufman, Rocky Mountain Research Lab., Boulder, CO, private communication, May 1995.

[8] Y. Yorozu, M. Hirano, K. Oka, and Y. Tagawa, "Electron spectroscopy studies on magneto-optical media and plastic substrate interfaces(Translation Journals style)," *IEEE Transl. J. Magn.Jpn.*, vol. 2, Aug. 1987, pp. 740–741 [*Dig. 9th Annu. Conf. Magnetics* Japan, 1982, p. 301].

[9] M. Young, *The Techincal Writers Handbook*. Mill Valley, CA: University Science, 1989.

[10] J. U. Duncombe, "Infrared navigation—Part I: An assessment of feasibility (Periodical style)," *IEEE Trans. Electron Devices*, vol. ED-11, pp. 34–39, Jan. 1959.

[11] S. Chen, B. Mulgrew, and P. M. Grant, "A clustering technique for digital communications channel equalization using radial basis function networks," *IEEE Trans. Neural Networks*, vol. 4, pp. 570–578, July 1993.

[12] R. W. Lucky, "Automatic equalization for digital communication," *Bell Syst. Tech. J.*, vol. 44, no. 4, pp. 547–588, Apr. 1965.

[13] S. P. Bingulac, "On the compatibility of adaptive controllers (Published Conference Proceedings style)," in *Proc. 4th Annu. Allerton Conf. Circuits and Systems Theory*, New York, 1994, pp. 8–16.

[14] G. R. Faulhaber, "Design of service systems with priority reservation," in *Conf. Rec. 1995 IEEE Int. Conf. Communications*, pp. 3–8.

[15] W. D. Doyle, "Magnetization reversal in films with biaxial anisotropy," in *1987 Proc. INTERMAG Conf.*, pp. 2.2-1–2.2-6.

[16] G. W. Juette and L. E. Zeffanella, "Radio noise currents n short sections on bundle conductors (Presented Conference Paper style)," presented at the IEEE Summer power Meeting, Dallas, TX, June 22–27, 1990, Paper 90 SM 690-0 PWRS.

[17] J. G. Kreifeldt, "An analysis of surface-detected EMG as an amplitude-modulated noise," presented at the 1989 Int. Conf. Medicine and Biological Engineering, Chicago, IL.

[18] J. Williams, "Narrow-band analyzer (Thesis or Dissertation style)," Ph.D. dissertation, Dept. Elect. Eng., Harvard Univ., Cambridge, MA, 1993.

[19] N. Kawasaki, "Parametric study of thermal and chemical nonequilibrium nozzle flow," M.S. thesis, Dept. Electron. Eng., Osaka Univ., Osaka, Japan, 1993.

[20] J. P. Wilkinson, "Nonlinear resonant circuit devices (Patent style)," U.S. Patent 3 624 12, July 16, 1990.

[21] *IEEE Criteria for Class IE Electric Systems* (Standards style), IEEE Standard 308, 1969.

[22] *Letter Symbols for Quantities*, ANSI Standard Y10.5-1968.

[23] R. E. Haskell and C. T. Case, "Transient signal propagation in lossless isotropic plasmas (Report style)," USAF Cambridge Res. Lab., Cambridge, MA Rep. ARCRL-66-234 (II), 1994, vol. 2.

[24] E. E. Reber, R. L. Michell, and C. J. Carter, "Oxygen absorption in the Earth's atmosphere," Aerospace Corp., Los Angeles, CA, Tech. Rep. TR-0200 (420-46)-3, Nov. 1988.

[25] (Handbook style) *Transmission Systems for Communications*, 3rd ed., Western Electric Co., Winston-Salem, NC, 1985, pp. 44–60.

[26] *Motorola Semiconductor Data Manual*, Motorola Semiconductor Products Inc., Phoenix, AZ, 1989.

[27] (Basic Book/Monograph Online Sources) J. K. Author. (year, month, day). *Title* (edition) [Type of medium]. Volume(issue). Available: http://www.(URL)

[28] J. Jones. (1991, May 10). Networks (2nd ed.) [Online]. Available: http://www.atm.com

[29] (Journal Online Sources style) K. Author. (year, month). Title. *Journal* [Type of medium]. Volume(issue), paging if given. Available: http://www.(URL)

[30] R. J. Vidmar. (1992, August). On the use of atmospheric plasmas as electromagnetic reflectors. *IEEE Trans. Plasma Sci.* [Online]. *21(3)*. pp. 876—880. Available: http://www.halcyon.com/pub/journals/21ps03-vidmar

First A. Author (M'76–SM'81–F'87) and the other authors may include biographies at the end of regular papers. Biographies are often not included in conference-related papers. This author became a Member (M) of IEEE in 1976, a Senior Member (SM) in 1981, and a Fellow (F) in 1987. The first paragraph may contain a place and/or date of birth (list place, then date). Next, the author's educational background is listed. The degrees should be listed with type of degree in what field, which institution, city, state or country, and year degree was earned. The author's major field of study should be lower-cased.

The second paragraph uses the pronoun of the person (he or she) and not the author's last name. It lists military and work experience, including summer and fellowship jobs. Job titles are capitalized. The current job must have a location; previous positions may be listed without one. Information concerning previous publications may be included. Try not to list more than three books or published articles. The format for listing publishers of a book within the biography is: title of book (city, state: publisher name, year) similar to a reference. Current and previous research interests ends the paragraph.

The third paragraph begins with the author's title and last name (e.g., Dr. Smith, Prof. Jones, Mr. Kajor, Ms. Hunter). List any memberships in professional societies other than the IEEE. Finally, list any awards and work for IEEE committees and publications. If a photograph is provided, the biography will be indented around it. The photograph is placed at the top left of the biography. Personal hobbies will be deleted from the biography.

Appendix C

FILE TEMPLATE FOR A THESIS, BOOK, OR LONG REPORT

Filename: ThesisTemplate.doc

Description: This template designed for long manuscripts, such as theses, dissertations, books, and reports. It is written in single-column format, with multi-level numbering (e.g., "Figure 3.2" as opposed to "Figure 7"). The template also contains extensive elements of front matter and back matter, rarely present in shorter documents, including dedications, acknowledgments, foreword, glossary, and index. Page numbering in the template follows the standard thesis page numbering, where front matter is numbered with roman numeral, and the rest of the manuscript with Arabic numerals.

Technical Writing for Teams: The STREAM Tools Handbook, by Alexander Mamishev and Sean Williams
Copyright © 2010 Institute of Electrical and Electronics Engineers

[Ph.D. Dissertation Title]

[Author Name]

A dissertation submitted in partial fulfillment of the requirements for the degree of
Doctor of Philosophy

University of Washington
2009

Program Authorized to Offer Degree: Department of Electrical Engineering

University of Washington
Graduate School

This is to certify that I have examined this copy of a doctoral dissertation by

[Author Name]

and have found it complete and satisfactory in all respects,
and that any and all revisions required by the final
examining committee have been made.

Chair of Supervisory Committee:

_____
[Committee Chair]

Reading Committee:

_____
[Committee Chair]

_____
[Committee member 2]

_____
[Committee member 3]

_____
[Committee member 4]

Date: _____

In presenting this dissertation in partial fulfillment of the requirements for a doctoral degree at the University of Washington, I agree that the Library shall make its copies freely available for inspection. I further agree that extensive copying of this dissertation is allowable only for scholarly purposes, consistent with "fair use" as prescribed in the U.S. Copyright Law. Any other reproduction for any purposes or by any means shall not be allowed without my written permission.

Signature_____

Date_____

University of Washington

Abstract

[Dissertation Title]

by [Author Name]

Chair of the Supervisory Committee

Associate Professor Alexander Mamishev
Department of Electrical Engineering

This is the abstract of the dissertation. The abstract of a Ph.D. dissertation cannot be longer than *350* words. The abstract section does not go into the table of contents.

TABLE OF CONTENTS

LIST OF FIGURES

LIST OF TABLES

ACKNOWLEDGMENTS

The acknowledgment section goes here. The acknowledgment section is not listed in the table of contents.

DEDICATION

[this page is optional and is not listed in the table of contents]

Chapter 1. Introduction

This is a template document for dissertations, master's theses, or other long manuscripts, including books. This document is specific to one institution, but the vast majority of universities use very similar formats.

1.1 Cover Page

The formatting of the cover page and first few pages needs to be followed exactly. There is no space to use creativity in this case. The degree name is strictly "Doctor of Philosophy," instead of "Doctor of Philosophy in Electrical Engineering." In the committee page, make sure you have the exact template as in this dissertation. The chair person should be listed twice, in a separate section and in the committee list. The acknowledgements, abstract, and vita sections should not show up in table of contents.

1.2 Table of Contents

The Table of Contents should be self-generated. The format of it can be changed through Insert-Index and Tables. The same is true for the List of Figures. The List of Tables can be generated in the same command window as the List of Figures.

In the Table of Contents, the list and pages of "List of Figures," "List of Tables," and "Reference" won't automatically generate. You can bookmark these titles at corresponding pages, and reference their page numbers in Table of Contents. In this way, you could auto generate the list in Table of Contents.

Do not forget to keep capitalization consistent in the Table of Contents. There should be at least two entries under each subheading (if you have 2.1, you must have 2.2). If you don't, reconsider your headings and organization scheme.

1.3 Chapter Title and Heading Title Style

Most universities have strict rules on the style of chapter titles and heading titles. The safest way is to follow this template and to consult with the appropriate parties who certify formatting of a thesis or dissertation.

1.4 Tables and Figures

Figure titles always go below the figure, while table titles always go above the table. This is a convention to be followed. In order to update numbering of all automated entries, click **Ctrl-A, F9**.

All figures should be numbered. To create a new figure, copy the existing figure (with the attached caption) and paste it to a new location. The figure template is designed in such a way that the caption stays with the image. Remember that letter and line thickness of each figure should be sufficiently large in order to be clearly legible in a double-column format.

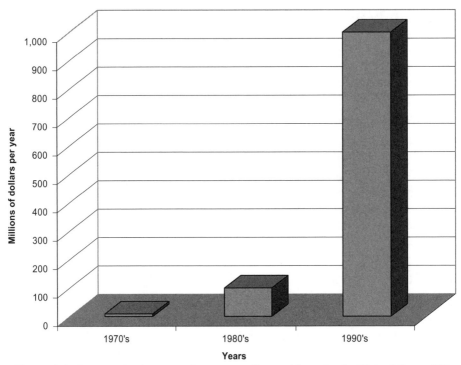

Figure 1.1. Increase in the cost of power quality problems in the United States [1].

Figure 1.1 is an example figure. In order to cross-reference a figure click **Insert-Cross Reference-Figure-Only label and number**, then select the appropriate figure. This procedure is the same for tables. Also, the caption of the figure is recommended to have indentation on both sides so to distinguish from normal text.

1.5   Equations

The equations should be created using the template below and MathType software. MathType is superior to Word's built-in equation editor because it allows exporting to LaTeX and is faster.

To cross-reference an equation, you must first create a bookmark by highlighting the equation number, clicking **Insert-Bookmark**, and giving that a unique identifier. All equation identifiers start with "eq". For example, eqColoumbForce. Pay attention to the font of your variables. It is not ok to have "V" in the equation and "V" in text. Auto-numbering of figures and tables that correspond to chapters (e.g., Fig 3.3) is discussed in the next section.

1.6   Chapter Heading

First, you can define the style of headings of a chapter. Right-click on the line of the chapter's title and choose "Bullets and Numbering," push "Outline Numbered" tab, to choose different sample styles. You can also "Customize" the style, like changing the "Number Format." For example, you can add "Chapter" in front of the chapter number to make this the format of Heading 1.

Next time, when writing a new chapter, just type in the chapter title, then choose "Heading 1." Your defined style will automatically appear.

Another method of adding "Chapter" in front of each chapter number is to create a "Chapter" character in other software, then copy it as a picture in front of the number.

If you make changes to the title format of one chapter, you can update all other chapters' title format at the same time, instead of redoing them one by one. Just re-click "Heading 1," a window of "Modify Style" pops up. Check "update the style to reflect recent changes."

1.6.1   Include Chapter Number in Figure Caption

To include the chapter number in a figure's caption, click "**Insert-Caption**" and choose label "**Figure**." Then click "**Numbering**," check "include chapter number" and also choose a desired format. Thus, the chapter number will be included.

1.6.2   Include Chapter Number in Equation Numbering

Normally only one number is assigned to one equation, as mentioned above. To include the chapter number, in front of the **original** equation number click "**Insert-Cross reference-Heading-Heading number,**" and then check the corresponding chapter. The chapter number will be present. Don't forget to add a "." between the chapter number and original equation number.

This is a sample equation [2]:

$$a = b- = c \qquad\qquad (1.1)$$

Equation counting does not restart from 1 in a new chapter. To solve this problem, in a new chapter (For example in Chapter 2, please refer to beginning of next chapter), right-click before the **original** equation number, check "Toggle Field Codes," the code will show up like "SEQ eq * MERGEFORMAT," add "2" after "eq" meaning the second (new) series of equation to "SEQ eq2 * MERGEFORMAT," then right-click "Toggle Field Codes" again, the second equation number in this new chapter will start from 1. For equations in the next chapter, just add "3" after "eq."

Also, it is very important to define every variable of the equation in the text nearby. If you use a lot of equations, it pays to learn shortcuts in MathType.

1.7   Section and Page Breaks

When writing a thesis, you are often required to use different styles of numbering for different sections. For example, Roman numerals are often used for preliminary pages, and Arabic numerals are used for text. You can achieve these differences by inserting section breaks: Insert-Break-Next Page (section break types). After that, you can adjust the numbering style freely in each section. If you just want to start writing a new chapter from the next page in the same section (you want to continue the sequential number-ing), you can just insert a Page Break.

1.8   Subsections

Please use the following style for the subsection heading titles.

1.8.1   Subsection Level 3

This section is just to show you how to make subsections.

1.8.1.1   Subsection Level 4

This section is just to show you how to make subsections.

1.9   Orphan Control

Orphan control is very important in order to pass the review of graduate school. Make sure that no page ends with a heading title (any level), and make sure the figure title and figure are on the same page. The same concept applies for tables and table titles.

Chapter 2. Complete Your Dissertation

Some professors use *Ph.D. dissertation* and *Ph.D. thesis* interchangeably, while some other professors do not feel comfortable with the wording *Ph.D. thesis*. So make sure you make all of them happy about this throughout your dissertation.

This is a sample equation [2]:

$$P(t, f) = \int_{-\infty}^{\infty} \int_{-\infty}^{\infty} A(\eta, \tau) \varphi(\eta, \tau) e^{j2\pi\eta t} e^{j-2\pi ft} d\eta d\tau \tag{2.1}$$

where t represents time, f represents frequency, η represents continuous frequency shift, and τ represents continuous time lag. The ambiguity plane $A(\eta, \tau)$ for a given signal $s(t)$ is defined as:

$$A(\eta, \tau) = \int_{-\infty}^{\infty} s(t) s*(t + \tau)^{j2\pi\eta t} dt \tag{2.2}$$

Here $s(t)$ represents the signal at time t, and $s(t+\tau)$ represents the signal at a future time $t+\tau$, and the $s*(t+\tau)$ means the complex conjugate of $s(t+\tau)$.

Table 2.1 is a sample table.

Table 2.1. A Sample Table Caption

Row 1	Value	Location
Row 2	1.89	Y
Row 3	1.94	N
Row 4	2.33	N
Row 5	1.45	N
Row 6	2.11	N

2.1   References

For literature citations, use EndNote software. The citations and references list should conform to the standards of your discipline.

It is very important to keep the consistency of the reference database file in the writing process, especially when you work on multiple computers.

2.2   Conclusions

This template document will be updated as more and more students start to work on Ph.D. dissertations. Please do note that the requirements for master's theses and Ph.D. dissertations are slightly different. Although this template may also be helpful for writing a master's thesis, it is important to identify the requirement differences and make appropriate changes.

End Notes

The current solution is to copy the whole reference section over.

References

[1] B. Kennedy, *Power Quality Primer*, McGraw-Hill, 2000.

[2] L. Cohen, *Time-Frequency Analysis*, Prentice-Hall, 1995.

Vita

A short bio of the author is required for a Ph.D. dissertation at the University of Washington. The vita section does not go into the table of contents. The formatting style follows the text of the dissertation.

Appendix D

IEEE TEMPLATE WITH *STREAM TOOLS* ENABLED

> REPLACE THIS LINE WITH YOUR PAPER IDENTIFICATION NUMBER (DOUBLE-CLICK HERE TO EDIT) <

Preparation of Papers for IEEE TRANSACTIONS and JOURNALS (October 2006)

First A. Author, Second B. Author, Jr., and Third C. Author, *Member, IEEE*

Abstract—**These instructions give you guidelines for preparing papers for IEEE TRANSACTIONS and JOURNALS. Use this document as a template if you are using Microsoft *Word* 6.0 or later. Otherwise, use this document as an instruction set. The electronic file of your paper will be formatted further at IEEE. Define all symbols used in the abstract. Do not cite references in the abstract. Do not delete the blank line immediately above the abstract; it sets the footnote at the bottom of this column.**

Index Terms—**About four key words or phrases in alphabetical order, separated by commas. For a list of suggested keywords, send a blank e-mail to keywords@ieee.org or visit the IEEE web site at** http://www.ieee.org/organizations/pubs/ani_prod/keywrd98.txt

I. INTRODUCTION

THIS document is a template for Microsoft *Word* versions 6.0 or later. If you are reading a paper version of this document, please download the electronic file, TRANS-JOUR.DOC, from http://www.ieee.org/organizations/pubs/transactions/stylesheets.htm so you can use it to prepare your manuscript. If you would prefer to use LATEX, download IEEE's LATEX style and sample files from the same Web page. Use these LATEX files for formatting, but please follow the instructions in TRANS-JOUR.DOC or TRANS-JOUR.DOC or TRANS-JOUR.PDF.

If your paper is intended for a *conference,* please contact your conference editor concerning acceptable word processor formats for your particular conference.

When you open TRANS-JOUR.DOC, select "Page Layout"

Manuscript received October 9, 2001. (Write the date on which you submitted your paper for review.) This work was supported in part by the U.S. Department of Commerce under Grant BS123456 (sponsor and financial support acknowledgment goes here). Paper titles should be written in uppercase and lowercase letters, not all uppercase. Avoid writing long formulas with subscripts in the title; short formulas that identify the elements are fine (e.g., "Nd–Fe–B"). Do not write "(Invited)" in the title. Full names of authors are preferred in the author field, but are not required. Put a space between authors' initials.

F. A. Author is with the National Institute of Standards and Technology, Boulder, CO 80305 USA (corresponding author to provide phone: 303-555-5555; fax: 303-555-5555; e-mail: author@boulder.nist.gov).

S. B. Author, Jr., was with Rice University, Houston, TX 77005 USA. He is now with the Department of Physics, Colorado State University, Fort Collins, CO 80523 USA (e-mail: author@lamar.colostate.edu).

T. C. Author is with the Electrical Engineering Department, University of Colorado, Boulder, CO 80309 USA, on leave from the National Research Institute for Metals, Tsukuba, Japan (e-mail: author@nrim.go.jp).

from the "View" menu in the menu bar (View | Page Layout), which allows you to see the footnotes. Then type over sections of TRANS-JOUR.DOC or cut and paste from another document and then use markup styles. The pull-down style menu is at the left of the Formatting Toolbar at the top of your *Word* window (for example, the style at this point in the document is "Text"). Highlight a section that you want to designate with a certain style, then select the appropriate name on the style menu. The style will adjust your fonts and line spacing. **Do not change the font sizes or line spacing to squeeze more text into a limited number of pages.** Use italics for emphasis; do not underline.

To insert images in *Word,* position the cursor at the insertion point and either use Insert | Picture | From File or copy the image to the Windows clipboard and then Edit | Paste Special | Picture (with "Float over text" unchecked).

IEEE will do the final formatting of your paper. If your paper is intended for a conference, please observe the conference page limits.

II. PROCEDURE FOR PAPER SUBMISSION

A. Review Stage

Please check with your editor on whether to submit your manuscript by hard copy or electronically for review. If hard copy, submit photocopies such that only one column appears per page. This will give your referees plenty of room to write comments. Send the number of copies specified by your editor (typically four). If submitted electronically, find out if your editor prefers submissions on disk or as e-mail attachments.

If you want to submit your file with one column electronically, please do the following:

--First, click on the View menu and choose Print Layout.

--Second, place your cursor in the first paragraph. Go to the Format menu, choose Columns, choose one column Layout, and choose "apply to whole document" from the dropdown menu.

--Third, click and drag the right margin bar to just over 4 inches in width.

The graphics will stay in the "second" column, but you can drag them to the first column. Make the graphic wider to push out any text that may try to fill in next to the graphic.

B. Final Stage

When you submit your final version, after your paper has been accepted, print it in two-column format, including figures and tables. Send three prints of the paper; two will go to IEEE and one will be retained by the Editor-in-Chief or conference publications chair.

You must also send your final manuscript on a disk, which IEEE will use to prepare your paper for publication. Write the authors' names on the disk label. If you are using a Macintosh, please save your file on a PC formatted disk, if possible. You may use *Zip* or CD-ROM disks for large files, or compress files using *Compress, Pkzip, Stuffit,* or *Gzip*.

Also send a sheet of paper with complete contact information for all authors. Include full mailing addresses, telephone numbers, fax numbers, and e-mail addresses. This information will be used to send each author a complimentary copy of the journal in which the paper appears. In addition, designate one author as the "corresponding author." This is the author to whom proofs of the paper will be sent. Proofs are sent to the corresponding author only.

C. Figures

All tables and figures will be processed as images. **However, IEEE cannot extract the tables and figures embedded in your document.** (The figures and tables you insert in your document are only to help you gauge the size of your paper, for the convenience of the referees, and to make it easy for you to distribute preprints.) Therefore, **submit, on separate sheets of paper, enlarged versions of the tables and figures that appear in your document.** These are the images IEEE will scan and publish with your paper.

D. Electronic Image Files (Optional)

You will have the greatest control over the appearance of your figures if you are able to prepare electronic image files. If you do not have the required computer skills, just submit paper prints as described above and skip this section.

1) Easiest Way: If you have a scanner, the best and quickest way to prepare noncolor figure files is to print your tables and figures on paper exactly as you want them to appear, scan them, and then save them to a file in PostScript (PS) or Encapsulated PostScript (EPS) formats. Use a separate file for each image. File names should be of the form "fig1.ps" or "fig2.eps."

2) Slightly Harder Way: Using a scanner as above, save the images in TIFF format. High-contrast line figures and tables should be prepared with 600 dpi resolution and saved with no compression, 1 bit per pixel (monochrome), with file names of the form "fig3.tif" or "table1.tif". To obtain a 3.45-in figure (one-column width) at 600 dpi, the figure requires a horizontal size of 2070 pixels. Typical file sizes will be on the order of 0.5 MB.

Photographs and grayscale figures should be prepared with 220 dpi resolution and saved with no compression, 8 bits per pixel (grayscale). To obtain a 3.45-in figure (one-column width) at 220 dpi, the figure should have a horizontal size of 759 pixels.

Color figures should be prepared with 400 dpi resolution and saved with no compression, 8 bits per pixel (palette or 256 color). To obtain a 3.45-in figure (one column width) at 400 dpi, the figure should have a horizontal size of 1380 pixels.

For more information on TIFF files, please go to http://www.ieee.org/organizations/pubs/transactions/informatio n.htm and click on the link "Guidelines for Author Supplied Electronic Text and Graphics."

3) Somewhat Harder Way: If you do not have a scanner, you may create noncolor PostScript figures by "printing" them to files. First, download a PostScript printer driver from http://www.adobe.com/support/downloads/pdrvwin.htm (for Windows) or from http://www.adobe.com/support/downloads/ pdrvmac.htm (for Macintosh) and install the "Generic PostScript Printer" definition. In *Word,* paste your figure into a new document. Print to a file using the PostScript printer driver. File names should be of the form "fig5.ps." Use Adobe Type 1 fonts when creating your figures, if possible.

4) Other Ways: Experienced computer users can convert figures and tables from their original format to TIFF. Some useful image converters are Adobe *Photoshop,* Corel *Draw,* and Microsoft *Photo Editor,* an application that is part of Microsoft *Office 97* and *Office 2000* (look for C:\Program Files\Common Files \Microsoft Shared\ PhotoEd\ PHOTOED.EXE. (You may have to custom-install *Photo Editor* from your original *Office* disk.)

Here is a way to make TIFF image files of tables. First, create your table in *Word.* Use horizontal lines but no vertical lines. Hide gridlines (Table | Hide Gridlines). Spell check the table to remove any red underlines that indicate spelling errors. Adjust magnification (View | Zoom) such that you can view the entire table *at maximum area* when you select View | Full Screen. Move the cursor so that it is out of the way. Press "Print Screen" on your keyboard; this copies the screen image to the Windows clipboard. Open Microsoft *Photo Editor* and click Edit | Paste as New Image. Crop the table image (click Select button; select the part you want, then Image | Crop). Adjust the properties of the image (File | Properties) to monochrome (1 bit) and 600 pixels per inch. Resize the image (Image | Resize) to a width of 3.45 inches. Save the file (File | Save As) in TIFF with no compression (click "More" button).

Most graphing programs allow you to save graphs in TIFF; however, you often have no control over compression or number of bits per pixel. You should open these image files in a program such as Microsoft *Photo Editor* and re-save them using no compression, either 1 or 8 bits, and either 600 or 220 dpi resolution (File | Properties; Image | Resize). See Section II-D2 for an explanation of number of bits and resolution. If your graphing program cannot export to TIFF, you can use the same technique described for tables in the previous paragraph.

> REPLACE THIS LINE WITH YOUR PAPER IDENTIFICATION NUMBER (DOUBLE-CLICK HERE TO EDIT) <

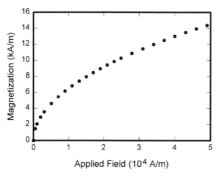

Fig. 1. Magnetization as a function of applied field. Note that "Fig." is abbreviated. There is a period after the figure number, followed by two spaces. It is good practice to explain the significance of the figure in the caption.

A way to convert a figure from Windows Metafile (WMF) to TIFF is to paste it into Microsoft *PowerPoint,* save it in JPG format, open it with Microsoft *Photo Editor* or similar converter, and re-save it as TIFF.

Microsoft *Excel* allows you to save spreadsheet charts in Graphics Interchange Format (GIF). To get good resolution, make the *Excel* charts *very* large. Then use the "Save as HTML" feature (see http://support.microsoft.com/support/kb/articles/q158/0/79.asp). You can then convert from GIF to TIFF using Microsoft *Photo Editor,* for example.

No matter how you convert your images, it is a good idea to print the TIFF files to make sure nothing was lost in the conversion.

If you modify this document for use with other IEEE journals or conferences, you should save it as type "Word 97-2000 & 6.0/95 - RTF (*.doc)" so that it can be opened by any version of *Word.*

E. Copyright Form

An IEEE copyright form should accompany your final submission. You can get a .pdf, .html, or .doc version at http://www.ieee.org/copyright or from the first issues in each volume of the IEEE TRANSACTIONS and JOURNALS. Authors are responsible for obtaining any security clearances.

III. MATH

If you are using *Word,* use either the Microsoft Equation Editor or the *MathType* add-on (http://www.mathtype.com) for equations in your paper (Insert | Object | Create New | Microsoft Equation *or* MathType Equation). "Float over text" should *not* be selected.

TABLE I
UNITS FOR MAGNETIC PROPERTIES

Symbol	Quantity	Conversion from Gaussian and CGS EMU to SI [a]
Φ	magnetic flux	$1 \text{ Mx} \rightarrow 10^{-8} \text{ Wb} = 10^{-8} \text{ V·s}$
B	magnetic flux density, magnetic induction	$1 \text{ G} \rightarrow 10^{-4} \text{ T} = 10^{-4} \text{ Wb/m}^2$
H	magnetic field strength	$1 \text{ Oe} \rightarrow 10^3/(4\pi) \text{ A/m}$
m	magnetic moment	$1 \text{ erg/G} = 1 \text{ emu}$ $\rightarrow 10^{-3} \text{ A·m}^2 = 10^{-3} \text{ J/T}$
M	magnetization	$1 \text{ erg/(G·cm}^3) = 1 \text{ emu/cm}^3$ $\rightarrow 10^3 \text{ A/m}$
$4\pi M$	magnetization	$1 \text{ G} \rightarrow 10^3/(4\pi) \text{ A/m}$
σ	specific magnetization	$1 \text{ erg/(G·g)} = 1 \text{ emu/g} \rightarrow 1 \text{ A·m}^2/\text{kg}$
j	magnetic dipole moment	$1 \text{ erg/G} = 1 \text{ emu}$ $\rightarrow 4\pi \times 10^{-10} \text{ Wb·m}$
J	magnetic polarization	$1 \text{ erg/(G·cm}^3) = 1 \text{ emu/cm}^3$ $\rightarrow 4\pi \times 10^{-4} \text{ T}$
χ, κ	susceptibility	$1 \rightarrow 4\pi$
χ_ρ	mass susceptibility	$1 \text{ cm}^3/\text{g} \rightarrow 4\pi \times 10^{-3} \text{ m}^3/\text{kg}$
μ	permeability	$1 \rightarrow 4\pi \times 10^{-7} \text{ H/m}$ $= 4\pi \times 10^{-7} \text{ Wb/(A·m)}$
μ_r	relative permeability	$\mu \rightarrow \mu_r$
w, W	energy density	$1 \text{ erg/cm}^3 \rightarrow 10^{-1} \text{ J/m}^3$
N, D	demagnetizing factor	$1 \rightarrow 1/(4\pi)$

No vertical lines in table. Statements that serve as captions for the entire table do not need footnote letters.

[a] Gaussian units are the same as cgs emu for magnetostatics; Mx = maxwell, G = gauss, Oe = oersted; Wb = weber, V = volt, s = second, T = tesla, m = meter, A = ampere, J = joule, kg = kilogram, H = henry.

IV. UNITS

Use either SI (MKS) or CGS as primary units. (SI units are strongly encouraged.) English units may be used as secondary units (in parentheses). **This applies to papers in data storage.** For example, write "15 Gb/cm² (100 Gb/in²)." An exception is when English units are used as identifiers in trade, such as "3½ in disk drive." Avoid combining SI and CGS units, such as current in amperes and magnetic field in oersteds. This often leads to confusion because equations do not balance dimensionally. If you must use mixed units, clearly state the units for each quantity in an equation.

The SI unit for magnetic field strength H is A/m. However, if you wish to use units of T, either refer to magnetic flux density B or magnetic field strength symbolized as $\mu_0 H$. Use the center dot to separate compound units, e.g., "A·m²."

V. HELPFUL HINTS

A. Figures and Tables

Because IEEE will do the final formatting of your paper, you do not need to position figures and tables at the top and bottom of each column. In fact, all figures, figure captions, and tables can be at the end of the paper. Large figures and tables may span both columns. Place figure captions below the figures; place table titles above the tables. If your figure has two parts, include the labels "(a)" and "(b)" as part of the artwork. Please verify that the figures and tables you mention in the text actually exist. **Please do not include captions as part of the figures. Do not put captions in "text boxes" linked to the figures. Do not put borders around the outside of your figures.** Use the abbreviation "Fig." even at the beginning of a sentence. Do not abbreviate "Table." Tables are numbered with Roman numerals.

Color printing of figures is available, but is billed to the authors (approximately $1300, depending on the number of figures and number of pages containing color). Include a note with your final paper indicating that you request color printing. **Do not use color unless it is necessary for the proper interpretation of your figures.** If you want reprints of your color article, the reprint order should be submitted promptly. There is an additional charge of $81 per 100 for color reprints.

Figure axis labels are often a source of confusion. Use words rather than symbols. As an example, write the quantity "Magnetization," or "Magnetization M," not just "M." Put units in parentheses. Do not label axes only with units. As in Fig. 1, for example, write "Magnetization (A/m)" or "Magnetization (A·m^{-1})," not just "A/m." Do not label axes with a ratio of quantities and units. For example, write "Temperature (K)," not "Temperature/K."

Multipliers can be especially confusing. Write "Magnetization (kA/m)" or "Magnetization (10^3 A/m)." Do not write "Magnetization (A/m) × 1000" because the reader would not know whether the top axis label in Fig. 1 meant 16000 A/m or 0.016 A/m. Figure labels should be legible, approximately 8 to 12 point type.

B. References

Number citations consecutively in square brackets [1]. The sentence punctuation follows the brackets [2]. Multiple references [2], [3] are each numbered with separate brackets [1]–[3]. When citing a section in a book, please give the relevant page numbers [2]. In sentences, refer simply to the reference number, as in [3]. Do not use "Ref. [3]" or "reference [3]" except at the beginning of a sentence: "Reference [3] shows ... ." Unfortunately the IEEE document translator cannot handle automatic endnotes in *Word*; therefore, type the reference list at the end of the paper using the "References" style.

Number footnotes separately in superscripts (Insert | Footnote).[1] Place the actual footnote at the bottom of the column in which it is cited; do not put footnotes in the reference list (endnotes). Use letters for table footnotes (see Table I).

Please note that the references at the end of this document are in the preferred referencing style. Give all authors' names; do not use "*et al.*" unless there are six authors or more. Use a space after authors' initials. Papers that have not been published should be cited as "unpublished" [4]. Papers that have been submitted for publication should be cited as "submitted for publication" [5]. Papers that have been accepted for publication, but not yet specified for an issue should be cited as "to be published" [6]. Please give affiliations and addresses for private communications [7].

Capitalize only the first word in a paper title, except for proper nouns and element symbols. For papers published in translation journals, please give the English citation first, followed by the original foreign-language citation [8].

C. Abbreviations and Acronyms

Define abbreviations and acronyms the first time they are used in the text, even after they have already been defined in the abstract. Abbreviations such as IEEE, SI, ac, and dc do not have to be defined. Abbreviations that incorporate periods should not have spaces: write "C.N.R.S.," not "C. N. R. S." Do not use abbreviations in the title unless they are unavoidable (for example, "IEEE" in the title of this article).

D. Equations

Number equations consecutively with equation numbers in parentheses flush with the right margin, as in (1). First use the equation editor to create the equation. Then select the "Equation" markup style. Press the tab key and write the equation number in parentheses. To make your equations more compact, you may use the solidus (/), the exp function, or appropriate exponents. Use parentheses to avoid ambiguities in denominators. Punctuate equations when they are part of a sentence, as in

$$\int_0^{r_2} F(r,\varphi)\, dr\, d\varphi = [\sigma r_2 / (2\mu_0)]$$
$$\cdot \int_0^{\infty} \exp(-\lambda\, |\, z_j - z_i\, |)\, \lambda^{-1} J_1(\lambda r_2) J_0(\lambda r_i)\, d\lambda\,. \quad (1)$$

Be sure that the symbols in your equation have been defined before the equation appears or immediately following. Italicize symbols (T might refer to temperature, but T is the unit tesla). Refer to "(1)," not "Eq. (1)" or "equation (1)," except at the beginning of a sentence: "Equation (1) is ... ."

Other Recommendations

Use one space after periods and colons. Hyphenate complex modifiers: "zero-field-cooled magnetization." Avoid dangling participles, such as, "Using (1), the potential was calculated." [It is not clear who or what used (1).] Write instead, "The potential was calculated by using (1)," or "Using (1), we calculated the potential."

Use a zero before decimal points: "0.25," not ".25." Use "cm^3," not "cc." Indicate sample dimensions as "0.1 cm × 0.2 cm," not "0.1 × 0.2 cm^2." The abbreviation for "seconds" is "s," not "sec." Do not mix complete spellings and abbreviations of units: use "Wb/m^2" or "webers per square meter," not "webers/m^2." When expressing a range of values, write "7 to 9" or "7-9," not "7~9."

A parenthetical statement at the end of a sentence is punctuated outside of the closing parenthesis (like this). (A parenthetical sentence is punctuated within the parentheses.) In American English, periods and commas are within quotation marks, like "this period." Other punctuation is "outside"!

---

[1] It is recommended that footnotes be avoided (except for the unnumbered footnote with the receipt date on the first page). Instead, try to integrate the footnote information into the text.

Avoid contractions; for example, write "do not" instead of "don't." The serial comma is preferred: "A, B, and C" instead of "A, B and C."

If you wish, you may write in the first person singular or plural and use the active voice ("I observed that ..." or "We observed that ..." instead of "It was observed that ..."). Remember to check spelling. If your native language is not English, please get a native English-speaking colleague to proofread your paper.

VI. SOME COMMON MISTAKES

The word "data" is plural, not singular. The subscript for the permeability of vacuum μ_0 is zero, not a lowercase letter "o." The term for residual magnetization is "remanence"; the adjective is "remanent"; do not write "remnance" or "remnant." Use the word "micrometer" instead of "micron." A graph within a graph is an "inset," not an "insert." The word "alternatively" is preferred to the word "alternately" (unless you really mean something that alternates). Use the word "whereas" instead of "while" (unless you are referring to simultaneous events). Do not use the word "essentially" to mean "approximately" or "effectively." Do not use the word "issue" as a euphemism for "problem." When compositions are not specified, separate chemical symbols by en-dashes; for example, "NiMn" indicates the intermetallic compound $Ni_{0.5}Mn_{0.5}$ whereas "Ni–Mn" indicates an alloy of some composition Ni_xMn_{1-x}.

Be aware of the different meanings of the homophones "affect" (usually a verb) and "effect" (usually a noun), "complement" and "compliment," "discreet" and "discrete," "principal" (e.g., "principal investigator") and "principle" (e.g., "principle of measurement"). Do not confuse "imply" and "infer."

Prefixes such as "non," "sub," "micro," "multi," and ""ultra" are not independent words; they should be joined to the words they modify, usually without a hyphen. There is no period after the "et" in the Latin abbreviation "*et al.*" (it is also italicized). The abbreviation "i.e.," means "that is," and the abbreviation "e.g.," means "for example" (these abbreviations are not italicized).

An excellent style manual and source of information for science writers is [9]. A general IEEE style guide, *Information for Authors,* is available at http://www.ieee.org/organizations/pubs/transactions/informatio n.htm

VII. EDITORIAL POLICY

Submission of a manuscript is not required for participation in a conference. Do not submit a reworked version of a paper you have submitted or published elsewhere. Do not publish "preliminary" data or results. The submitting author is responsible for obtaining agreement of all coauthors and any consent required from sponsors before submitting a paper.

IEEE TRANSACTIONS and JOURNALS strongly discourage courtesy authorship. It is the obligation of the authors to cite relevant prior work.

The Transactions and Journals Department does not publish conference records or proceedings. The TRANSACTIONS does publish papers related to conferences that have been recommended for publication on the basis of peer review. As a matter of convenience and service to the technical community, these topical papers are collected and published in one issue of the TRANSACTIONS.

At least two reviews are required for every paper submitted. For conference-related papers, the decision to accept or reject a paper is made by the conference editors and publications committee; the recommendations of the referees are advisory only. Undecipherable English is a valid reason for rejection. Authors of rejected papers may revise and resubmit them to the TRANSACTIONS as regular papers, whereupon they will be reviewed by two new referees.

VIII. PUBLICATION PRINCIPLES

The contents of IEEE TRANSACTIONS and JOURNALS are peer-reviewed and archival. The TRANSACTIONS publishes scholarly articles of archival value as well as tutorial expositions and critical reviews of classical subjects and topics of current interest.

Authors should consider the following points:
1) Technical papers submitted for publication must advance the state of knowledge and must cite relevant prior work.
2) The length of a submitted paper should be commensurate with the importance, or appropriate to the complexity, of the work. For example, an obvious extension of previously published work might not be appropriate for publication or might be adequately treated in just a few pages.
3) Authors must convince both peer reviewers and the editors of the scientific and technical merit of a paper; the standards of proof are higher when extraordinary or unexpected results are reported.
4) Because replication is required for scientific progress, papers submitted for publication must provide sufficient information to allow readers to perform similar experiments or calculations and use the reported results. Although not everything need be disclosed, a paper must contain new, useable, and fully described information. For example, a specimen's chemical composition need not be reported if the main purpose of a paper is to introduce a new measurement technique. Authors should expect to be challenged by reviewers if the results are not supported by adequate data and critical details.
5) Papers that describe ongoing work or announce the latest technical achievement, which are suitable for presentation at a professional conference, may not be appropriate for publication in a TRANSACTIONS or JOURNAL.

IX. T-MAGIC SYSTEM

This word file has been preset for compatible use with the T-MAGIC template designed for creating well-formatted reports and papers using the automatic formatting features of Microsoft Word. The template is fully explained in *Writing for Research Teams: Tools and Techniques* by A. V. Mamishev and D. K. Farkas, published by the IEEE Press. This template is one of a set. Depending on the document you are creating, you may want to use one of the following: the Double-Column Template, the ThesisOrBook Template, or the Instructions Template.

A. Headings

To add a new heading to your document:

1. Choose the placeholder heading in this whose heading level matches the heading you wish to add. Four heading levels are provided.

2. Copy this placeholder heading and paste it in the desired location. The newly pasted heading will take on the appropriate heading number.

3. Replace the placeholder text with your own heading text

B. Figures and Captions

To add a new figure and caption to your document:

4. Select and copy the placeholder figure (see below) and its accompanying caption.

5. Paste to the desired location in your document.

6. Copy and paste the figure you wish to add to the **Clipboard.**

7. Select the placeholder figure so that you will overwrite it when you paste in your figure.

8. On the **Edit** menu, click **Paste Special.**

9. In the **Paste Special** dialog box click **Picture (Windows Metafile)** and click **OK.**

10. Replace the placeholder caption text with your own caption text.

11. If desired, update all your figure numbers with the **Global Update** command: Press **CTRL+A** to select the entire document and then **F9** to update all updatable components.

C. Cross References for Figures and Tables

There are many occasions when you need to refer the reader from the text of your document to the caption of a figure or table.

To add a cross reference to a figure or table:

12. Place the mouse pointer at the location where you wish to add the cross reference.

13. On the **Insert** menu, click **Reference** and then **Cross Reference**.

14. In the **Cross Reference** dialog box, click the caption to which you are building the text reference.

15. In the case of a figure, under **Reference Type** click **Figure** and under **Insert Reference To**, click **Only Label and Number.**

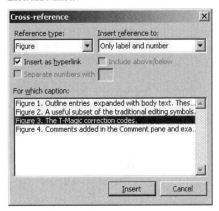

OR

In the case of a table, under Reference Type click Table and under Insert Reference To, click Only Label and Number.

16. Click **Insert.**

An autonumbered cross reference (such as **Figure 13** or **Table 4**) will appear in the text. Remove the boldfacing and write the figure or table cross reference text.

17. If desired, update all your table numbers with the **Global Update** command: Press **CTRL+A** to select the entire document and then **F9** to update all updatable components.

X. CONCLUSION

A conclusion section is not required. Although a conclusion may review the main points of the paper, do not replicate the abstract as the conclusion. A conclusion might elaborate on the importance of the work or suggest applications and extensions.

APPENDIX

Appendixes, if needed, appear before the acknowledgment.

ACKNOWLEDGMENT

The preferred spelling of the word "acknowledgment" in American English is without an "e" after the "g." Use the singular heading even if you have many acknowledgments.

Avoid expressions such as "One of us (S.B.A.) would like to thank ... ." Instead, write "F. A. Author thanks ... ." **Sponsor and financial support acknowledgments are placed in the unnumbered footnote on the first page.**

REFERENCES

[1]   G. O. Young, "Synthetic structure of industrial plastics (Book style with paper title and editor)," in *Plastics*, 2nd ed. vol. 3, J. Peters, Ed. New York: McGraw-Hill, 1964, pp. 15–64.

[2]   W.-K. Chen, *Linear Networks and Systems* (Book style). Belmont, CA: Wadsworth, 1993, pp. 123–135.

[3]   H. Poor, *An Introduction to Signal Detection and Estimation*. New York: Springer-Verlag, 1985, ch. 4.

[4]   B. Smith, "An approach to graphs of linear forms (Unpublished work style)," unpublished.

[5]   E. H. Miller, "A note on reflector arrays (Periodical style—Accepted for publication)," *IEEE Trans. Antennas Propagat.*, to be published.

[6]   J. Wang, "Fundamentals of erbium-doped fiber amplifiers arrays (Periodical style—Submitted for publication)," *IEEE J. Quantum Electron.*, submitted for publication.

[7]   C. J. Kaufman, Rocky Mountain Research Lab., Boulder, CO, private communication, May 1995.

[8]   Y. Yorozu, M. Hirano, K. Oka, and Y. Tagawa, "Electron spectroscopy studies on magneto-optical media and plastic substrate interfaces(Translation Journals style)," *IEEE Transl. J. Magn.Jpn.*, vol. 2, Aug. 1987, pp. 740–741 [*Dig. 9th Annu. Conf. Magnetics* Japan, 1982, p. 301].

[9]   M. Young, *The Techincal Writers Handbook*. Mill Valley, CA: University Science, 1989.

[10] J. U. Duncombe, "Infrared navigation—Part I: An assessment of feasibility (Periodical style)," *IEEE Trans. Electron Devices*, vol. ED-11, pp. 34–39, Jan. 1959.

[11] S. Chen, B. Mulgrew, and P. M. Grant, "A clustering technique for digital communications channel equalization using radial basis function networks," *IEEE Trans. Neural Networks*, vol. 4, pp. 570–578, July 1993.

[12] R. W. Lucky, "Automatic equalization for digital communication," *Bell Syst. Tech. J.*, vol. 44, no. 4, pp. 547–588, Apr. 1965.

[13] S. P. Bingulac, "On the compatibility of adaptive controllers (Published Conference Proceedings style)," in *Proc. 4th Annu. Allerton Conf. Circuits and Systems Theory*, New York, 1994, pp. 8–16.

[14] G. R. Faulhaber, "Design of service systems with priority reservation," in *Conf. Rec. 1995 IEEE Int. Conf. Communications*, pp. 3–8.

[15] W. D. Doyle, "Magnetization reversal in films with biaxial anisotropy," in *1987 Proc. INTERMAG Conf.*, pp. 2.2-1–2.2-6.

[16] G. W. Juette and L. E. Zeffanella, "Radio noise currents n short sections on bundle conductors (Presented Conference Paper style)," presented at the IEEE Summer power Meeting, Dallas, TX, June 22–27, 1990, Paper 90 SM 690-0 PWRS.

[17] J. G. Kreifeldt, "An analysis of surface-detected EMG as an amplitude-modulated noise," presented at the 1989 Int. Conf. Medicine and Biological Engineering, Chicago, IL.

[18] J. Williams, "Narrow-band analyzer (Thesis or Dissertation style)," Ph.D. dissertation, Dept. Elect. Eng., Harvard Univ., Cambridge, MA, 1993.

[19] N. Kawasaki, "Parametric study of thermal and chemical nonequilibrium nozzle flow," M.S. thesis, Dept. Electron. Eng., Osaka Univ., Osaka, Japan, 1993.

[20] J. P. Wilkinson, "Nonlinear resonant circuit devices (Patent style)," U.S. Patent 3 624 12, July 16, 1990.

[21] *IEEE Criteria for Class IE Electric Systems* (Standards style), IEEE Standard 308, 1969.

[22] *Letter Symbols for Quantities*, ANSI Standard Y10.5-1968.

[23] R. E. Haskell and C. T. Case, "Transient signal propagation in lossless isotropic plasmas (Report style)," USAF Cambridge Res. Lab., Cambridge, MA Rep. ARCRL-66-234 (II), 1994, vol. 2.

[24] E. E. Reber, R. L. Michell, and C. J. Carter, "Oxygen absorption in the Earth's atmosphere," Aerospace Corp., Los Angeles, CA, Tech. Rep. TR-0200 (420-46)-3, Nov. 1988.

[25] (Handbook style) *Transmission Systems for Communications*, 3rd ed., Western Electric Co., Winston-Salem, NC, 1985, pp. 44–60.

[26] *Motorola Semiconductor Data Manual*, Motorola Semiconductor Products Inc., Phoenix, AZ, 1989.

[27] (Basic Book/Monograph Online Sources) J. K. Author. (year, month, day). *Title* (edition) [Type of medium]. Volume(issue). Available: http://www.(URL)

[28] J. Jones. (1991, May 10). Networks (2nd ed.) [Online]. Available: http://www.atm.com

[29] (Journal Online Sources style) K. Author. (year, month). Title. *Journal* [Type of medium]. Volume(issue), paging if given. Available: http://www.(URL)

[30] R. J. Vidmar. (1992, August). On the use of atmospheric plasmas as electromagnetic reflectors. *IEEE Trans. Plasma Sci.* [Online]. *21(3).* pp. 876—880. Available: http://www.halcyon.com/pub/journals/21ps03-vidmar

First A. Author (M'76–SM'81–F'87) and the other authors may include biographies at the end of regular papers. Biographies are often not included in conference-related papers. This author became a Member (M) of IEEE in 1976, a Senior Member (SM) in 1981, and a Fellow (F) in 1987. The first paragraph may contain a place and/or date of birth (list place, then date). Next, the author's educational background is listed. The degrees should be listed with type of degree in what field, which institution, city, state or country, and year degree was earned. The author's major field of study should be lower-cased.

The second paragraph uses the pronoun of the person (he or she) and not the author's last name. It lists military and work experience, including summer and fellowship jobs. Job titles are capitalized. The current job must have a location; previous positions may be listed without one. Information concerning previous publications may be included. Try not to list more than three books or published articles. The format for listing publishers of a book within the biography is: title of book (city, state: publisher name, year) similar to a reference. Current and previous research interests ends the paragraph.

The third paragraph begins with the author's title and last name (e.g., Dr. Smith, Prof. Jones, Mr. Kajor, Ms. Hunter). List any memberships in professional societies other than the IEEE. Finally, list any awards and work for IEEE committees and publications. If a photograph is provided, the biography will be indented around it. The photograph is placed at the top left of the biography. Personal hobbies will be deleted from the biography.

Appendix E

POWERPOINT SLIDES FOR TEACHING *STREAM TOOLS* BASICS IN 30 MINUTES

Technical Writing for Teams: The STREAM Tools Handbook, by Alexander Mamishev and Sean Williams
Copyright © 2010 Institute of Electrical and Electronics Engineers

30-minute fast track to STREAM Tools

Alexander V. Mamishev and Sean D. Williams

email: streamtools@gmail.com

Motivation

- Compatibility
  - Internal (reuse, sharing)
  - External (extraction, sharing)
- Streamlining of information processing
- Automation of routine functions
- Rigor in writing and in typesetting

(c) Alexander V Mamishev and Sean D. Williams

Requirements for a Typesetting System

- Auto-numbering of headings, figures, tables, equations, and references
- Auto-numbered text can be reused in manuscripts of different format
- The system is based on commonly available software
- The system can be learned quickly by all co-authors

(c) Alexander V Mamishev and Sean D. Williams

STREAM Tools Highlights

- Use BasicTemplate files that suit your manuscript
  - BasicTemplateSingleColumn.doc
  - BasicTemplateDoubleColumn.doc
  - BasicTemplateThesisOrBook.doc
- Use templates for headings, figures, tables, equations
- Use End Note for references
- Use color-coding and comment codes for communication between co-authors

(c) Alexander V Mamishev and Sean D. Williams

Software

- Required
  - Microsoft Word
- Recommended
  - End Note – for references
  - MathType – for equations
  - CorelDraw – for figures

(c) Alexander V Mamishev and Sean D. Williams

Templates

- Template files – download them
- Template manuscript elements – reuse the ones provided in the file
- General approach:
  - 1) Copy the entire template for each manuscript element
  - 2) Paste the template at the new desired location
  - 3) Replace the old text with the new text, but do not touch the auto-features
  - 4) Press **Ctrl-A, F9** for updates across the entire document

(c) Alexander V Mamishev and Sean D. Williams

Elements of a Manuscript

- Headings
- Equations
- Figures and Tables
- References
- Miscellaneous

Headings

- Reuse the template or change paragraph style
- To update Table of Contents, press **Ctrl-A, F9**
- To cross-reference a heading
  - ➤ Click **Insert, Reference, Cross-Reference**
  - ➤ Select: *Reference type:* **Heading**
  - ➤ Select: *Insert reference to:* **Heading number**
  - ➤ Unselect: *Insert as hyperlink*
  - ➤ Select the desired heading from the list
  - ➤ Click **OK.**

Equations

- Reuse the template, remember to copy the entire line
- It is better to use MathType, but one can do without it in many cases
- To update the equation number, press **Ctrl-A, F9**

Cross-Referencing an Equation

- To prepare for cross-referencing
  - ➤ Bookmark the equation number
  - ➤ Give the bookmark a descriptive name, that starts with eq
    - • good example: eqMagneticField
    - • bad example: eq4
- To cross-reference
  - ➤ Click **Insert, Reference, CrossReference, Bookmark**
  - ➤ Unselect *Hyperlink*
  - ➤ Click **OK.**
  - ➤ Add parentheses manually as needed

Figures and Tables

- Reuse the template, copying both the graphics and the caption
- To update numbering, press **Ctrl-A, F9**
- When pasting new graphics, especially Line Art *do not* use **Paste** or **Ctrl-V**
- Instead, click **Edit, Paste Special, Picture (Enhanced Metafile)**

Pasting a Figure

- Copy/Paste the figure template
- **Paste Special as Picture**
- To adjust settings if needed
  - ➤ Right-click on the graphics
  - ➤ Click **Format Picture, Layout, In line with Text** (little rectangles change from outline to black)
  - ➤ Center the figure
- Adjust figure size
- Type in a new caption

Cross-Referencing a Figure or a Table

- To insert cross-reference
  - Click **Insert, Reference, Cross-reference**
  - Select *Reference type:* **Figure**
  - Select **Only Label and Number**
  - Uncheck Hyperlink
  - Pick the desired figure from the list
- If figure is far from the reference, you may choose to cross-reference the page as well: "Figure 3 on page 12"
- Remove or add bold and italics as needed

References

- Use EndNote or Reference Manager
- The subject is beyond the short introduction
- EndNote and Reference Manager are very similar packages. In an ideal world, there would be only one of them, and compatibility would be less of an issue

Conclusions

- *STREAM Tools* system provides writers with LaTeX-like capabilities while preserving the convenience of Microsoft Word
- *STREAM Tools* is not about individuals mastering typesetting, its main benefit is in streamlined collaborative writing
- Auto-features maybe confusing, but they are very useful in the long term
- Learning *STREAM Tools* beyond basics takes several hours, and can be done in steps

Appendix F

TEN COMMANDMENTS OF *STREAM TOOLS*

Commandment #1: Team members should use compatible tools.

Commandment #2: Your boss is not your English teacher.

Commandment #3: Use document templates.

Commandment #4: Use automatic formatting features.

Commandment #5: Use modern communication tools.

Commandment #6: Do not assume that others know what you expect them to know.

Commandment #7: Never start from scratch.

Commandment #8: Iterate.

Commandment #9: Never underestimate the power of superficial appearance.

Commandment #10: "Better" is the enemy of "good."

Technical Writing for Teams: The STREAM Tools Handbook, by Alexander Mamishev and Sean Williams
Copyright © 2010 Institute of Electrical and Electronics Engineers

INDEX